Why Music Matters

Why Music Matters

David Hesmondhalgh

WILEY Blackwell

This edition first published 2013
© 2013 David Hesmondhalgh

Blackwell Publishing was acquired by John Wiley & Sons in February 2007. Blackwell's publishing program has been merged with Wiley's global Scientific, Technical, and Medical business to form Wiley-Blackwell.

Registered Office
John Wiley & Sons, Ltd, The Atrium, Southern Gate, Chichester, West Sussex, PO19 8SQ, UK

Editorial Offices
350 Main Street, Malden, MA 02148-5020, USA
9600 Garsington Road, Oxford, OX4 2DQ, UK
The Atrium, Southern Gate, Chichester, West Sussex, PO19 8SQ, UK

For details of our global editorial offices, for customer services, and for information about how to apply for permission to reuse the copyright material in this book please see our website at www.wiley.com/wiley-blackwell.

Library of Congress Cataloging-in-Publication Data
Hesmondhalgh, David, author.
  Why music matters / David Hesmondhalgh.
     pages   cm
  Includes bibliographical references and index.
  ISBN ISBN 978-1-4051-9241-5 (pbk. : alk. paper) – ISBN 978-1-4051-9242-2 (cloth : alk. paper)   1. Music–Social aspects.   2. Music–Philosophy and aesthetics.   I. Title.
  ML3916.H47 2014
  781.1'7–dc23

                                              2013006642

A catalogue record for this book is available from the British Library.

Cover image: Top image © Atlantide Phototravel/Corbis. Bottom image © Klaus Hackenberg/Corbis
Cover design by Simon Levy Design Associates

Set in 10.5/13pt Minion by SPi Publisher Services, Pondicherry, India

Contents

1

Music as Intimate and Social, Private and Public

Music matters because it has the potential to enrich people's lives, and enrich societies. But in what ways does it enrich them, why, and in what circumstances? Just as importantly, what constrains music from doing so? These questions, which I hope to address in this book, are big ones, and even they are only one aspect of a broader problem: the role of aesthetic experience in modern life. So my examination of the value of music draws upon wider debates about the value of art and culture in the modern world, and it also seeks to contribute to those discussions.

Music as an example of aesthetic experience raises further questions, concerning the specificity of music. What distinguishes musical practices and experiences from other artistic, cultural, and social practices? What is distinctive about music as a form of communication? These issues are addressed across the book as a whole, but in this introductory chapter I want briefly to give some indication of my particular approach to them, before outlining the essays that follow.

The fact that music matters so much to so many people may derive from two contrasting yet complementary dimensions of musical experience in modern societies. The first is that *music often feels intensely and emotionally linked to the private self*. As one writer has put it, music is a set of cultural practices that have come to be intricately bound up with the realm of the personal and the subjective (Martin, 1995: 2). This includes the way in which music provides a basis for intimate relations with others: a parent singing a child to sleep; three sisters expressing their feelings for a fourth by singing to her on her birthday; two lovers in bed hearing a song that they will forever associate with each other. The second is that *music is often the*

Why Music Matters, First Edition. David Hesmondhalgh.
© 2013 David Hesmondhalgh. Published 2013 by John Wiley & Sons, Ltd.

basis of collective, public experiences, whether in live performance, mad dancing at a party, or simply by virtue of the fact that thousands and sometimes millions of people can come to know the same sounds and performers.

These private and public dimensions of musical experience may support and reinforce each other. Our excitement or sadness at hearing a song can be intensified through the sense that such emotions in response to a particular piece of music are shared by others, or even just that they *might* be shared. This feeling can be especially strong at a live performance, but it is just as possible when seeing someone perform on television or on YouTube. Listening to music through headphones as you wait for a bus, you might, however semi-consciously and fleetingly, imagine others – a particular person, or untold thousands – being able to share that response. That sense of sharedness is one of the pleasures of pop music, and many people are suspicious of it, perhaps because the feeling of community involved may seem to derive from sentimentality or even from a loss of individuality. But communal sentiment also derives from music's capacity for enhancing experiences of collectivity, and there are reasons to value that.

Music, then, represents a remarkable meeting point of intimate and social realms. It provides a basis of self-identity (this is who I am, this is who I'm not) and collective identity (this is who we are, this is who we're not), often in the same moment. All cultural products have this potential – films, television programs, even shoes and cars. Yet music's seemingly special link to emotions and feelings makes it an especially powerful site for the bringing together of private and public experience.

This is where things start to get complicated. The relations between public and private realms have always been complex and contested. But in modern times, the private self has never been, in Eva Illouz's words, "so publicly performed and [so] harnessed to the values of the economic and public spheres" (2007: 4). It is no longer possible to sustain the idea that "private" spheres such as the home and family offer some kind of opposition to, or protection from, a world of public power, with the private understood as "warm" and intimate, and the public realm as a "cold," rational, administrative domain. Of course, many people cope with the demands of their working lives by telling themselves that their private realm offers a "haven in a heartless world" (Lasch, 1977), and arguably a number of political interests encourage this privatization of people's feelings of attachment and belonging (an argument made by, among others, Berlant, 1997). But in reality, those realms we think of as "personal" – our inner selves internal conversations and relationships with families, lovers, and close friends – are hugely affected by the world beyond them, and can be just as troubled as the workplace (see Hochschild, 1983). This may be more so now than ever before, as powerful commercial and state institutions in advanced industrial countries increasingly require autonomy, creativity, and emotional roundedness in their employees and citizens.

So this book examines the social value of music by exploring the relationships between music, history, society, and the self. It does so by offering *a critical defense of music*. Why on earth, you might ask, would music need defending? Who could possibly be against music, other than religious fanatics and disgruntled parents? Well, a variety of people and institutions are skeptical about the relative value of artistic forms such as music compared with other social practices. I mean "artistic" here in a broad sense: the use of skills to produce works of the imagination, to invoke feelings of pleasure, beauty, shock, excitement, and so on, rather than some rarified notion of "high art." The social value of artistic practices and experiences, like that of other potentially important things such as education, has come under attack in recent years. Some trace such attacks to the 1970s. During that decade, faced by an increasing sense of economic crisis, many politicians and commentators began to argue more strongly than ever for the view that economic prosperity should be the central goal of governments and of many other public institutions, including those involved in education, health, and culture. This was an old viewpoint, of course, and has existed in various forms since the eighteenth century. But a contemporary version of this type of thinking, often called neo-liberalism, was argued for with particular force from the 1970s onwards, and with great success (see Crouch, 2011). Government policy towards culture was increasingly guided by economic conceptions of what was best for individuals and society, and many economic approaches implicitly or explicitly assumed that the life-enhancing properties of art and culture were less important than the goal of economic prosperity. Although there have undoubtedly been strong counter-tendencies, that devaluation and implicit denigration of culture and art has continued. In the wake of the post-2008 economic crisis unleashed by the unregulated venality of the financial services and banking sectors, savage cuts were made to education, library, and arts funding in England, where I live and work, and in many other places too.

This is one very significant way in which the value of art (again, I stress that I am using this term in a broad sense), and of music, has been questioned, and with enormous consequences for musicians and other cultural practitioners, and for ordinary people. There is, however, another way in which the value of art (and music) has been questioned, and I have much more sympathy with it. Some are skeptical not about artistic practice and experience per se, but about the particular forms that artistic practices such as music take in modern societies. A number of writers, perhaps most notably the sociologist Pierre Bourdieu, have focused on the way in which divisions between "high" and "low" culture draw upon and reinforce patterns of social inequality, and on how therefore the dominant ways of thinking about beauty and pleasure in modern societies are deeply compromised. This view has merit, because there are good reasons to think that culture should not be thought of as autonomous of society, or of power relations. For example, cultural forms associated with societies in the global south are often considered less worthy than those of the global north, or, almost as bad, are elevated above them on dubious grounds. Such evaluations are surely connected to long histories of inequality and violence. Gender and class inequality infect prevailing judgments of aesthetic worth.

Recognizing the ways in which cultural practices are imbricated with social dynamics means that critics are right to be suspicious of certain ways of celebrating artistic practices and experiences. That is partly why I use the phrase *critical defense* of music, because I want to take into account the way that music is imbricated with society and the self, with all their problems.

But in some quarters, a critique of the power dynamics involved in culture has led to a strange situation. Many intellectuals who are rightly critical of existing social relations enjoy and gain enrichment from artistic and cultural experience in their own lives. They buy DVD box sets, download films and music, and discuss them heatedly with friends. They have strong opinions about the value of the particular cultural products they love. But they seem unable or unwilling in what they write and say to provide an account of how art, culture, entertainment, and knowledge might enhance people's lives more generally, and why these domains might need defending from the kind of denigration and lack of public support that I noted earlier.

Alternatively, some intellectuals can only defend whatever they define as *popular* culture – perhaps because popularity among "ordinary" (or working-class?) people is felt to reflect an implicit democratic appeal. But such uncritical populism (McGuigan, 1992) is bad politics and bad aesthetics. It appears egalitarian, but often ends up enacting a reversal of the exclusion and snobbery involved in the preference for high culture over low culture. It submits to notions of quality that may be determined to a large degree by powerful cultural corporations that dominate the production and dissemination of cultural goods.[1] What I want to do is provide a critical defense of music, by explaining why it matters, and to do so by looking and listening across a range of different genres and experiences, including "popular" forms, but others too.

This is an academic book, based on my own research, and drawing on research that others have carried out in a range of disciplines, mainly in the social sciences, but also in the humanities. The main ones are sociology; social and political theory; media, communication, and cultural studies; anthropology and ethnomusicology; musicology and music history; philosophy (aesthetics in particular); psychology, especially the burgeoning field of music psychology; and social history. Nevertheless, I have tried to keep my explanations as clear and as simple as possible, while staying true to the main goal of academic life: to enhance knowledge by providing a rigorous examination of difficult issues.

How then do I mount my critical defense of music in this book? In short, I investigate why music matters at the level of the individual self (Chapter 2), in our intimate relations with others (Chapter 3), in constructing and enhancing experiences of sociability and "co-present" community (Chapter 4), and in building experiences of solidarity, commonality, and publicness across space and time (Chapter 5).

Chapter 2 begins by arguing that music's relationships to affective experience, to emotion and feeling, are distinctive and are important for music's ability to contribute to human flourishing. I draw on the work of the feminist, neo-Aristotelian philosopher Martha Nussbaum who argues that music, like stories and play, can enhance our lives by helping us understand our emotions better, and that music communicates emotions in a particular way, and can therefore perform a distinctive ethical role in our lives. Importantly, Nussbaum's account relies on an understanding of the self as vulnerable, which is partly derived from object–relations psychoanalysis. I then outline the concept of human flourishing, defend it against potential criticisms, and relate it to artistic and musical practice, using "the capabilities approach" to questions of human needs and social justice. Nussbaum's

---

[1]   I use this somewhat cumbersome phrase rather than saying "by markets" because of my view that markets are not in themselves the problem with modern society, it is the particular way that markets are organized; see Keat (2000). For fuller analysis of relations between economics and culture than is possible in the current book, see Hesmondhalgh (2013).

perspective is too centered on classical music, contemplative listening, and the cognitive aspects of emotion. It downplays other, more somatic, affective, and bodily experiences of music. So, to supplement Nussbaum's account of how music's crystallization of emotion can enhance life, I discuss the kinds of affective rewards that people might get from dancing to music, and I draw upon the philosophical tradition known as pragmatist aesthetics to understand the contribution such experiences might make to human flourishing. These include revitalization and a healthy loss of self-consciousness. (Remember my focus is on the individual here, and that collective aspects of flourishing through music are discussed in later chapters.)

I then go on to complement Nussbaum's approach further by examining one of the most important developments in social science of music over the last 20 years: a tide of analysis of "music in everyday life." This, however, is where I begin to introduce the social and psycho-social factors that might severely constrain the ways in which music enriches people's lives in modern societies (hence a *critical* defense of music, because there is much to criticize in the way the world is). I argue that the major social scientific approaches to music in everyday life, from sociology, anthropology, and psychology, overestimate people's freedom to use music, and understate ways in which music is tied up with social problems such as inequality and suffering. Another, separate problem is that some of these accounts implicitly downplay the importance of aesthetic experience by focusing excessively on uses of music as a resource for mood regulation. So in order to construct a better social scientific approach to music, centered on *music's constrained contributions to human flourishing*, I examine some problems of self-realization in modern life and their relation to music, and I look at ways in which competitive individualism – which I believe to be an important feature of modern societies – is apparent in people's relations to music. I draw on interviews that I and colleagues conducted with a number of people about their musical practices, and interpret them using critical social theory. In spite of this emphasis on critique, my overall perspective is not a pessimistic one (though it is one troubled by aspects of contemporary society and culture) and in a final section, I summarize some aspects of what I call music's *constrained enrichment* of people's individual lives.

Chapter 3 then moves beyond the individual level to people's intimate relations, and asks: what means has popular music culture provided for enhancing people's experiences of sexual love? My focus in this chapter is historical and roughly chronological, concentrating on the period from

1945 to the present, and it is genre-based, examining the prevailing ways in which particular genres encoded ideas of sex, sexuality, and gender. I confine myself in this chapter to the "mainstream" popular music genres of rock and pop in the Anglophone world, their various sub-genres, and black musical genres of soul, R&B, and hip hop. I begin by distinguishing my approach from the main ways in which questions of sex and sexuality have been approached in music studies: critical musicology's appropriation of post-structuralist theory, and neo-Deleuzean ideas of rock as a music of bodily desire. Instead, I focus, in line with the approach developed in Chapter 2, on the affective experiences that music can help generate in ordinary life, here looking at how different genres have involved diverse configurations of emotion and feeling at discrete stages in their historical development. I listen to a range of musical examples, but the approach remains sociological in orientation, examining the ways in which sexual desire and vulnerable needs for attachment to others become institutional-ized into historically changing processes of courtship, romance, and marriage.

The chapter takes the "countercultural moment" of the 1960s as pivotal and relates this to the rock/pop division that is crucial to understanding popular music culture in the late twentieth century, and which lingers today. Against notions that music is valuable because of its close links to sexual freedom, I show that a much wider range of emotions and feelings have been apparent in a great deal of popular music, not only in the lyrics to popular songs, but in the way that these emotions and feelings were embodied in music, and combined with words and images. I trace the origins of rock countercultural notions of sexual freedom in bohemianism's view that personal sexuality is compromised by convention. In doing so, I criticize some major ways in which those notions of sexual freedom were articulated, but I also criticize conservative thinking. What we need, I argue, is a conception of the ordinary pleasures of music in relation to sex and love. (Here, as throughout the book as a whole, my argument shows the influence of certain versions of cultural studies, most notably the kind of respect for "ordinary" and working-class experience apparent in the work of writers such as Raymond Williams.) Against rock's rejection of various genres for their lack of authenticity, I show that much (though by no means all) post-war popular music made available a rich commentary on questions of sex, romance, and intimacy – and "commentary" here includes the articulation of emotion and feeling through musical sound. I show this mainly through a defense of popular music's relations to sex and love. This includes consideration of recent pop music that has been lambasted in the media for its sexual explicitness, and scrutiny of debates about hip hop's supposed misogyny. This is no populist celebration of pop however. Pop music has reflected, and constituted, troubling aspects of modern culture: misogyny, narcissism, and excessive sentimentality. We would flourish through music more, I argue, if music addressed a wider variety of emotional contexts and psychic dynamics. The ambivalence of music's ability to contribute to human flourishing is therefore re-emphasized.

Chapters 4 and 5 turn to the question of how we might flourish *together* in modern societies. Chapter 4 focuses on co-present sociability and publicness, and also the related question of locality (which is a kind of extended co-presence). The guiding question is as follows: how might music enhance collective experience among people who share the same space? I begin the discussion by analyzing the work of three writers who have made important contributions to understanding music's relationships to community and social life. In particular, they offer ways of understanding the social value of musical participation. I argue, however, that each of these writers seeks a notion of community that is not feasible under conditions of capitalist modernity, and is unlikely to be recoverable in complex modern societies, even in more equal and emancipated ones. Christopher Small underestimates the ways in which the Afro-diasporic forms he values are a product of modernity, and he assumes that musical practices directly reflect the fundamental features of the societies from which they derive. Charles Keil draws too strong a line between participations that "revitalize, equalize and decentralize" (Keil , 1994/1966: 98) and negative forms, underestimating ambivalence. He bases his views of participation on a Freudo-Marxian politics that is too optimistic about human psychology and too pessimistic about modern societies. Finally, Thomas Turino shows such a deep yearning for experiences of (comm)unity that he finds valuable forms of musical practice only in restricted pockets of modern life. My claim, in response to these authors, is that we need to look for beneficial experiences of sociability in life as it is currently lived, and not aspire to impossible levels of communality. For this reason, I then turn to accounts of the pleasurable and life-enriching sociality people experience when they sing together, dance together, and play music together in modern societies. There is, I argue, considerable evidence of rich music-related sociability that should not be overlooked in a quest for ideal forms of communal existence. If music is already, here and now, providing such experiences, though in constrained ways, how might we theorize music's continuing ability to enhance sociality and sociability in ordinary life, even amidst sometimes appalling and often troubling circumstances? I offer three routes (noting limitations where appropriate): phenomenological sociology's attention to the way in which music offers shared experiences of time; ideas from anthropology and Durkheimian sociology concerning a primal need in humans for intense experiences of collectivity; and the capabilities approach discussed in Chapter 2, which emphasizes human needs for affiliation, and our interdependence and shared vulnerability. The capabilities approach has the advantage of directing our attention to questions of social justice, and of encouraging accounts of how some social and institutional arrangements might be more effective than others in enhancing music's contribution to social life. In line with this focus on social justice, I discuss the way in which social class inhibits access to the benefits of amateur music-making; examine what conditions might allow particular cities or towns to develop as thriving musical places; and, finally, discuss how cultural production in capitalist modernity distorts musical labor markets, allowing a certain musical diversity, but inhibiting people's chances to make a living out of music-making, other than a lucky few.

Chapter 5 moves away from co-present forms of sociality and publicness to mediated ones. It addresses the role that aesthetic experience and musical experience might play in establishing relations of commonality in complex modern societies. The chapter moves from philosophy and the history of ideas to more concrete and sociologically informed case studies. I begin by discussing post-Enlightenment hopes that aesthetic experience might establish a basis for people to live together peacefully, across different communities. Such thinking has been thoroughly critiqued by Marxists, post-structuralists, and social scientists. In order to defend aesthetic experience, there have recently been some efforts to reconstruct an emancipatory conception of aesthetic experience based on commonality across different communities. Clearly, such efforts are relevant to a consideration of the value of aesthetic experience, and of music. However, from my perspective, these efforts (e.g., by Rancière and Garnham) lack concreteness and an adequate attention to the institutions that sustain publicness. So, to explore how we might construct better understandings of music's contribution to a commonality that valuably transcends social difference (rather than violently suppresses or dismisses it), I make a number of moves. First of all, given that emancipatory conceptions of the aesthetic are often understood as being based upon the value of aesthetic deliberation, or at least reflection, I examine some of the ways in which people talk about why they value music. The problem though is that the value of aesthetic experience is not at all easily captured by language. So I make a second move: to consider the idea that music's most valuable contribution to collective human life might be to advance political struggles for a better distribution of flourishing. My claim is that music's most significant effects on the world are not directly political, in the sense of contributing to forms of publicness that involve deliberation, or that advance political struggle, but instead relate to the sustenance of a public sociability, which keeps alive feelings of solidarity and community. In this and in other ways too, musical culture develops values and identities that feed into deliberation, democracy, and politics in substantial but rather indirect ways.

The rest of the chapter then concretizes the discussion of aesthetics, commonality, and publicness by looking at a number of case studies, concentrating on different forms of musical collectivity. First of all, I examine collectivities based on shared enjoyment of particular genres (such as extreme metal) and star performers. Although not without significance and value, I argue, such musical collectivities offer too fragmented a means of assessing music's relation to collective human flourishing. It is to the crucial institution of the nation that we must turn for evidence of how musical-aesthetic experience might fare in terms of enhancing meaningful community across space and time. I examine case studies of various relations between music and identity in modern nations, concentrating on questions of nationalism and cosmopolitanism. I criticize an account that finds significant musical cosmopolitanism in international flows of rock music. I find hope for music's ability to transcend difference in the perhaps surprising context of Afghanistan. Latin America provides a number of examples of where music associated with marginalized ethnic and class groups came to be identified as "national" music. Turkey offers a striking example of music's ability, in the right institutional circumstances, to bridge differences of religion and sexuality. Finally, and more pessimistically, drawing on the work of Paul Gilroy, I discuss how the inspiring cosmopolitanism of Afro-diasporic music has been affected by commercialization and globalization in the neo-liberal era. Music's ability to unite people across space and time, and thereby enable their collective flourishing, I conclude, is real, but specific, and highly vulnerable to systemic changes, such as increasing consumerism, commodification, and competitiveness. A final section briefly rehearses the perspective of the book as a whole.

2

Feeling and Flourishing

2.1 Music, Affect, Emotion

Nearly everyone agrees that music is a cultural form that has strong connections to emotions, feelings, and moods: the realm of affect. It is not surprising then that for hundreds of years considerable attention has been paid to the relations between music and affect. Here I briefly examine approaches from philosophical aesthetics, cultural theory, and psychology in order to contextualize my own approach, which, as I made clear in Chapter 1, examines music's capacity to enrich our lives via the feelings and emotions it engenders, and the limits of this capacity in modern societies.

Debates in philosophical aesthetics have centered on issues such as how music, as a non-sentient object, can possibly "express" emotion; on understanding how listeners might be able to feel emotions that mirror those expressed in music, such as feeling sadness in response to sad music, when they lack the beliefs that usually go with emotions such as sadness; and on why listeners would seek out negative emotions such as sadness in music.[1] These are intellectually interesting questions but they often seem far removed from the questions of value and experience that are central to my approach in this book. Philosopher Kathleen Marie Higgins (2011) has shown how, in the nineteenth and twentieth centuries, serious aesthetic

---

[1] See Davies (2010) who provides a helpful summary of philosophical theories of music and emotion. Musicologists have recently turned their attention to emotion (see Spitzer, 2009), but the shadows of formalism and structuralism, discussed later in this paragraph, still loom. See also Cook and Dibben (2010) for a good survey of musicological approaches to music and emotion.

thought moved away from earlier concerns with values and ethics, and she attributes this drift to the rise of a type of aesthetics that was centered on the question of how form creates beauty: a formalism derived from Kantian aesthetics and shaped by the concerns of the nineteenth-century German writer Hanslick with musical structure. Higgins outlines three predominant historical Western explanations of the relationship between music and emotion: that music *imitates* or *represents* emotions, that it *arouses* them, and that it *expresses* them (the first two of these have often overlapped and interacted). For ancient and medieval thinkers, relations between music and feelings were understood as strongly intersubjective, and with significant ethical implications. Imitation theory, for example, emphasized music's profound impact on character and on society; medieval arousal theorists such as Augustine emphasized the mixed blessings of music's appeal to the emotions, in terms of its ability to foster virtue or vice. Higgins shows how, from the eighteenth century onwards, especially under the influence of Kantian forms of formalist structural analysis, understandings of musical emotion lost this connection to ethics and intersubjectivity. Imitation, arousal, and expression theory were all revived in the twentieth century, but on formalist terms. Oriented towards analytical precision, the primary interest was in how the formal structure of music afforded emotions. For Higgins, the roles of "context" and "association" of meaning in producing emotions in listeners were sidelined. Even where association and context were discussed, as in musicologist Leonard Meyer's highly influential *Emotion and Meaning in Music* (1957), they were generally treated as an afterthought to questions of structure. Association and context were overshadowed by analysis of structural arousals of anticipation and deferral, and affective responses were often undifferentiated.

Higgins provides a philosophical account of musical affect which emphasizes its value in enriching people's lives, and in particular how people might live their lives together.[2] In this respect, she provides a corrective to dominant trends in philosophical aesthetics of music and in musicology. Her approach, and that of other writers who seek to reconnect affect with ethics, intersubjectivity, and value (see following text), also suggests some limitations of

---

[2] I think that Higgins is too optimistic about music's ability to transcend the limitations of the societies that produce it, a fault her excellent book shares with other writers that I discuss later. Also, I use Nussbaum's account of music and emotion, rather than Higgins', because I find the former's psychoanalytically informed model richer, and more able to address the complexity of human subjectivity.

the recent "affective turn" in cultural theory. Theorists of culture and affect have usefully pointed beyond the limitations of an excessive focus on signification, meaning, and discourse (apparent in media and cultural studies) towards the complex bodily effects of cultural experience.[3] The affective turn in cultural theory has the benefit of recognizing that sensations, moods, and feelings are a key part of cultural experience alongside emotion, and that there are important somatic dimensions to affect. This is good, because responses to culture should not be treated primarily as a matter of intellectual interpretation and evaluation. However, some affective cultural theorists are too inclined to dismiss emotion as a category of affect. For example, some researchers influenced by Deleuze differentiate affect, defined hazily as a "pre-personal intensity," from emotion as something "owned and recognised" (Massumi, 1995: 84). The implication is that emotion is a category primarily of interest to liberal-humanist conceptions of subjectivity, which need to be transcended. In my view, neither humanism nor emotion, nor the rich history of thinking about affect in philosophy, should be dismissed quite as easily as that. Emotions matter, in part because they potentially provide appraisals of our situation in life – they are linked in complex, opaque but important ways to ethics and intersubjectivity.

From a very different standpoint from cultural theory, music psychology has also indicated the very wide range of affective experiences that people in modern societies have in relation to music. In order to understand musical affect, some psychologists and other writers have paid special attention to strong emotional experiences. Undoubtedly, the most notable is Alf Gabrielsson, who, with colleagues, has collated over 1300 accounts of strong musical experiences, and has provided an elaborate system to categorize them. Listing just some of the categories and sub-categories gives a flavor of the richness of the material, and the variety of strong experiences that people report: when music takes over; merging with the music; feeling light, floating, leaving one's body; the content and meaning of life; presence in life, ultimate moments; changed view of oneself and one's life; music and transcendence; contact with divinity; making contact with one's innermost self; confirmation through music (Gabrielsson, 2011).

---

[3] See, for example, Grossberg (1992) and Gilbert (2004) who explains how the conception of affect in cultural theory might help illuminate cultural experience, using examples from music. Against those theorists of affect who claim that signification has been overemphasized in much cultural theory, Gilbert argues that we need to understand both meaning and affect. See also Gregg and Seigworth (2010) for a collection of "affect theory."

Gabrielsson is aware that many experiences of music are not of this kind. But does a focus on strong experiences present a distorted understanding of relations between music and affect in general? Other analysts suggest that this is the case. According to John Sloboda (2010), summarizing a large number of studies, everyday (a significant word which we shall return to later in this chapter) musical emotions tend to be of low intensity rather than high, to be mostly unmemorable, and to be short-lived and multiple rather than sustained. Furthermore, they often involve negative emotions such as irritation, disapproval, and dislike, and prioritize basic rather than complex emotions. What is more, many everyday musical experiences are hardly *aesthetic* experiences at all, in the sense of experiences oriented towards beauty, pleasure, and other forms of reward from the perceptions of artistic objects. They tend to involve other goals rather than aesthetic satisfaction. Sloboda distinguishes four recurring features of self-chosen music use: distraction, energizing, entrainment (using music to achieve synchronization, e.g., aerobics classes), and meaning enhancement. A social-scientific account of ways in which music might enrich people's lives needs to take account of these very divergent relations to musical experience.

This brief survey only touches the surface of a vast body of writing and research about music and affect. Nevertheless, I draw two implications from it. First, we need a broad understanding of musical affect, one which would include aesthetic experiences (where people primarily seek beauty or other aesthetic responses from music) but also other affective states that are not primarily aesthetic, such as relaxation or invigoration. Second, as Higgins suggests, understanding of musical affect needs to be related to questions of value and ethics. This would involve considering how we might value music's contribution to the affective dimensions of people's lives, to their moods, feelings, and emotions. I would also add that musical affect needs to be linked to questions of power and politics, to the ways in which musical experience in modern societies is deeply influenced by social forces.

2.2   Emotions, Narrative Play, and Music

In her book, *Upheavals of Thought* (2001), the philosopher Martha Nussbaum provided an account of the ethical importance of emotions, which illuminates the relationship of culture and music to emotions, and in turn advances our understanding of how musical experience might enhance people's lives.

Emotions have a narrative structure. "The understanding of any single emotion is incomplete," Nussbaum writes, "unless its narrative history is grasped and studied for the light it sheds on the present response" (236). This suggests a central role for the arts in human self-understanding, because narrative artworks of various kinds (whether musical or visual or literary) "give us information about these emotion-histories that we could not easily get otherwise" (236). So narrative artworks are important for what they show the person who is eager to understand the emotions, and also because of the role they play in people's emotional lives.

Nussbaum grounds her conception of emotions in a psychoanalytically informed account of subjectivity. Rather than the bizarrely non-feeling subject to be found in the Lacanian tradition favored by much post-structuralist cultural studies, she draws on writings by the British psychotherapist D.W. Winnicott (1971), associated with the "object relations" approach. For Nussbaum and Winnicott, the potentially valuable role that artistic experience might take in people's lives is suggested by studies of children playing. Storytelling and narrative play cultivate the child's sense of her own aloneness, her inner world. The capacity to be alone is supported by the way in which such play develops the ability to imagine the good object's presence when the object is not present, and play deepens the inner world. Narrative play can help us understand the pain of others, and to see them in non-instrumental ways. Children can be given a way of understanding their own sometimes frightening and ambivalent psychology, so that they become interested in understanding their subjectivity, rather than fleeing from it. Stories and play can militate against depression and helplessness, by feeding the child's interest "in living in a world in which she is not perfect or omnipotent" (237). They contribute to the struggle of love and gratitude versus ambivalence, and of active concern against the helplessness of loss. These dynamics continue into adult life – this, of course, is a fundamental insight of psychoanalytically informed thought – and adults too benefit from narrative play.

How might this relate to music as a particular type of cultural and aesthetic experience? Nussbaum claims that much music, in most modern societies, is closely connected to emotions, or at least is ideally thought to be so. A problem though is that music as such does not contain representational or narrative structures of the sort that are the typical objects of concrete emotions in life, or in other kinds of aesthetic experience such as films or novels. This makes it less obvious how music itself can be about our lives. Music is of course often linked to stories – in songs, operas, ballads, and so on – and, even when it is not, is often highly discursively mediated, by the use of titles, instructions on scores, or critical discourse that seeks to interpret what music means. But we still need an account of the way musical sounds per se encourage emotion and feeling.

Nussbaum delineates a number of ways in which narrative fiction, such as novels, films, and plays, allows for emotion on the part of the reader/ spectator. Emotions can be felt

- towards characters, sharing emotion through identification or reacting against the emotions of a character;
- towards the sense of life embodied in the text as a whole, reacting to it sympathetically or critically;
- towards one's own possibilities;
- in response to coming to understand something about life or about oneself (272).

Music can allow for emotional responses in similar ways, says Nussbaum, but with the emotional material embodied in peculiarly musical forms. Music's distinctive language is one of compressed and elliptical reference to our inner lives and our prospects; for Nussbaum, it is close to dreaming in this respect. Our responses to music are crystallizations of general forms of emotion, rather than reactions to characters, as in narrative fiction. So most musical emotions, for Nussbaum, fall into the second and third of the categories just listed. Nussbaum agrees with Schopenhauer that music is "well-suited to express parts of the personality that lie beneath its conscious self-understanding" (269), bypassing habit and intellect. Music "frequently has an affinity with the amorphous, archaic, and extremely powerful emotional materials of childhood" (269). Its semiotic indefiniteness gives it a superior power to engage with our emotions.

Using examples from Mahler, Nussbaum claims that musical works can contain structures in which great pain is crystallized and construct "an implied listener who experiences that burning pain" (272); or they may "contain forms that embody the acceptance of the incredible remoteness of everything that is good and fine" and construct a listener who experiences desolation. Or a musical work may contain forms that embody the "hope of transcending the pettiness of daily human transactions." Music is somehow able to embody "the idea of our urgent need for and attachment to things outside ourselves that we do not control" (272). Its capacity to do so is not natural; it is the product of complex cultural histories, and experience of such emotions depends on familiarity with the conventions that allow them, either through everyday contact with musical idioms or through education. These emotions might be hard to explicate as they happen, and Nussbaum is clear that not all works invoke deep emotion – they can just be enjoyable or interesting.

Nussbaum does not provide, and does not seek to provide, a complete theory of musical value. She does not explore the importance of enjoyment, pleasure, and sociability, or the rewards of "interestingness." Music that attempts to innovate, and to explore new forms of sound, can valuably add to the diversity of expression in a society; such music will often need, and deserve, public support.[4] But Nussbaum helps us see that one important way in which music matters is that it can provide its own version of the ways that stories and plays potentially enhance our lives, by cultivating and enriching our inner world and by feeding processes of concern, sympathy, and engagement, against helplessness and isolation.

2.3 Human Flourishing, Aesthetic Experience, and Music

Nussbaum offers a perspective that relates the value of aesthetic experience to emotion and human well-being, and which also addresses the specificity of music as part of that account. Of course, music might fail to enhance flourishing much of the time. Nussbaum is suggesting what music *can* offer, how it *might* add to prospects for living different versions of a good life.

This idea of living a good life, or flourishing, is fundamental to the Aristotelian tradition in philosophy, but has only rarely been addressed in critical social sciences and humanities in recent decades, perhaps because of some misunderstandings about the concepts. I will say just three things about these ideas here, although they underpin my approach throughout this book. The first point is that flourishing is not the same thing as happiness or pleasure. Although pleasure and happiness can be important elements of flourishing, they are better thought of as occasional (and desirable) results of a flourishing life. But if they are perceived as the main goals of life, then

---

[4] As well as being valuable for its avoidance of stale convention, musical innovation can also lead to new articulations of emotion. My view is that music that is both innovative and evocative of strong emotion has a greater potential to contribute to human flourishing than music that is merely innovative.

there is a danger of underestimating the rewards associated with loyalty, tenacity, sacrifice, courage, and even love. What is more, as social theorist Andrew Sayer points out, flourishing has connotations of activity, whereas happiness merely connotes a state of mind (Sayer, 2011: 234).

This leads to the second point, which is that the correct way to understand flourishing does not in itself imply an individualistic or subjectivist conception of ethics and politics. We need an objectivist understanding of well-being, to avoid the emphasis on personal pleasure and happiness that makes many kinds of modern thinking so limited. Well-being or flourishing should not be thought of merely as a subjective state of mind. As the Indian philosopher and economist Amartya Sen (1999) has shown, the poor often lower their expectations. We are often unsure of why we feel good or bad, but we can usually give some sort of account of what has been happening to us and what matters to us. The presence of these factors, and our ability to take them into account, means that we can often realize that our evaluations were mistaken – "that we had a false sense of security, or that we had underestimated how much we were appreciated, and so on" (Sayer, 2011: 134). Our subjective assessments of our well-being are deeply fallible. So flourishing is better thought of "in terms of objective states of being which people strive to discover, achieve or create" (134). But, as Sayer emphasizes, it is vital to realize that this objectivist conception of well-being does not mean that there is "only one good way of living" (135). We should take a pluralist, but not relativist, view that there are many kinds of well-being, but "not just any way of life constitutes well-being." What is good is not simply relative to one's point of view – and social science can help develop ways of thinking about what might be good in a more objective way. That is one of the things this book seeks to do.

This leads to my third point, which is that while the concept of flourishing should not be linked to one conception of goodness, such as a Western ethnocentric one, the best conceptions of flourishing recognize that fundamental human characteristics and needs are widely shared, though they may take very different forms in different societies. Nussbaum herself has contributed to the development of recent thinking on this subject, along with Sen. In his work, Sen questioned the emphasis on income and wealth in understanding the goals of addressing global inequality through "development" (e.g., Sen, 1999). He also questioned happiness, utility, and pleasure as the basis for understanding a good life, by emphasizing the importance of freedom and justice. For Sen, what people are able to do is more important than states of mind in assessing the good life. For this reason, Sen developed the term "capability" to refer to the ability of people to do certain things, should they choose to. The goal of development should be to enable such functionings. Nussbaum developed this approach and in her book *Frontiers of Justice* (2006) went so far as to make a list of 10 central human capabilities she thought were generally necessary for well-being and a life with dignity (Nussbaum, 2006: 76–77 – all the quotations from Nussbaum in the following text are from these pages). It includes fundamental capabilities such as not dying prematurely, having good health and shelter, bodily integrity (including security against violent assault), and control over one's political and material environment. Needless to say, a flourishing musical life is greatly inhibited in situations where people are deprived of the aforementioned capabilities. But a number of Nussbaum's capabilities relate more directly to understanding the value of aesthetic experience in modern societies, and the value of music. I shall comment on them here, as a way of indicating the normative basis underlying my analysis of music in the rest of this chapter and throughout the book.

The most directly relevant of Nussbaum's list to the discussion so far is her fifth:

> Being able to have attachments to things and people outside ourselves; to love those who love and care for us, to grieve at their absence; in general, to love, to grieve, to experience longing, gratitude, and justified anger. Not having one's emotional development blighted by fear and anxiety.

As we have already seen, in *Upheavals of Thought*, Nussbaum suggested how access to a rich set of aesthetic experiences (including musical ones) might help us to understand and enhance these vital emotional capabilities, in ourselves. That is not a solipsistic or liberal–individualist conception, because the key emotions here are other-directed. And in this later discussion, the purpose is one of social justice: considering how everyone should be able to live lives that incorporate such capabilities, if they choose to. That means making certain musical resources available in all societies.[5]

But Nussbaum does not imply that the value of the arts and of music should be thought of purely, or even primarily, in terms of its ability to

---

[5] This, of course, raises the question of whether some capabilities might need to be prioritized over others, and what implications this may have for the allocation of scarce resources in societies.

enhance our emotional lives. Capability 4 lists the following elements of the importance of "senses, imagination, and thought":

> Being able to use the senses, to imagine, think and reason – and to do these things in a "truly human way," a way informed by and cultivated by an adequate education, including, but by no means limited to, literacy and basic mathematical and scientific training. Being able to use imagination and thought in connection with experiencing and producing works and events of one's own choice, religious, literary, musical, and so forth. Being able to use one's mind in ways protected by guarantees of freedom of expression with respect to both political and artistic speech, and freedom of religious exercise. Being able to have pleasurable experiences and to avoid nonbeneficial pain.

And capability 9 suggests the intrinsic importance of "being able to laugh, play, to enjoy recreational activities," which takes into account issues of sensuousness, pleasure, and enjoyment more than Nussbaum's rather intellectualist discussion of music and emotion, outlined earlier, was able to do. This is an issue that I pursue in the following text and in Chapter 3.

Finally, capability 7, affiliation, concerns "being able to live with and toward others, to recognize and show concern for other human beings, to engage in various forms of interaction." Another way we can build on Nussbaum's approach, then, is to consider ways in which music might valuably enhance such interactions, and our ability to live with and towards others, to recognize them and to show concern for them. This takes us beyond any sense of capabilities as somehow individualistic. These are topics that I return to in Chapters 4 and 5.

2.4   Musical Flourishing Beyond Contemplative Cultivation

So far, I have sought to defend a notion of the good life and human flourishing as the basis of an account of the value of music's relation to affective experience, and to give indications of why the capabilities approach developed by Sen, Nussbaum, and others offers the best understanding of such human flourishing available. To recap, this is because that approach is objectivist and pluralist, and takes into account both our individual needs and our needs for affiliation with others. In its attention to social justice, it also valuably suggests the need to consider what social arrangements are needed to allow humans to flourish, and this draws our attention to the question of how to create thriving musical cultures where people can flourish musically.

However, as I have been suggesting, Nussbaum's account of music and emotion, while it helpfully clarifies how music might (valuably) crystallize emotion in particular ways, lacks attention to some important aspects of musical flourishing. I shall suggest three objections to Nussbaum's approach to music and emotion here, as a way of recognizing its limits, but also in order to complement the valuable insights it carries, and thereby build up a more comprehensive model of music's relations to affective experience and the good life.

A first objection is that Nussbaum's account depends on an appreciation of high culture, and so is not applicable to the more ordinary aesthetic experiences that might be available to most people. I defend her account by showing that her delineation of emotional responses by listeners might also be applied to more "accessible" forms of popular music. A second potential objection is that her account relies on notions of self-cultivation which are discredited; I defend a particular conception of self-realization through culture. A third concerns the way in which Nussbaum's model equates good experiences of music with emotionally enriching contemplation and self-analysis. I agree with this objection, and discuss other aspects of music's value in this section, and the next.

Emotional resonances in popular music

Nussbaum offers a rather specific and possibly high-minded understanding of musical emotion, based on the case of Mahler, a composer of music that was explicitly intended to provide deep and enriching musical experiences of a particular kind. Arguably, given the way in which education and cultural consumption work in highly marketized modern societies, this leaves self-realization through culture in the hands of the highly educated bourgeoisie (and a shallow cultural populism that suggests that there are no worthwhile rewards to be gained from classical music only makes this problem worse). But I want to suggest that Nussbaum's approach, or something like it, could be extended to music that might more easily be understood by a wide range of people, across different social classes. Nussbaum needs complementing with the kind of approach to culture that is apparent in the best versions of cultural studies, where art and culture are understood as fundamentally rooted in "ordinary" experience (see Williams,

1965/1961), and where the complex social forces that shape that experience are explored.[6] This means taking seriously music that may be dismissed as mere entertainment or as "popular culture."[7] A character in Noel Coward's play *Private Lives* (1930) remarks "Strange how potent cheap music is," but we can go beyond the patronizing ways in which this observation has been used – as if popular music's emotional power is somehow surprising or contradictory. All kinds of popular culture allow for rich reflection on our own emotional lives, and on those of others.

Considering popular music brings another benefit. It allows us to go beyond Nussbaum's concern with the "purely musical" by considering how musical sources of affect combine with other sources. Nussbaum is right, given her philosophical concerns, to try to separate out what is specific to music in terms of its emotional qualities, as opposed to the various other forms of communication with which music is often combined, such as lyrics, or "secondary texts" concerning performers and writers. However, in reality, the experience of music is nearly always inseparable from these and other semiotic resources, and a consideration of the value of music needs to understand that music takes many different forms in modern societies, and that these different mediations interact in complex ways.[8] To put it simply,

---

[6] My own approach is strongly influenced by certain versions of cultural studies. But cultural studies and cultural theory have made only limited advances in theorizing affect, in spite of the admirable efforts of Eve Kosofky Sedgwick (2002) and others – see my discussion of the "affective turn" in footnote 3 of this chapter. The most famous reference to emotion and feeling in cultural studies is Raymond Williams' concept of "structure of feeling" (Williams, 1965/1961; Williams, 1977). So it might be worth briefly explaining to Williams' admirers why this concept is not particularly relevant to the questions of musical value, affect, and flourishing that I address in this book (though Williams' approach is in general a big underlying influence). That concept was developed by Williams (1977: 130–135) as a way of referring to the character of life in a particular place and time, as part of a methodological discussion of how that character might best be reconstructed historically, as Paul Jones (2004: 20–23) convincingly shows. There is much to learn from and be inspired by in Williams' historical methodology. But the "feeling" part of Williams' phrase is only very briefly elaborated by him; it refers in an intriguingly loose way to "the felt sense" of life as a whole.

[7] That includes taking seriously not only popular musical artifacts, but also, as we shall see in Chapter 5, though rather briefly, the ambivalent concept of the popular.

[8] The most valuable theorization of the multiply mediated nature of modern music culture is that of Georgina Born. "Since meaning inheres in the social, theoretical, technological and visual mediations of music as well as in the musical sound, and since these all play a part in the construction of the musical sound, we should consider the musical object as subsuming these mediations" (Born, 1995: 23). See also Born (2005) for a later development of her ideas in terms of historically shifting "assemblages" of musical creativity.

our understanding of good experiences of music should not be artificially distilled down, so that only "the music itself" is considered to be relevant. Music is always embedded within complex networks of meaning and affect.

Because so much of popular music revolves around the song, rather than instrumental music, this allows us to think about the way in which songs allow for a conjunction of the emotional effects of music with those produced by words, narratives, and visuals. I want to explore the emotional potential of popular music, and its intertextual combination of music and narrative, through a consideration of Candi Staton's 1976 hit "Young hearts run free." This was a product of the genre dubiously known as disco, which has often been interpreted as a perversion of more politically conscious soul music. Here, in this despised form of music, as in soul music, there are rich resources for considering emotions about issues such as love, fidelity, and personal resilience. I begin from lyrics, but I also show that music is vital in producing the emotions that the song makes available to those who hear it.

Most modern music tends to be connected to a variety of discourses and meanings. Perhaps the most notable source of extra-musical meaning in popular music is lyrics. We might also read or hear stories about performers. In the era of YouTube, many of us have regular access to recordings of performances, including clips from old television programs, promotional videos, and live shows filmed on mobile phones. Listeners (who are often spectators too) can therefore often engage in the activity covered by the first of Nussbaum's categories of where emotion might be directed in artworks: we react towards characters, sharing emotion through identification or reacting against the emotions of a character. "Young hearts run free," like many popular songs, is a first person song: it explicitly uses an "I." A central character, a first-person narrator "played" by Candi herself,[9] dispenses advice to young women to be true to themselves and to follow their desires.

---

[9] In songs that use the first person, there is a range of relationships between the "I" and "we" in the lyric, on the one hand, and the singer on the other. In songs performed by well-known artists and strongly associated with them, there is often a strong sense that the song is a sincere expression of the singer's own feelings. An example might be Beyoncé's "Crazy in love" (2003), partly because it also features a rap by her then new partner Jay-Z; it feels as though this is a song about Beyoncé's feelings about being newly in lustful love with a man. In some songs, such as "Young hearts run free," there is a greater sense of a persona being adopted. Even there, though, the conventions of emotional intensity make it feel as though this is an expression of the singer's actual feelings – though, in fact, "Young hearts run free" was written by its producer Dave Crawford.

This is feminism with an individualistic twist: self-preservation should be the goal, and this is what is really going on today. But the lyrics are clever, because there is a poignant undertow: what sounds like a call for liberation is actually (or also) an expression of pain. While the words of the title refrain encourage freedom, the lead to the chorus enacts a struggle within Candi/the character: a hundred times a day, she says she is going to "turn loose" (leave), but she just cannot break away – perhaps because of her children. It is clear that the character "played" or embodied by Candi Staton wishes she had been able to enjoy the sexual freedom that she entreats her younger sisters to relish. And the sadness of her advice is also clear: if they do not, they will merely end up another lost and lonely wife. They'll count up the years, and they will be filled with tears.

I think I can hear in the music of "Young hearts run free" something of that tension between freedom and constraint, vitalization and sadness. The lead-in to the chorus is at the top of Candi's range, emphasizing her struggle. In the passage immediately before the chorus, the backing singers build our sense of anticipation for the "resolution" of the chorus by singing "oh, oh, oh" in a pentatonic ascent. But when that resolution comes, it is melancholy. After "Young hearts run free," the payoff is "never be hung up, hung up like my man and me." Rather than a straightforward celebration of liberation, the song is a dramatization of the tug between freedom and obligation, and about disillusioned love, about what happens when love really does not love you. Sadness is reinforced by the melancholy timbre of Candi Staton's voice, an edge of roughness that implies a mixture of vulnerability and experience.[10]

My claim is that the song encourages strong emotion in many listeners, and some might find that it opens a door to their inner lives. It covers all four of the ways in which emotions are evoked, in Nussbaum's discussion of music and emotion. In terms of identifying or reacting against the emotions of a character, listeners might pick up on the fact that the song involves a woman who has had children talking about women who do not yet have kids, and they might therefore identify with the character's regrets. Or some may react against this yearning for freedom, and feel more at peace with their own decision to commit to a long-term relationship. Some may feel anger as they identify with Candi's emphatic singing of "While he's busy

[10] This was apparent on the soul recordings that Candi Staton made in the late 1960s, even as a very young woman. Thanks to Dai Griffiths and an anonymous reader for help with "Young hearts."

loving every woman that he can" – followed by a "huh huh" that suggests "you know how it is" – and come to know more about their rage at a partner's infidelity. Remembering that this is a song from the 1970s, women and men of a certain age might reflect on the struggles of their own mothers and fathers, or even grandparents; some may feel a sense of forgiveness or anger as they follow that emotional pathway in the song. As I have tried to explain, I experience the sense of life embodied in the text as the tussle between freedom and obligation. Listeners who feel the same way might become aware of their feelings about their own version of this struggle, feeling anger, compassion, or guilt. They may experience secondary feelings of release or tension as they come to understand this aspect of themselves, if only temporarily. Some listeners, aware that the 1970s were the era when feminism was beginning to challenge long-standing assumptions about women and men in the West, may reflect on what it was like for a generation of older women to see younger women gain increasing opportunities for freedom; here emotions that are more directly engaged with social and political issues might be invoked.

Of course, such responses will often occur at a sub-conscious level, especially if the song is heard in relatively distracted settings. But even the fragments that one might pick up, listening to the song on the radio, or dancing to it at a party (when people are often highly focused on songs), might elicit versions of these various emotions in response to the song. Candi Staton teaches us that a four-minute disco recording can allow a listener to explore their own emotions and to imagine the emotional lives of others.[11]

However, it may be the case that my choice of a well-constructed popular *song* with rather intelligent lyrics to illustrate the emotional resonances of popular music may involve an excessive focus on semantic and narrative meaning rather than musical meaning. Popular music where lyrics are nonexistent (relatively rare in the most popular music of many societies in recent decades) or unimportant may also be rich in emotional effects. A classic jungle track can illustrate this: "We are ie" by Lennie De Ice (originally released in 1992; the version I have is on a 1995 CD compilation called *Routes from the Jungle*, where the title is given as "We are E"). This track involves only two sung phrases, both of them repeated many times: a phrase

---

[11] Even if I am right to detect emotional depth in Candi Staton's recording, however, how typical is it of modern popular song? Might the intense focus on love, sex, and relationships in commercial song make available to popular audiences a narrow, debased, distorted, and/or negatively sentimental set of emotions? I discuss these issues in some detail in Chapter 3.

that sounds like "We are E" but is actually a sped-up sample of an Arabic phrase from a rai track by Cheba Fadela and Cheb Sharaoui, and "Let me hear you scream" – though the "m" is cut off. One way to read the tune is to see it as taking the famous "Amen break" sample loop used in many hip hop and hardcore recordings – which is taken from an obscure 1969 funk b-side by the African-American band, the Winstons – and mixing it with a bass line taken from the Caribbean genre of ragga, and a vocal sample from an Algerian rai piece: a nice melange of musical multiculturalism. But the emotional effects are as interesting as the diverse sources. The feeling generated by the Amen break sample and the bass is one of energetic forward propulsion – this is music intended for clubs. The phrase of the title invokes the ecstatic unity of rave culture, under the influence of the drug MDMA, or ecstasy, or E. Yet the track is actually full of urban anxiety, even fear, not only through the minor key synth stabs, but also by the use of non-musical sounds sampled into the record: gunshots, and the repeated use of a tape recorder rewinding. "Rewind" in Caribbean dance music indicates pleasure – this is what the crowd shouts when they want to hear a particularly good bit of music again. But here it is a disorienting squiggle generating a mood of anxiety. And the "let me hear you scream" sample adds considerably to that feeling. It is slightly cut off, requiring the listener to wonder, "is he really saying 'scream'?" "We are E" sounds like what it is – a strange piece of found language. Sadness, strangeness, melancholy, excitement, danger, and anxiety are all mixed. What fears and thrills lurk in the club, and in the urban world outside? "We are ie" asked us to feel that confusion, if only for a fleeting moment, and this seemed more interesting and more appropriate to the environments where it was heard than music which celebrated loved-up unity on the dance floor.

Self-cultivation as bourgeois and ethnocentric?

Even if Nussbaum's ideas can be applied to music from beyond the high culture examples she employs, does her approach assume individuals who are oriented to self-realization, and thereby exclude most ordinary experience of music? Related to this, does her model reproduce the emphasis on self-cultivation in supposedly discredited notions of culture?

The fact that not all experiences of music lead to emotional self-enrichment is not in itself a problem for my argument. To value music for its *potential* to contribute to such emotional self-enrichment does not require the idea that *all* music should be capable of this, all or even most of the time. What matters is that some kinds of music offer this capacity for much of the time to many listeners – and across different social groups. Mahler's *Kindertotenlieder* (*Songs on the Death of Children*) and "Young hearts run free" may be wonderful pieces of music, but modern life offers many opportunities for people to collate music that they find emotionally powerful. However, my argument about the value of music takes into account the way that social forces affect music. Opportunities for emotional enrichment are unevenly distributed. People might be too busy, distracted, or depressed to make the most of them, even if they feel that they would benefit from better musical experiences. These are issues to which I shall return in discussing constraints on music's emancipatory potential. In historical terms, however, I think it is plausible to suggest that there are now unprecedented technological opportunities for individuals to find emotionally resonant music.

Is the very idea of a subject who develops herself through culture compromised by its links to Western, bourgeois notions of selfhood and of aesthetic canons? Might such a model as Nussbaum's be guilty of ethnocentrism and a submerged class politics? For some, her ideas may smack of a line of thinking about culture that goes back to nineteenth-century traditions of the German idea of *bildung* (self-cultivation) and the poet and essayist Matthew Arnold's adaptation of it for British cultural education. From a leftist perspective, literary historian Martin Ryle and philosopher Kate Soper have defended against postmodernist attack the goal of self-realization through learned culture.[12] They are clear that cultural self-realization "requires intellectual effort, and may come about only under a certain duress" (9). It depends on "resisting or deferring easier or less exacting types of engagement or gratification in the interests of an ultimately more memorable and cherishable satisfaction" (9). In this respect, it clearly has origins in certain types of religious thought. However, it offers rewards in this world not in another. The individualistic interpretation of self-realization can lead to a blithe indifference to the realities of life. But Ryle and Soper also see self-realization through culture as having a potentially strong social orientation, when it is combined with "a more historical, intersubjective and critically-honed sense of one's own identity and society,"

---

[12] For discussion of why the value of the concept of self-realization might still be valuable, in spite of the individualism and narcissism attached to certain uses of it, such as appropriations of the work of Abraham Maslow, see Hesmondhalgh and Baker (2011: 33–34), where the context is the possibilities or otherwise of self-realization through labor, and "creative labor" in particular. I have disgracefully forgotten the name of the person who recommended Ryle and Soper's book to me at a conference at London Metropolitan University in September 2011.

of a type explored in much culture. Furthermore, "cultural reflection helps
to awaken forms of sensibility which are immanently in contradiction with
instrumental economic 'ends'" (12). As part of their discussion, Ryle and
Soper raise an issue that I will return to in Chapter 5 regarding the
ambivalence of the category of the aesthetic as it developed in modern
Western thought after Kant. For them, the aesthetic confirms bourgeois
sensibility but, because it is grounded in a common human sensibility,
gestures towards a common culture. They make a convincing case that the
democratization of cultural self-realization, especially through educational
institutions, is not only possible and coherent, but desirable, and that attacks
on self-realization based on excessive critique of subjectivity leave little
ground upon which to defend culture, or indeed the idea that people should
live their lives well.

Beyond contemplative aesthetic experiences

There can be no doubt, however, that Nussbaum's perspective is centered
on a model of a listening self that is contemplative and self-analytical. She
offers an account of music and emotion centered on subjects who actively
seek self-realization through art. There are surely other ways to think about
the value of music in people's everyday lives, and indeed of the value of life
itself, than this contemplative ideal. Reflection is good but Socrates was
surely wrong when, according to Plato, he said that for human beings
"the unexamined life is not worth living" (Plato, *Apology*, 38). There are
many valuable experiences in life that do not involve contemplation or
introspection.

As we shall see shortly, recent leading contributions to the social science
of music have paid significant attention to the uses people make of music in
everyday life, at the more mundane levels of mood-enhancement, relaxation, invigoration, and so on. This turn to the everyday in social analysis of
music valuably moves discussion of music's positive effects into the realm of
mood and sensation, in a way that can complement the rather intellectualist
account of musical emotion offered by Nussbaum.

This attention to mood and sensation as well as emotion is also apparent
in some rival philosophical accounts of affect in relation to aesthetic experience, such as that of Jenefer Robinson in her book *Deeper Than Reason*
(2005). Robinson offers a fuller account than Nussbaum of musical affect,
and points to multiple sources of affective responses to music, including
more directly physiological reactions that do not necessarily involve

the kind of "appraisal" that Nussbaum and others see as important to understanding the ethical importance of emotions. Drawing on a range of psychological studies, Robinson suggests that it is mood, rather than emotion, which is commonly evoked by music. Even if Robinson's account of musical affect is fuller and more accurate than Nussbaum's, however, it is not necessarily inconsistent with Nussbaum's ideas about the value of how certain kinds of music can invoke life-enriching emotions.[13] In Section 2.6, I will argue that many of the recent social scientific accounts of music in everyday life suffer from an overly "thin" conception of the self, in contrast with Nussbaum's richer psychoanalytically informed notion. They also lack a critical historical account of the problems of subjectivity. Nevertheless, these accounts point to the somatic and physical aspects of music in ways that Nussbaum's approach fails to do. In this respect, Nussbaum is in danger of reproducing a neglect of embodied aspects of music which has generally characterized a great deal of musicology, and of arts scholarship more generally, perhaps influenced by the emphasis on the mind in the mainstream traditions of Western aesthetics since Kant. For example, here is aesthetician Roman Ingarden's seeming dismissal of the importance of the body for understanding music:

> We may doubt whether so-called dance music, when employed only as a means for keeping the dancers in step and arousing in them a specific passion for expression through movement, is music in the strict sense of the word (Roman Ingarden, quoted by McClary and Walser, 1994: 75).

In fact, as we shall see in discussing music's relationship to intimate experiences of love and sex in Chapter 3, some of the ways in which the body has been reinserted into discussions of music are as dubious as its exclusion by overly cognitivist analysis. Nevertheless, somatic experience matters in music. Many people value music for the way it allows for aesthetic experiences that combine bodily invigoration and emotional intensity. Paying proper attention to this fact may take us more into the realm of the demotic, the carnivalesque, and somatic, in ways that can complement Nussbaum's rather intellectualist focus on self-cultivation. Perhaps the foremost among these more somatic aesthetic experiences of music is dancing, and so

---

[13] Robinson's attention to physiological effects is valuable but she risks reducing emotion to physiology. Nussbaum's view is that emotions usually have a physiological character, but not always, and that seems correct to me.

I devote the next section to that topic, as a way of exploring the positive potential of music-related experiences beyond the contemplative self.

2.5   Musical Aesthetics and Bodily Experience: Dancing

What do people find pleasurable, rewarding, and even life-enhancing in dance?[14] Dancing, writes geography researcher Ben Malbon (1999: 86), involves a transformation that takes a person out of his or her ordinary world "and places them instead in a world of heightened sensitivity and altered perception of self, others and/or the environment." Cultural studies writer Iain Chambers eloquently captures the way in which dancing can transcend mere escape:

> Dancing, where the explicit and implicit zones of socialized pleasures and individual desires entwine in the momentary rediscovery of the "reason of the body" (Nietzsche), is undoubtedly one of the main avenues along which pop's sense "travels." Suspended over the predictable rhythms of the everyday, to dance often involves loaded steps, a pattern of obliquely registered tensions. These represent not only the contradictory pulls between work and pleasure, but also between a commonsensical view of pleasure ("letting off steam," "a well-earned break," "enjoying yourself") and a deeper, internalized moment where a serious self-realisation – sexual and social, private and public – is being pursued (Chambers, 1986: 17).

Malbon's informants and those of other analysts (such as Pini, 1997; Jackson, 2004) provide a valuable window on people's understanding of how dance enriches their lives. This man, interviewed by Phil Jackson, spoke about the way dancing allowed him to feel his body again:

---

[14]   I concentrate here on contemporary dancing in modern societies, partly because many of the main sources relate to contemporary clubbing. Typically for contemporary social science, interviewees are often committed aficionados – probably because it is easier to get people to speak about their enthusiasms. There seems to be a surprising dearth of research on other forms of social dancing, including dancing at private parties, weddings, and so on. I have sought to fill the gap with some of my own observations. I am referring here mainly to noncompetitive dancing. Of course, dance floors are never without an element of competitiveness, and dancing competitions undoubtedly have their pleasures, but their adherence to a system of rules brings them closer to sport.

> I work in front of a computer all week, sitting on my bum staring at this headache-inducing screen with one eye on my boss. … Then I get to go out at the weekend and dance and it's stunning, just moving and the music and the heat and my body feels like mine again (Jackson, 2002: 20).

This ability of dance to help people pleasurably to connect to their own physicality leads to a frequent comparison with sex. One woman told Jackson that "dancing allows me to enter a wonderful sensual place. It's almost as good as sex in terms of making your body feel fabulous" (21). Another woman told Jackson, "I get to be sexy. It seems silly, but I really enjoy it. When I'm in a club dancing my whole body feels hot and horny and alive." The same woman emphasized the need for the public sexual element in dance to be safe, playful, and contained. And as Vivienne Griffiths (1988: 118) explains, "the sensual pleasure young women derive from dancing is not simply directed at men." One woman told researcher Griffiths of the "free" feeling that dance gave her in the more ordinary surroundings of a simple disco: "You just hear the music and it completely takes over. It's very relaxing as you use every part of your body and move freely." Although people often talk of being taken over by music, this does not mean that reflexivity is abandoned altogether, in such a way that anyone should discount such experiences as merely automatic. A steady tempo and an interestingly patterned beat, observes Simon Frith (1996: 144), enable listeners to respond actively and to experience music "as a bodily as well as a mental matter." This is often as much about order and control as much as going wild – a pronounced steady beat often underlies dance music. Frith rightly points out too that dancers are often the most attentive of listeners. Malbon echoes this when he comments that dancing is "an expressive form of thinking, sensing, feeling and processing" (Malbon, 1999: 87). But Malbon makes a further move, which is surprisingly rare in writing on music and dance, when he refers to how dance is also a "source of personal and social *vitality*" (87, emphasis added). The concept he uses to understand such vitality is "flow," as developed by the psychologist Mihaly Csikszentmihalyi: the holistic sensation that people feel when they act with great involvement in something.

One of Csikszentmihalyi's earliest efforts to understand such flow experiences was a study of what he called rock dancing (Csikszentmihalyi, 1975) – the kind of free-form dancing that prevails in many non-competitive dance situations in the West. Csikszentmihalyi noted that such dancing involved a number of characteristics rather similar to other activities he studied, such as climbing and chess. Action and awareness were merged. Dancers centered their attention on a limited set of stimuli, allowing an immersion in the present. There was a loss of self-consciousness, but with it a heightened awareness of internal processes. People felt simultaneously in control of and yet merged with their environment. The demands made on participants were coherent and non-contradictory. It is, of course, music that allows dancers to focus their awareness on that limited set of stimuli, and so the value of dance is intimately related to that of music.

However, as Csikszentmihalyi (1975: 107) points out, there are a number of features of dancing which limit flow, and for some people, make it difficult to enjoy dancing at all. One is a lack of direct, ambiguous feedback; people are unsure how they are doing, and most of us need to be in a situation of relative sociable trustfulness to achieve flow. Another is that, because, as Csikszentmihalyi notes, dancing is often more strongly linked to social activities than the other flow activities he studied (and music's sociability is something we return to in Chapter 4), it takes place in contexts where loss of self-consciousness is difficult to achieve in a sustained way.[15] Nevertheless, for the millions of people who enjoy it, dancing is an activity that allows for richly shared experiences of flow. And it seems to me that Csikszentmihalyi and Malbon are absolutely right to consider flow as life-enhancing (see also Csikszentmihalyi, 1990). Composing, performing, and listening to music also, in different ways, allow for flow.

Dance is a form of play, as writers such as Csikszentmihalyi make clear, but it is also an aesthetic experience. More than the instances of listening discussed by Nussbaum, dance provides musical experiences of a bodily kind. Emotions involve physiological processes, to different degrees. Some music is more kinetic and somatic than others, and this requires a somewhat different understanding of relations of music, emotion, and aesthetics than a focus on emotion-as-cognition can provide. The most notable contribution in philosophical aesthetics to an understanding of the ways in which somatic aesthetic experiences might be valuable in people's lives

---

[15] Loudness matters at parties, clubs and gigs. I've been at parties where the music is so quiet that you can not only hear conversation, which is bad enough, you can also hear feet moving on the dance floor, and fellow dancers singing the wrong words to the song. For most people, only a great deal of alcohol and other stimulants can preserve flow in such a situation – and this can lead to other problems that then destroy it (bumping into others, falling over, fighting).

comes from American pragmatism.[16] The American pragmatist philosopher and educationalist John Dewey argued that art's special function and value lie (in Richard Shusterman's gloss) "not in any specialized particular end but in satisfying the live creature in a more global way, by serving a variety of ends, and above all by enhancing our immediate experience which invigorates and vitalizes us, thus aiding our achievement of whatever further ends we pursue" (Shusterman, 2000: 9). Art is thus at once instrumentally valuable and a satisfying end in itself. Art "keeps alive the power to experience the common world in its fullness," in Dewey's words (1980/1934: 138), and provides the means to make our lives more meaningful and tolerable through the introduction of a "satisfying sense of unity" into experience. This does not mean that pragmatist aesthetics relies on a model of an integrated subject, or organic unity, though some pragmatists may veer in that direction. But it does defend the idea that it might be desirable for people, at least some of the time, to feel a sense of unity and wholeness about aspects of their experience. Such unity should not be dismissed as an ideological attempt to block people's sense of the diversity of their personal identity, or a dubious habit of Western metaphysics (see Shusterman, 2000: 62–83). To live without *some* stability or centeredness would be intolerable for nearly everyone. Nor does pragmatism depend upon on a dubious notion of immediacy as the basis of art's power. Such an approach would merely mirror one which overly valued intellectual or formal complexity. Some romantic, populist, and even some neo-Deleuzean approaches to culture might be accused of a fetishization of immediacy, or at least of non-reflective somatic experience. Dewey's pragmatism certainly focuses on aesthetic experience (Jay, 2006: 161–169) but as Scott Stroud (2011) makes clear, this emphasis on art's heightening of experience in no way precludes the importance of meaning and reflection. Some experiences invite an enjoyable and enriching lack of self-consciousness (as in flow), while others have a puzzling quality which invites us to reflect on what is valued.

There are problems with the legacy of pragmatist aesthetics (as there are with all traditions of thought). In spite of his desire to convey that "art is a part of the natural range of experiences" (Stroud, 2011: 5), and that "art is a continuation, by means of intelligent selection and arrangement, of natural tendencies of natural events" (Dewey, quoted by Stroud, 2011: 4), Dewey focused heavily on experiences of fine art, and did not adequately clarify what

[16] Like Nussbaum's neo-Aristotelianism, this is a resource that has been neglected in sociology and cultural studies.

distinguished such experiences from aesthetic experiences in general (such as finding a person or a landscape deeply attractive). There are important ways in which somatic aesthetic experience is tied up with some of the most disturbingly instrumentalized and commodified aspects of modern societies, in ways that Dewey failed to consider (unlike writers such as Foucault, Bourdieu, and Bataille). Nevertheless, pragmatist aesthetics makes room for forms of artistic expression and entertainment involving energetic kinaesthesis, and engagement of the body – such as popular dance. A pragmatist aesthetics, therefore, allows a fuller understanding of some of the dimensions of music sidelined by Nussbaum. This includes its ability to enhance feelings of sociality, community, and collectivity, issues that are addressed in Chapters 4 and 5. But it also involves the ways in which music might valuably add to our sense of flourishing by invigorating our sense of vitality and aliveness.

Is this notion of vitality a mystificatory abstraction, a form of new-age tosh? Emphatically not. The following quotation from the British psychotherapist Adam Phillips gives a strong sense of its concrete reality, in a way that I think is consistent with the approach outlined earlier:

> I think the experience of aliveness is an ordinary experience. It is, nevertheless, sometimes difficult to articulate it. One is aware that when one is doing something that one finds genuinely pleasurable or intriguing, that really engages one's curiosity or passion, or something which one becomes absorbed in – or indeed when one is with people that one loves, or desires, or likes – there is a different quality to one's sense of oneself. One of the causes is that one forgets oneself, one loses a certain amount of self consciousness. In such situations or experiences questions like "Is my life worth living?" or "Do I love my life?" disappear because they are, in a way, answered by the experience. They don't require a justification (from an interview with Jonathan Rutherford, in Rutherford, 2000: 183–184).

For many people, then, music valuably provides the basis for a pleasurable forgetting of oneself, a loss of self-consciousness which is never complete, but which is beneficial. A whole range of musics offer deeply pleasurable, feelingful, and absorbing experiences. Yet I want to emphasize that a balanced approach should not neglect some of the problems of this aspect of music. The philosopher Andrew Bowie indicates one notable problem concerning emotion and affect in the following passage:

> Music can give rise to affective states which transcend conceptual reflection in a manner that constitutes a valuable new dimension of experience of the

world, but it can also just entail the surrender of rational justification to emotions that are derived from mere socially conditioned prejudice. The question is how to sustain the aspect of aesthetic value based on this immediacy of feeling, at the same time as finding ways of being critical when this source of value becomes perverted (Bowie, 2003: 19).

It is this kind of balance that the current book seeks to strike. But the value of music, as we have seen, consists in other dimensions than its transcendence of reflection. Equally, the perversion of its value takes other forms than the surrender of rationality to negative emotion – and we shall explore some of these in the next section.

2.6 Approaches to Music and Emotion in Everyday Life: Contributions and Limitations

I have been drawing on a variety of different philosophical, intellectual, and political traditions to examine a number of ways in which musical experience, and artistic-aesthetic experience more broadly, might be appreciated in modern societies. But none of these traditions provides a *critical* aesthetics of the kind that this book seeks to construct. How might a more critical orientation towards culture, and towards music, balance the claims we might want to make for its emancipatory potential to allow human flourishing? To put this another way, how might we incorporate into our analysis the recognition that the world is severely marred by injustice, inequality, alienation, and oppression, and that music is unlikely to remain unaffected by these broader social dynamics? Perhaps the most durable body of critical writing on culture and music in modernity is that of Theodor Adorno. No one applied a historical understanding of power and subjectivity so relentlessly to musical culture as a whole than did Adorno. For him music could only contribute to bettering the world through "the coded language of suffering" (Adorno, 2002/1932: 393). From the perspective I am seeking to develop here, the usefulness of Adorno's work is limited by its excessive austerity, by his idealist requirement that art should aspire to extremely demanding levels of autonomy and dialectic, by his failure to recognize adequately the ambivalence in both "high culture" and "popular culture" and, linked to all this, by his seeming contempt for everyday cultural experience in modern societies.

A significant challenge for this book, then, is to produce a historically informed, and critical, but *non-Adornian*, account of the relations between music, power, subjectivity, and value, in the context of ordinary experience of music. Ordinary experience has been a matter of major interest in recent social scientific approaches, often through the lens of the concept of "the everyday." I want now to develop my perspective further by examining perspectives on music, emotion, and experience from three major contributors to social science of music, one each from anthropology, psychology, and sociology.

The first figure is Ruth Finnegan, an anthropologist whose book, *The Hidden Musicians* (1989), is probably the most important detailed account of the ordinary experience of making music within a particular locale. I discuss this book in some detail in Chapter 4. Here, though, I want to focus on a survey by Finnegan of ethnomusicological research on music and emotion. Finnegan rightly argues that more attention needs to be paid to emotion in music. She valuably outlines a number of ways in which anthropologists have analyzed the centrality of emotion in a range of musical settings. As an anthropologist, her interest is not in "trying to penetrate and pin down hidden internal states" but in "the manner, variably practiced and conceptualized in different contexts, in which people are personally involved in their musical engagements" (Finnegan, 2012: 355). Finnegan emphasizes the sheer range of emotions at work in musical performance and practice:

> It is not so much self-conscious internalized "feelings" – though in some cultural settings that is indeed one element – as the contextualized manner of people's musical engagements: joyfully, fearfully, attentively, reflectively, proudly; in a spirit of exaltation or energy or irritation; in sorrowful, celebratory or nostalgic mood; with boredom (that too!), with dance, with tranquillity (Finnegan, 2012: 355).

Finnegan then summarizes her view of how music itself figures in people's emotional lives.

> Whether in deeply intense fashion or more light-touch action, music provides a human resource through which people can enact their lives with inextricably entwined feeling, thought and imagination (Finnegan, 2012: 355).

Music here is seen as a *resource*, at the disposal of humans conceived in a particular way: creative, active, imbued with agency. I think we have to see musical agency as more constrained and contradictory than this, and I shall develop this theme in what follows. Also striking is how Finnegan sees emotion primarily as a matter of public display, which ultimately serves to bind people together. The difficult relations of the self to affect, stressed by psychoanalysis and by other approaches to subjectivity, do not seem to be of interest here; nor are less positive aspects of aesthetic experience in relation to a person's emotional life. Such questions raise a crucial issue for a critical social science: how to connect problems of the self with problems of the social?

The second major figure I consider here is Tia DeNora. In two insightful, readable, and stimulating books, *Music in Everyday Life* (DeNora, 2000) and *After Adorno: Rethinking Music Sociology* (DeNora, 2003), DeNora has made an extremely important contribution to the sociology of music. As with my discussion of Finnegan, it is her account of music, emotion, and the self that I am particularly interested in here and so her chapters on "Music as a technology of self" (DeNora, 2000: 46–74) and "How does music 'channel' emotions?" (DeNora, 2003: 83–117) are most relevant. In these chapters, self-identity is understood as a production of the continuing activity of individuals, rather as a fixed inner essence, as in older conceptions of "personality." The title of the first of these chapters recalls Foucault's use of the term "technologies of the self" (Foucault, 2000) but in fact DeNora's approach to subjectivity is very un-Foucauldian and owes more to interactionism, pragmatism, and Anthony Giddens's conception of modern self-identity as based upon reflexivity (Giddens, 1991; DeNora, 2000: 46). Drawing on interviews and ethnography, DeNora aims to show music

> in action as a device for ordering the self as an agent, and as an object known and accountable to oneself and others ... Music is a material that actors use to elaborate, to fill out and fill in, to themselves and to others, modes of aesthetic agency and, with it, subjective stances and identities (DeNora, 2000: 73–74).

Again, as with Finnegan, there is a strong sense of music as a resource to be used: "music is a resource for modulating and structuring the parameters of aesthetic agency – feeling, motivation, desire, comportment, action style, energy" (53). DeNora's account helpfully transcends the cognitivist bias of some discussions of musical emotion by reminding us of music's power to enhance people's lives in all kinds of routine, humdrum ways, for example by re-energization or relaxation. And DeNora helpfully puts the emphasis of her sociological account not on the *expression* by music of internal emotional states (though this aspect might actually be of greater interest than she implies) but on the way that music reflexively *constitutes* emotional states in people (57). DeNora calls this kind of reflexive activity "emotion work" (DeNora, 2000: 53; DeNora, 2003: 96). And as with Finnegan, the attitude is overwhelmingly positive. Time and again, for DeNora, music is found to be enriching experience, adding to agency, enhancing dimensions of people's everyday lives. It can be used for attaining and maintaining states of feeling, for aiding concentration, and more generally for retrieving memories and therefore "remembering/constructing who one is" (DeNora, 2000: 63).

A third major figure is John Sloboda, who in the 1990s and 2000s was probably the Anglophone world's leading psychologist of music. As with DeNora, the relationship of music and emotion has been central to his work (see Juslin and Sloboda, 2001; Juslin and Sloboda, 2010). And like DeNora, an issue of central concern is *everyday* experience. I should note that while Sloboda is an eminent psychologist of music, he is not necessarily typical or representative of this sub-discipline. Because the psychology of music, and in particular music therapy, has made rather major contributions to understanding the value of music in recent years, I consider it separately in Box 2.1. My main focus here though is on Sloboda's concern with ordinary, routine, habitual, musical experience. Like DeNora's work, Sloboda's helpfully qualifies the assumption made by philosophical aesthetics and by a great deal of musicology that musical experience only matters when people pay very high levels of attention to music. A socially oriented psychology can, in this respect, help us to inject a healthy dose of reality into our conception of why music matters. There is also a welcome quest for scientific precision and hard evidence, compared with the fluffy speculations of some cultural studies and even some sociological accounts. In one book chapter, Sloboda (2010) outlines a number of propositions about emotion in everyday music, and tests them against findings in research on the psychology of music. As we saw earlier, Sloboda's overall argument is that most experiences of music are mundane and individualistic, rather than special and sociable. That seems highly plausible, at least when it comes to "developed," industrialized countries. But in emphasizing the *functions* of music for individuals in this way, Sloboda fails to get at what is most interesting about music's tangled relationships to emotion, personal experience, and community in modern societies. By privileging the "everyday" so much, he ignores the possibility that we might find significance too in experiences that are not exceptional, but which are not altogether mundane either: "everyweek" or "everymonth" ventures into sonic emotion that involve negotiations with our sense of self and our varied senses of collective identity.

Box 2.1   Music psychology, music therapy, and the value of music

Music psychology has boomed in recent years. This extremely diverse field has analyzed music in a number of ways.[17] At times, this has included discussion of how music might enhance people's lives. A report by Susan Hallam for the UK Performing Rights Society, for example, ably discussed some of the main facets of "the power of music" (Hallam, 2001), though a more accurate title might have been "the value of music." Drawing on numerous psychological studies, Hallam summarized how music can be used by people to manipulate their moods, alleviate boredom, and create environments appropriate for particular social events; music's role in enhancing child development, and in increasing self-esteem in young people; and its ability to "promote relaxation, alleviate anxiety and pain, promote appropriate behaviour in vulnerable groups and enhance the quality of life of those who are beyond medical help." While some of the conceptualization used by Hallam and other psychologists echoes the functionalism of research on music and everyday life criticized earlier, the therapeutic and developmental aspects of music are worthy of further consideration. They have been addressed in detail in music therapy research and practice. In the work of writers such as Gary Ansdell (1995), there are compelling and at times moving indications of how music can enhance the lives of people who need help most: the seriously depressed or severely ill.

Music therapy, and the research that helps sustain it, makes a more direct contribution to human well-being than my musings ever will. Yet perhaps my more sociological, historical, and cultural focus might complement the best work in music psychology and music therapy. I hope, for example, that this book might help advance understanding of ways in which the social and historical shaping of our selves might

---

[17]   See Clarke, Dibben, and Pitts (2010) for a good overview, one which makes connections with other fields such as musicology and ethnomusicology. The authors address questions of how individuals and groups "use" music in their Chapters 6 and 7, including some discussion of emotion and mood, but the focus is on how music induces emotion, and how it "regulates" mood, rather than on musical emotion in relation to flourishing, as here.

influence experiences of music, and in some cases put limits on music's capacity to contribute to life. I believe that music therapy (and music psychology) might benefit by drawing on perspectives that examine concepts of "quality of life," human flourishing, and self-realization in greater philosophical depth than has been the case in the research so far. In this respect, however, it has to be said that my approach draws on conceptions of subjectivity in which a great deal of music psychology and even music therapy usually seem rather uninterested – psychoanalytical understandings of the self that emphasize the constraints on human efforts at self-realization (paradoxically, psychoanalysis emphasizes these constraints so that more people might achieve more meaningful self-realization).

I believe that these leading social science writers on music and society are right to consider aspects of the ordinary, everyday, experience of music. They are also right to pay attention to the agency of people as they seek to use music in a range of settings. Their focus on emotion and mood is welcome and often insightful. But in addition to the comments I have already made about their limitations, I want to point to some problems in the way they conceive of music and affect in modern societies and to ways in which we need to go beyond such approaches in order to build a historically informed critical defense of music.[18]

One major problem is their limited conception of agency in relation to self and society. I agree that we need to understand people as individuals able to reflect upon and alter their actions, and to make positive use of cultural resources. But we need a sense of *constrained agency*, of the ways in which social and psychological dynamics might limit people's freedom to act. We should not underestimate the psychic difficulties that individuals face in constructing a coherent and healthy self-identity. It is true that humans can act on their environment and upon their selves, but they surely do so in ways that are limited not only

---

[18] In an article on music and everyday life, Simon Frith (2002: 46) finds that DeNora and Sloboda are too individualistic, that they tend to "refer musical meaning to its emotional function for individuals" when music "remains equally important as a means of communication and a form of sociability." I agree with this criticism, and my account in this book seeks to balance the individual and social aspects of the value of music. My criticisms here particularly concern the sidelining of questions of *power* in work on music and everyday life.

by social and historical factors (such as poverty, deprivation, lack of education, or training) but also by their own personal biographies. You do not have to subscribe to unreconstructed Freudianism to recognize that damaging experiences in infancy can place severe constraints on what it is possible to do in later life – including the way we interact with music, and how we might use it to shape our selves. It seems obvious to me that this is the case. As I suggested in discussing Nussbaum's use of Winnicott, the best versions of psychoanalysis still offer the most coherent accounts of human subjectivity and its constraints, especially when combined with insights drawn from philosophy and social science.

A second major problem that really derives from the first is that these accounts are very positive depictions of the role of music in modern societies (though Sloboda is more neutral than Finnegan and DeNora). They risk downplaying various ways in which music may become implicated in less pleasant and even disturbing features of modern life. There is a proper emphasis on the social nature of music and of self-identity, but if music is as imbricated with social processes as these writers suggest, then it is hard to see how people's engagements with music can be so consistently positive in their effects, when we live in societies that are marked by inequality, exploitation, and suffering. While it is true that people have been miserable and mistreated in all human societies, it is also the case, as numerous sociologists have taught us, including Georg Simmel and C. Wright Mills, that private lives, personal biographies, and mental states cannot be detached from history. Can music really be so autonomous that it floats free of social forces? And, turning to self-identity, might not people's projects of self-creation (to use DeNora's term), *and therefore their uses of music as part of these projects*, have some more difficult and troubling dimensions than emerges in such accounts?

A third problem concerns the underdeveloped account of the *aesthetic* elements of musical experience in these social scientific approaches. De Nora, Finnegan, and Sloboda offer social analysis of music which floats free of debates about what aesthetic experience contributes to human life. They also sideline questions concerning how people bring values of various kinds to music, and make judgments about what pleases and moves them, and what does not.

This book represents my attempt to develop a different approach, one based in social science, which would allow for a critical but ultimately positive of music. I begin by offering, in the next section, what I hope is a balanced critical account of the place of the self in modern societies. This emphasizes the importance and the possibility of self-realization, but it also shows how self-realization is deeply compromised by certain conditions of capitalist modernity. This allows us to build on the positive account of musical-aesthetic experience based on emotion and human flourishing, by relating aesthetic experience to historical developments in modern societies.

2.7   Problems of Self-realization in Modern Life and Their Relation to Music

To understand how emotions and self-identity might become bound up in problematic aspects of modern societies, in ways that have relevance to the case of music, in this section I now examine a number of contributions from critical sociology and social theory.

In her well-known study, *The Managed Heart*, Arlie Hochschild (1983) analyzed workers' experiences of service employment. These jobs appeared comfortable and rewarding, but for Hochschild they involved new and distinctive forms of control and alienation, whereby workers were being required to internalize at the deepest level the emotional responses required *to look as though they love their jobs*. Her most striking example was the way that flight attendants are trained to smile by airlines that promote their service on the basis that "our smiles are not painted on." One implication of Hochschild's study was that the emotional self-management made possible by new forms of self-identity in capitalist modernity can be appropriated in dubious ways by powerful interests. If this is true, then this suggests that the use of music to achieve emotional self-management may not always be healthy either.[19]

My main interest here though is in the *historical* dimensions of the corruption of goals of self-realization and autonomy in capitalist modernity. The German social theorist Axel Honneth has argued that increasingly, in modernity, "members of Western societies were compelled, urged or encouraged, for the sake of their own future, to place their very selves at the centre of their own life-planning and practice" (Honneth, 2004: 469). As a result,

[19]   DeNora refers explicitly to Hochschild's studies (DeNora, 2003: 96; DeNora, 2000: 53), including her concept of "emotional work," yet she does not register Hochschild's critical orientation, or her contrastive concept of "emotional labour."

individual self-realization becomes linked to "institutionalized expectations" and "transmuted into a support of the system's legitimacy" (467). Honneth does not sufficiently specify what this might mean in his suggestive article, but a more thorough sociological account, compatible with Honneth's, is provided by Luc Boltanski and Eve Chiapello in their tour de force *The New Spirit of Capitalism* (2005). Boltanski and Chiapello differentiate two principal ways in which capitalist societies have been criticized – social critique and artistic critique. Social critique emphasizes poverty, inequality, the opportunism and egoism of private interests, and the destruction of social bonds brought about by capitalism. Artistic critique, with its roots in bohemianism and romanticism, instead stresses capitalism as a source of disenchantment and inauthenticity, and the limits it places on freedom, autonomy, and creativity (Boltanski and Chiapello, 2005: 35–38). Boltanski and Chiapello trace how, faced with a crisis of legitimacy and motivation in the late 1960s, under pressure from both the social and artistic critiques (coming together in the events of 1968 in France and across much of the world), capitalist institutions responded by validating the artistic critique, especially critical demands for autonomy in working life. Measures aimed at providing security for workers were replaced by measures aimed at relaxing hierarchical control and allowing people to fulfil their individual potential (Boltanski and Chiapello, 2005: 190). The result is a society based on a "connexionist" model where the self is an individual enterprise, and where transitory relationships and commitments are considered more legitimate than stable ones – because rapidly changing one's connections can supposedly lead to personal growth and greater self-realization. In this connexionist society, individuals are increasingly expected to take responsibility for their own self, even though that self is borne down upon by all kinds of social pressures. Honneth, Boltanski, and Chiapello all write about the potentially damaging effects of that pressure on individuals. However consciously skeptical individuals may be, "the ideal of self-realization is experienced … subliminally … as posing demands upon the manner in which one's subjectivity is to be formed," as Honneth puts it (Honneth, 2004 467). The result, Honneth claims, drawing on a variety of sources, is a rise in the levels of depression in society – though depression is not necessarily to be understood in clinical terms here. It may involve a combination of "symptoms of inner emptiness, of feeling oneself to be superfluous" with "hectic and enervating activities" (478). Boltanski and Chiapello (2005: 420–424), meanwhile, place greater stress on anxiety and anomie, citing statistics on rising numbers of suicide. In a widely read book, British sociologists Richard

Wilkinson and Kate Pickett (2010: 66–69) showed a very strong association between mental illness and social inequality: countries with far higher levels of social inequality, such as the United Kingdom, the United States, and Australia, had far higher levels of mental illness than more equal countries such as Japan, Germany, and Spain.

There are reasons to be suspicious, then, of the account of self-fashioning implicitly assumed by writers on music and society cited earlier. For Honneth, a key basis of "organized self-realization" was that individuals in the twentieth century increasingly felt compelled "to seek an intensification of one's own feeling of being alive in the consumption of cultural products." In his view, this derives from a protestant undercurrent in which an "uncommon state of emotional excitement was taken to be a sign of God's goodness and grace" (Honneth, 2004: 478), which co-existed with the protestant work ethic and did not necessarily contradict it. For Honneth, drawing on the historian Colin Campbell, this protestant undercurrent eventually becomes the basis for "a massive investment in intensity-enhancing consumer goods" (478). Daniel Bell's thesis that modern individualistic hedonism contradicts the functional demands of capitalism, leading to crisis, has not been borne out. Rather, for Honneth, it has only strengthened capitalism. The presence of shorter and more fragile bonds between people (powerfully analyzed by Sennett, 1998, among others), and the tendency for leisure to be seen as a key means of self-definition, do not radically conflict with the needs of the capitalist economy. Indeed, according to Honneth, these facets of modern societies have become a productive force in their own right, in that they fuel cultural consumption. Similarly, for Boltanski and Chiapello (2005: 437), in the new connexionist society that has arisen in the wake of capitalism's appropriation of the artistic critique, "People's aspirations to mobility, to multiply their activities, to greater opportunities for being and doing, emerge as a virtually boundless reservoir of ideas for conceiving new products and services to bring to the market." Innovation is strongly connected to this need for liberation, including transport and automation, but it now includes devices which allow people to be active while mobile.[20]

---

[20] The ambivalent qualities of consumer uses of mobile music devices are well-captured by Michael Bull (2007). For Bull, users employ iPods and so on to reclaim urban space, but they do so by privatizing it.

However, there is another way in which music is connected to these developments, which neither Honneth's article nor *The New Spirit of Capitalism* comment upon. This is music's own active role in fuelling capitalism's incorporation of autonomy; in Boltanski and Chiapello's terms, its centrality to the artistic critique. The most prominent musical genres in Europe and North America of the last century – jazz, rock, soul, and hip hop – have all been strongly tied up with romantic notions of personal autonomy. Rock in particular accompanied the kind of historical changes tracked by Boltanski and Chiapello, producing a culture that was centered on values of rebellious creativity, but which, in retrospect, was assimilated very quickly to values of commercialism. The mainstream rock music of the 1980s on, with its often unchallenging celebrations of mobility and unfettered individuality, can be seen to conform closely to Boltanski and Chiapello's connexionist world.[21] When dozens of nostalgic rock documentaries look back to the glory years of rock rebellion (see Reynolds, 2011: 28–31) they provide a picture of the cultural turbulence of the 1960s and 1970s for older viewers, in which, like documentaries of the Second World War, there is a comforting sense that victory was achieved in the end.

Such critical perspectives on consumption and self-identity are missing from social science approaches that see music as a positive resource for self-making or, more basically, as a tool for functioning in everyday life. Admittedly, however, these perspectives involve large-scale sociological–historical claims. A great challenge is to apply these perspectives to ordinary experience, without doing violence to the specificity of people's lives, or without implicitly denying the undoubted truth that people do have some freedom to shape their own cultural practices. While the fundamental aim of this chapter is primarily to question the *theoretical* assumptions regarding emotion and self-identity underlying studies of musical consumption, in Box 2.2 I reflect on these issues using empirical case studies, in the manner of DeNora's micro-sociological analyses, but examined from a perspective influenced by the critical and historical accounts outlined earlier.

---

[21] The best accounts of this aspect of rock culture are by Simon Frith (1981) and Keir Keightley (2001).

Box 2.2   Case study: a collector

As we have seen, both Honneth and Boltanski/Chiapello point to ways in which the quest for personal meaning and self-realization in capitalist modernity helps to fuel consumption, and also to how "organized self-realization" (partly through consumption, but also through the development of more formally autonomous types of labor) seems to be resulting in greater society-wide levels of anxiety and depression. It is interesting in this context to consider those people who seem to place a particularly strong emphasis on self-realization through musical consumption, if only as a limit case, while recognizing their atypicality.

Paul, for example, a 40-year-old hairdresser, was interviewed in a room lined with hundreds of CDs and records. His main loves were rock, R&B, soul, and reggae, but his collection included other material too. What united them was music that was in some way "challenging" (The Rolling Stones, Neil Young, and Prince were his favorites). He had contempt for music that was "empty," with "no real feeling." At the salon where he worked, Paul was well-known for being a musical aficionado, and his conversations with customers often centered on music. However, Paul's collecting was a source of real tension in his relationship with his wife. In Paul's presence, his wife Helen told the interviewer that she found his record collecting and his playing of loud music obtrusive and irritating. She expressed anger concerning the sheer amount of money Paul spent on music and music equipment. And in the salon where he worked, although he was well-liked by customers and colleagues, Paul could be very forward in asserting his views about what kind of music should be played. Paul's relationship to music seemed a defiant statement about his independence – both within the family and within society. He acknowledged that his desire to buy music constantly, to accrue amounts of music that he could not possibly play more than once or twice, was irrational, but he revelled in that irrationality.

Paul's love of music, then, provided an important part of his identity. Whether his pleasure in music might be understood via DeNora's concept of reflexive "emotional work" (see DeNora, 2000: 53–58), however, is another matter. Or at least there were uncomfortable aspects to his relationship with music, of a kind which barely seem to appear in the conception of music and self-identity apparent in the social science of music in everyday life. Active and positive self-making may have been involved here, but some other, more ambivalent aspects were also at work.

It might be objected that Paul's "problems" have nothing to do with music, that music was simply a vehicle through which he and his wife found a reason to express their ambivalence towards each other. If music had not been there, one might say, they would have found other ways to quarrel with each other. But this is to see music as passive, as dead matter with no consequence, rather as active material that has an effect upon the world, when combined with human agency. It is surely more interesting to ask: what is it that made music the basis of this disagreement? Why music and *not* something else? And here it is important I think that Paul was drawn to rebellious, individualistic music and expressed disdain for music he considered conformist. Somehow, the notion of music as (at its best) intensely and genuinely expressive came to stand for Paul as a defense against what he portrayed as the emptiness of much of the rest of the world. This attitude, it seems, may indeed have helped him in certain situations in his life (after all, music undoubtedly has positive uses) but it is also likely to lead to some psychological trouble too – of a kind that is not adequately recognized in some of the accounts discussed earlier. In Paul's case, the quest for personal authenticity through music had become so important that it almost seemed to fill his house, in spite of the objections of his partner. Yet this authenticity was somehow transferred on to the record collection. Music can sometimes seem elusive compared with the solidity of these ordered and alphabetized commodities.

This raises the issue of the gendered nature of record collecting – and arguably collecting more broadly. It is not fair to interpret Paul's motivations on the basis of a short period of time spent with him (in interview and in the salon where he worked), but it seems reasonable to think that at the very least the obsessive pursuit of completeness and order exhibited by collectors such as Paul might also be an example of disavowal, in that huge amounts of time, effort, and feeling are devoted to categorization and knowledge, rather than to music as a source of emotional self-management (in DeNora's sense). In fact, almost inevitably, most of the records and CDs in Paul's vast collection went unplayed, and he admitted to having difficulty in discussing his emotional engagement with music. There are strongly gendered dimensions to such disavowal; boys are often strongly discouraged from open displays of emotion. But, combined with the dynamics of social power that are somewhat underplayed in studies of music and everyday life, this can lead to exclusions. As Will Straw (1997: 15) has incisively discussed, the "nerdish homosociality" of record collectors, while relatively harmless compared with more blatant displays of masculinist power in popular music cultures, is as fundamental to the unequal gender politics of pop as any phallic guitar strutting.

2.8   Competitive Individualism and Status Competition Through Music

I turn now to another problematic aspect of music–self–society relations downplayed by theorists of music, emotion, and everyday life, where music is seen as a positive resource for forging self-identity. This is the way that the use of music for self-management can be bound up with the competitive individualism that is prevalent throughout modern societies. The work of Pierre Bourdieu is relevant here. Where writers from various academic disciplines and traditions (including "consumer culture theory" and media studies of "active audiences") see an abundance of creative agency in contemporary cultural consumption, Bourdieu's *Distinction* is well-known for stressing its darker, competitive aspects. In fact, as we shall see in Chapter 5, Bourdieu singles out music from all other forms of culture in terms of its power to act as a marker of class differentiation. And this link between music and symbolic power was bound up, for Bourdieu, with a number of factors: the way in which music is particularly associated with "interiority"; an emphasis on the value of "listening" in modern societies – including in psychoanalysis (which Bourdieu distrusted); and the socially imputed purity of music, its tendency to slip towards negation of the world.[22]

---

[22]   There have been various responses to Bourdieu from sociologists of music. Some question Bourdieu's pessimism and/or his neglect of the aesthetic properties of works or texts (Frith, 1996; Hennion, 2012). Some do so while wanting to hold on to many of his central insights about power (Prior, 2011). Born (2010) critiques his conceptions of subjectivity, agency, and the aesthetic. I have written on Bourdieu's limited treatment of popular culture as manifest in his studies of cultural production (Hesmondhalgh, 2006).

In my view, Bourdieu is too cynical about the role of aesthetic experience, and this may in part derive from his excessively sociological analysis, which is also curiously lacking in any consideration of the emotions when it comes to cultural consumption. Nevertheless, Bourdieu helps us to see that cultural consumption cannot be so easily separated from the competitive individualism of modern societies as writers such as Finnegan and DeNora imply.

In his article, "On status competition and emotion management" (1992), the historical sociologist Cas Wouters offers a perspective on modern competitive individualism that in my view is more useful for considering music consumption in relation to emotion and self-identity than Bourdieu's work. Wouters traces how in some respects it has become increasingly difficult for powerful groups to show superiority through traditional means such as "birth," displays of wealth, and physical violence. Instead, displays of efforts to experiment with new lifestyles and tastes become increasingly important in the everyday lives of many people in advanced industrial societies, and so too does an awareness and knowledge of emotions. In some circles and some situations, we might say, being a sensitive emotional individual is a key marker of superiority. Such superiority needs, at its best (its most superior), to come naturally – and this means, for Wouters, that much of the work involved is done in secret in order to conceal from others the effort needed to articulate oneself as an authentic individual. Wouters does not say in his article how the dynamics he observes may take different forms in different social spaces – for example, amongst different social classes. Nevertheless, I think that there is something suggestive here for the study of music. Music can be part of status battles to show one's openness to a variety of lifestyle pleasures and one's superior emotional range. After all, music has come to be linked, perhaps more than any other cultural form, with the emotional dimensions of our selves.

Competitive individualism is also a relevant frame for examining how people talk about music's capacity to intensify sociality, celebrated in much of the literature (Filmer, 2003). Whether in the dance club, at a funeral, or on a radio show inviting its audience to look back nostalgically on past times, music offers the emotional intensity craved by modern consumerism (recalling Honneth's account mentioned earlier). This can be about sadness, catharsis, and self-awareness; but it can also be about fun, pleasure, and sociality. In a hedonistic society of the kind hypothesized by Honneth, then, music may actually be attached even more strongly than other socio-cultural forms to a certain *duty to have pleasure*.[23] I use this phrase to refer to the way modern individuals compete over who is having the most fun, who is gaining most from life.

I am suggesting, then, that there are two ways in which music might be the basis of status battles in modern society: in terms of the emotional sensitivity of its consumers, and in terms of its basis for hedonistic pleasures. To investigate these issues, I now turn again to interview material, here in terms of competitive individualism over "emotional sensitivity." I want to examine some different ways in which middle-class people are able to present themselves to interviewers as rounded, musically sensitive individuals, taking three examples: James, a retired university lecturer; Ian, a social worker; and Lauren, a church minister. In all three cases, I discuss how these people have successfully incorporated a critique of snobbery or exclusion into their accounts, in order to present themselves as open-minded and sensitive people. (And this is one of the factors that makes Wouters a more appropriate lens through which to view this material than Bourdieu.)

First, James, a retired university lecturer in metallurgy, who talked about a favorite Mozart piece (K563): "it's called a divertimento which suggests something light but it's actually a most profound piece of chamber music, fully the equal of any of his string quartets and of course they are as lovely as anything in the world." There are echoes here of some of Bourdieu's respondents in *Distinction* (e.g., the case study of the "truly classical" university teacher: see Bourdieu (1984: 288–290)). But James was doing more than just displaying his cultural capital – he was also making an implicit set of claims about his emotional sensitivity to music, and the way it fitted into his relations with others. In talking about music he does not like, James was extremely careful to qualify his comments ("I mean it's always it's all right for you, it's easy for you to talk, you've had a silver spoon in your mouth all your life"). He also differentiated himself from a "cold," technical or intellectual approach to loving music, embodied in the figure of a piano teacher he knew from church (and this anecdote was followed immediately by "I like her very much as a person"):

> I think she probably thinks I'm a frivolous old devil but she teaches a lot of the youngsters and [...] every now and then she puts on little concerts of her protégés in church after the Sunday service with proceeds to a charity or

---

[23] Bourdieu discusses "pleasure as a duty" in discussing the emerging cultural habits of "the new petite bourgeoisie" (1984: 367). Also relevant here is Featherstone's notion of "calculating hedonism" (1991).

something like that. And I remember going up to her once after a concert which I had been very impressed by and amongst other things I said – meaning it entirely as a compliment to her – "Well, [...] you have achieved something because your pupils obviously enjoy making music." She looked at me and she almost spat and said "music isn't about enjoyment it's about understanding."

What better way of illustrating one's own capacity for enjoyment and enrichment than by invoking the figure of someone who is devoted entirely to a *dutiful* notion of musical understanding?

Second, Ian, a social worker from London. Ian was one of a number of respondents who emphasized how his tastes had expanded over time, and who was therefore able to put together a personal narrative based on a growing aesthetic consciousness. Ian emphasized his growing omnivorousness ("I've always been interested in literature and music I would say, I've always been interested in most things really, and I suppose what you would call current affairs and what's going on in the world and that kind of thing"). The thread through his expanding musical tastes, beginning with rock ("it was actually more in my mid to late teens that I got into music, you know like we used to listen to [BBC radio presenter] John Peel late at night and heard stuff like Captain Beefheart and Kevin Coyne and the Soft Machine"), and expanding into contemporary music, was the idea of "weird" sounds. Ian set this against the "blandness" of "boring" music, across a wide range of musical genres, from soft rock ("when I was in Mozambique, there was a guy who was particularly into *Hotel California* by the Eagles, which I absolutely hated and despised") to traditional rock and roll ("I just found it utterly boring, utterly tedious" – as opposed to the "magic" of blues artists like Robert Johnson) to Mozart ("there was a bit of Mozart on the radio and I was saying how fucking boring it sounded, and how tedious Mozart was"). But Ian displayed his musical – and emotional – sensitivity by showing that he was able to find value in unlikely places, claiming a growing openness that comes with age:

> Ian: [...] his ex-partner was really into the Pet Shop Boys and we had this argument about the Pet Shop Boys, he was telling me how they actually have really good well-put-together pop songs – which actually I can hear. You know stuff I would have really hated in the past, I've had my ears opened to, bits of George Michael you know.

Finally, Lauren, an American woman in her forties but who had lived in an English city for 25 years and who was working as an ordained minister at a local church. Lauren expressed her sadness and anger at the legacy of imperialism via music ("it saddens me no end when I hear Indian and African Victorian hymns, I think 'where's their music, where's their culture?'") and, when asked to play us a piece of music that she had recently enjoyed, chose a track called "Oh Robin," from an album called *Music for a Harmonious World*. This featured singers from England singing in collaboration with singers from South Africa. What Lauren valued was how the music "allowed each other's genres to be there, the English people are singing English style music, the Africans singing African music and the way it moves together is just stunning." This is not just an aesthetic experience, Lauren is saying, it is also ethical, tied to concerns about imperialism and oppression.

All these people are involved in using music to construct self-identity. All of them do so sincerely. All of them eschew snobbery by opposing symbols of high culture (the cold, technical piano player; Mozart, hailed as a genius, is in fact "boring"; the Victorians who could not accept otherness). It seemed to me, in considering our interviews with these people, that they were engaged in a new form of status seeking, which has displaced the "sense of distinction" analyzed by Bourdieu (1984). Important contributions to the sociology of consumption have drawn attention to some of these changing dynamics, including how omnivorousness has replaced snobbery as the goal of "highbrow" taste.[24] Here I am trying to capture changing dynamics that are specific to music. The point is that analysis of qualitative interviews can lead to very different conclusions about music, emotion, and self-identity from those drawn by the leading social science of music writers discussed earlier.

A further point is worth noting briefly. It is difficult to imagine working-class people telling stories of self-realization through music in quite this way. Rather, our working-class interviewees tended to be flummoxed by attempts to articulate what they like in music. This means that relying on interviews with middle-class subjects in examining musical self-identity in music – as DeNora does, for example – is likely to lead to an incomplete sociology of music.

---

[24] A seminal example is Peterson and Kern (1996). However, see Warde, Martens, and Olsen (1999) for a helpful survey and critique of some of this American empirical work on the sociology of consumption.

2.9 Review: Music's Constrained Enrichment of Lives

In the final section of this chapter, I want to bring together the positive and critical elements in my discussion, and to make my normative position more concrete, by laying out some of the ways in which music might contribute to people's lives, at the individual level, and how that potential might be both aided and constrained by social factors. There are, of course, many other ways in which music might contribute to human well-being, yet is constrained in doing so. My emphasis here tends towards the role of music in individual lives, because later chapters deal more with the collective and sociable aspects of music, but it would be wrong in any case to have too dualistic a conception of the relationship between individuals and society.

First, music can *heighten people's awareness of continuity and development in life*. It seems powerfully linked to memory, perhaps because it combines different ways of remembering: the cognitive, the emotional, and the bodily–sensory (Van Dijck, 2006). It allows us to remember things that happened, how we felt, and what it is like to move, dance, and feel to a certain set of sounds, rhythms, and textures. This ability for music to get stuck in our minds has surely been enhanced by recording technologies: most of us hear a lot more music now than most of our ancestors, and we are likely to hear some of it repeatedly, often in great bursts of repetition over a few weeks when a recording is initially a hit, when it is played regularly in public spaces. This tends to happen to people more when they are young, and so for older people, music can be powerfully evocative of loss as well as continuity. Nostalgia is neither good nor bad in itself, as it has the potential to make us aware of things that we might be justified in regretting (Boym, 2001). But it can involve a negatively sentimental relationship to our past: for example, older people might project on to their youth the feeling that things were better then, when in fact life involved a mixture of different emotions and processes, and may often have been extremely difficult. Attachment to the familiar records of the past can crowd out the inclination and desire to add new experiences to people's lives, inhibiting development and flourishing. Arguably, the commodification of music has encouraged that negative sentimentality through economics and aesthetics that make it cheaper and easier to invoke musical pasts than to encourage an enriching emotional engagement.

Second, music can combine *a healthy integration of different aspects of our being, combining reflection and self-awareness with kinetic pleasure*, as

Shusterman (2000) suggests. Shusterman (2000: 184) gives the example of how funk embodies an aesthetic, which he sees as derived from Africa, of "vigorously active and communally impassioned engagement." Shusterman is rather too inclined to dismiss other experiences of music as "dispassionate, judgemental remoteness" in his efforts to defend popular culture. My view is that contemplative and bodily engaged experiences both have a great deal to offer. Popular and classical music each offer both of these. Musicians consciously and sub-consciously seek to produce certain moods in those who are hearing or who at some time will hear their music. In moving to music, from almost imperceptibly tapping a foot or a steering wheel while the radio plays at a traffic light, through swaying at a concert, to full-on dancing at a club or party, people are both thinking and feeling. Of course, those thoughts might involve the mind wandering along a chain of associations; and they will feature preoccupations that have nothing to do with the music at all. It often takes us a while at concerns to "attune" ourselves to music, and, in a live music setting, after the initial rush of excitement when a band or orchestra begin playing, we might lose our way for a while. But when certain kinds of music *work*, they put mind and body together. This is one of the reasons why "the primitivist understanding of black music" (Danielsen, 2006: 27) is so objectionable. It reduces the complex interplay of thought, reflection, and skilful practice in the varieties of African-American music she examines to an unmediated expression of some inner essence, and in so doing often reduces people of color to one aspect of themselves: their sexuality. As Anne Danielsen shows, the skill of great funk musicians is to conceal the remarkable amount of work that goes into making their music sound as though it flows naturally from the impulse to dance. But the common misreading of such forms of music suggests, again, how difficult it is for even the most remarkable genres and practices to escape the effects of the inequality and racism that so profoundly scar modern societies.

Third, music can *heighten our understanding of how others might think and feel*. It can do so because music encodes human emotions into sounds that can be transmitted and transported across time and space, and because the understanding of these sounds is not limited by the need to learn verbal languages (which makes it easier to transmit than stories and poems). This has synchronic and diachronic dimensions. Synchronically, it is true of our potential understanding of music that comes from other societies in our own time; diachronically, it is true of music that comes from previous eras. This potentially *sympathetic* (sym = with, pathetic = related to feeling) quality of music is severely limited, however, by the deceptively conventional nature of musical communication. All communication, including spoken language, relies on convention. When we hear a foreign language, of which we have no knowledge, we are completely reliant for our interpretation of what is happening on the paralinguistic features of speech – tone and volume of voice, and so on. We will always be aware of the "gap" left by not knowing the language. When we hear music from a society that we do not know well, by contrast, we may often be deceived into thinking we understand its resonances and potential meanings better than we really do. Of course, some musical features may "translate" – certain combinations of musical sounds may reliably indicate happiness or sadness whether emanating from Nigeria or Nebraska. But many more subtle indications of mood, emotion, and purpose will be much more elusive. The sympathetic quality of music – its potential heightening of our understanding of how others think and feel – is also limited by the same dangers of projection that I discussed in the previous point: inequality and ideology might mean that musical practices and values are radically misunderstood, either devalued, or highly valued for the wrong reasons. This is one reason why education about culture might be life-enhancing. The sensitive teaching of conventions and discourses can help us to get more realistically at what kinds of experiences and emotions are being coded into music.

Fourth, and this is an aspect that I have not had the chance to pursue here, but will return to in Chapter 4, music provides considerable rewards to those who play it regularly. One way of conceiving this value is to see it as offering the rewards associated with *practices* in the Aristotelian sense, where practice is used to mean co-operative activities which involve the pursuit of excellence, and which emphasize the "internal" rewards of achieving standards appropriate to those forms of activity, rather than external compensations of money, power, prestige, and status (MacIntyre, 1984; Keat, 2000). Music-making is an activity loaded with ethical significance for many people. Musicians put enormous amounts of time into practising (in the everyday rather than the philosophical sense) so that they can be adept in making the sounds that they are required to make, and this is often for the intrinsic rewards associated with making music, rather than for fame itself. As Mark Banks (2012) has aptly put it, jazz is a particularly acute example of a practice because of the "sharply delineated contrast and tension between the durable ethical pull of the internal goods of the practice (the virtues of community participation and engagement and the 'good of a certain kind of life' that jazz provides) against the contingent external goods that musicians and institutions might seek to accumulate in jazz." But this emphasis on intrinsic rewards can lead to self-exploitation in artistic labor markets characterized by massive over-supply of willing workers, and reward systems hugely skewed towards the successful few. Chapter 4 discusses this issue (and see also Hesmondhalgh and Baker, 2011).

All the aforementioned potential contributions of music to people's efforts to live good lives combine individual and social dimensions. However, there is a key aspect of music which, for the purposes of clarity, I need to address separately. This aspect involves music's enhancement of *our sense of sociality and community*, because of its great potential for providing shared experiences that are corporeal, emotional, and full of potential meanings for the participants. Yet, just as self-realization is a highly ambivalent pursuit in modern life, so too are community and sociability. This is the subject of Chapters 4 and 5. First, though, I focus on the tangled relations of music with the intimate spheres of love and sex.

3
Love and Sex

3.1 Sex and Love and Rock and Roll

We live in an era, a conjuncture, where there is unprecedented sexual explicitness in public communication. There is also a strong and possibly unprecedented emphasis on self-realization through erotic experience.

Music, in many historical periods, has often been considered to have a close relationship to sex and sexuality. When I told one friend that I was trying to write about music and sex, he said "but that's the whole of music, isn't it? It's *all* about sex." That might be overstating it, but many people would agree with Suzanne Cusick (1994: 71) that music and sexuality are "psychically right next door" to each other. There might be various reasons for this link, including historically constituted ideas that both music and sex are both forms of pleasurable experience that can somehow bypass thought and various other troublesome forms of mediation. But music and sex have both become linked to rebellion and transgression, and via this to marginalized and disempowered groups. This raises interesting issues, and politically and culturally significant ones, concerning music's relationships to power at the meeting point of the public and the private. However, in considering such questions, as in life more generally, sex is made more complicated by love; and as in life there may be reasons to think that the complications love brings are sometimes good ones. One problem with overstating the relationship of music to sex is that this can cloud the importance of love. It would be better to consider music, sex, and love together in order to assess music's complex possibilities in spheres of intimacy.[1]

The guiding question that the chapter seeks to answer is as follows: what means did popular music culture provide for enhancing human experiences of love and sex in the second half of the twentieth century and the first decade of the twenty first? My focus is historical, and I look at prevailing norms and mores, influential framings of the meanings of sexuality and romance, and on the recordings that millions of people were hearing in Anglophone countries.[2]

3.2 Two Approaches to Music, Sex, and Sexuality

How have these various issues been approached in relation to music? I will discuss two interesting approaches here. The first derives from critical musicology, where the stress has been upon how gender and sexuality have been encoded in musical meanings and conventions. The most influential and widely cited version of this approach has probably been that of the musicologist Susan McClary (1991), who provided readings of the sexual politics of a number of musical forms, exposing the elements of male paranoid fantasy in *Carmen*, and praising Madonna's "counternarratives of female heterosexual desire." This emphasis on the gendered coding of sexual politics into musical form and style has been taken up by a number of other musicologists.[3]

Critical musicology has made great advances in terms of understanding the sexual politics of difference in music. The theoretical underpinnings for the most prominent analyses have been provided by Lacanian psychoanalytical theory, as mediated through film theory. Richard Middleton

---

[1] Briefly, some terminological issues. Sex as a domain of human activity (sexual acts, sexual practices, sexual feelings) inevitably raises questions about sex as a characteristic of species based on reproductive functions (some people are male, some female), which in turn raises questions about gender (sex as expressed in social and cultural distinctions) and about sexuality in two senses: the capacity for sexual feelings, and the fact that people differ in their preferences and orientations, most notably about whether they prefer to have sex with people of the opposite sex, the same sex or a mixture of both, or not at all (see Everett Maus, 2012).

[2] I concentrate on the Anglophone countries here, but some of these issues are discussed in a more international context in Chapter 5. For rich commentary on related issues in other countries, see Stokes (2007) on sentimental song in the Egyptian context, and Yano (2002) on Japanese *enka*.

[3] See, among numerous others, Whiteley (2000), Scott (2003), Everett Maus (2012).

(2006) has provided a challenging and brilliant account of the sexualized and gendered nature of vocality in popular music, through analyses of Patti Smith, Nina Simone, Diamanda Galas, Michael Jackson, and others. Drawing on theorists such as Lacan, Žižek, and Judith Butler, Middleton (2006: 92) provides a warning against facile conceptions of agency that would ignore how the subordination of women is "deeply embedded in the historically constituted structures of socialized subjectivity and will not easily go away." So, for example, Middleton shows how Patti Smith's performance of "Gloria," for all its celebration of lesbian sexual pleasure, marked by jouissance-inducing falsetto shrieks, remains haunted by the Lacanian "law" of sexual difference.

For all its valuable contributions and insights, especially as practised by scholars such as McClary and Middleton, this body of work has its limitations in enabling us to understand the value of music, as conceived in this book. With few exceptions, analysis of the sexual politics of music has been overwhelmingly dominated by perspectives oriented to textual analysis in the name of this kind of politics of difference. Even on its own terms, as textual analysis, the dominant approach to music and sexuality in music studies has shortcomings that have not been sufficiently acknowledged. These include a reliance on concepts such as *jouissance* (from Barthes) and *excess* (from Lacan). As Georgina Born points out, these notions are limited by their ineffability – they are simply not describable. Another is that "both are defined by negation, so that their positivity is impossible to grasp."

> [O]n both rests so much – a vast psychic space of inchoate resistances, of escapes from ideology, of desires, of forms of the sublime, and so on. The ultimate irony is that the rhetoric of "jouissance/the body/desire/excess" – especially given its disregard for cultural and aesthetic differences, and for the historical and cultural specificity of subjectivity – often amounts to a powerful instrument of closure (Born, 1992: 84).[4]

Middleton is certainly alive to cultural specificity, but in spite of his deep historical knowledge, the Lacanian theory he employs runs the risk of going beyond the challenge to sovereign notions of subjectivity and dispensing with agency altogether.

---

[4] This is as part of a review that is broadly (and, in my view, rightly) sympathetic to McClary's achievements in bringing sexual politics to bear on a range of genres across the field of music. Born also criticizes McClary's "lack of attention to the socio-economic and institutional aspects of musical practice" (83).

A second approach we might call neo-Deleuzean, because of the way it picks up themes and ideas from the French thinker Gilles Deleuze. Its best-known exponent is the cultural studies analyst Lawrence Grossberg. Rock, Grossberg once wrote, is "a music of bodily desire. There is an immediate material relation to the music and its movements. This relation, while true of music in general, is foregrounded in rock and roll" – by which Grossberg meant rock music right through to the time of his writing in the 1980s (Grossberg, 1984: 238, 239). In his early writings, Grossberg created a curious hybrid of British cultural studies and Deleuzean theory to argue for the corporeal, invasive, non-representational, yet ultimately empowering properties of rock. Rock and roll released energy by rearranging the sites "at which pleasure can be found and energy derived" (Grossberg, 1990: 115). In its focus on energy, desire, and pleasure, this conception of rock and pleasure is actually rather close to the rock counterculture's own under-standing of its sexual politics, a familiar story whereby Elvis released us from lingering Victorian sexual constraints before Hendrix and the Stones took us further along the road to transgression. Grossberg was too smart not to see that this narrative of liberation was easily incorporated into something more conservative. Nevertheless, even the more sophisticated versions of this attitude to musical politics, such as Grossberg's, miss a great deal of the strangeness and variety of sexual feelings and practices, and of music's relationships to them.

My approach here then is to stand back from these ways in which debates about music and sexuality have generally been conducted to consider music and sex in rather different terms. One way I do this is to pay more attention to the question of love, and the broader issue of the relationship of popular music to erotic and intimate experience in modern societies. Linked to this, we need to consider, consistent with the approach outlined in Chapter 2, the *emotions and feelings* that different genres of music seek to draw upon and construct, in historical terms, rather than refer to generalized theoretical ideas of affect or jouissance or excess. A third move this chapter makes is to take into account the ways in which sexual desire is *institutionalized* into historically changing processes of courtship, marriage, and so on. As much as the corporeal desire that is supposedly expressed most directly in musical form in rock, music in modern life also concerns the vast emotional apparatus that we build around desire: melancholy, envy, abandonment, rejection, and shame; feelings of attraction, commitment, reliance, vulnerability, control, and repulsion. And in fact if we turn our attention away from heroic narratives of rock's liberation of desire, we can see and hear this in pop music and non-rock genres of various kinds, as I shall show in this chapter.

Nevertheless, I treat the countercultural moment of rock as pivotal. This is partly because rock came to pre-eminence at a time of unprecedented public debate about the proper role of sexuality in human life, and the meaning of "sexual freedom." There was a very strong association of rock with ideas that sex should be *empowering* (even if that involved a liberating self-shattering) and in particular with the idea that music is at its most politically potent when it encourages the transgressive unleashing of desire, especially sexual desire. This thread of discussion picks up from my suggestion, in Chapter 2, that we need to take seriously the ways in which the bodily aesthetic experiences afforded by music might enhance people's lives. But at the same time, I look at rock's constitutive other: pop. In assessing changing relationships between music, sex, and love, I want to invoke a wider terrain of experience and everyday life, and to examine it historically, while inevitably focusing on a small number of genres and emotions. I begin by looking at the two "super-genres" of rock and pop which dominated popular music in the period from the 1950s to the 1980s, and which emphasized different notions of personal erotic fulfilment.

3.3 The Pop-Rock Divide and Rock's Sexual Politics

By the middle of the twentieth century, popular music was overwhelmingly concerned with love and romance (Horton, 1957). This fact was often treated as a simple sign of music's industrialization and commodification. In an age when the purchase of music was increasingly driven by a newly independent and burgeoning youth in the United States, and in other countries, the music business was seen as exploiting the interest of teenagers, especially teenage girls, in intimacy. Some on the Left developed ideological critiques. Love songs were distractions from the real business of changing the world, which rock was felt to be better equipped to do, or they reinforced feminine passivity.[5] It is certainly true that the focus on intimacy in twentieth-century pop depended on a massive shift in consumption patterns, and that the youth audience, especially girls, were fundamental to the focus on

---

[5] Though feminists pointed out that dismissal of girls' culture (such as pop) could be just as much a product of sexism as the banal assumptions about girls evident in many commercial songs (McRobbie, 1991).

love and romance in pop. And the venality of music entrepreneurs is not in doubt. But the shift also reflected a new individualization, as working-class young people gained increasing independence in an era of new economic concessions to their parents. As traditional forms of collective identity and experience diminished in importance, there were liberating effects and a new (compromised) sexual freedom. We should not overstate the emancipation here. It was accompanied by a rise in narcissistic conditions and social behavior (Sennett, 1974; Lasch, 1977). Narcissism, which is understood here in a psychotherapeutic sense, "treats the body as an instrument of sensual gratification, rather than relating sensuality to communication with others" (Giddens, 1991: 170).[6] Self-realization becomes an unrelenting quest for personal gratification, often at the expense of commitment and genuine intimacy with others. Change was messy and compromised.

In popular music, pop and rock each articulated, reflected, and shaped two conflicting ethics of sex and love. In pop, commitment, trust, and sympathy were valued, while rock emphasized freedom, authenticity, and "honest" self-expression. This division had roots in historical developments. Simon Frith (1981: 240–241) points out that teenage culture was already sexualized by the time rock and roll spread across the industrialized world, and the 1920s were as significant as the 1960s in the history of modern sexuality. For it was then that the ideology of sentimental love was fused with a new kind of advocacy of sexual pleasure; in historian Paula Fass's words, it was the early twentieth century that saw a "dual process of the sexualization of love and the glorification of sex" (quoted by Frith, 1981: 237), made possible by contraception and popular versions of sexology and psychoanalysis, but with marriage envisaged as where the best sex could take place. Post-war pop culture drew on these conceptions in articulating teenage sexuality in terms of commitment and eventual matrimony.

Jazz, folk, and rock – the main genres in which anti-pop views were crystallized in the post-war period – tended to dismiss such views as hollow ideology or shallow sentimentalism, and saw their own music as better because they were more adventurous, in tune with "the people," or more earthily sexual. The rock counterculture crystallized these issues in a particular way, derived from influential thinkers and public intellectuals. These visions of sexual freedom influenced rock's sexual politics, but they had serious limitations.

---

[6] See also Craib (1998). Narcissism in this sense can involve self-loathing just as much as self-love (the popular sense of the term).

One of the great transformations in twentieth-century Western societies was the rise of the view that "the glorification of sex" (Fass's words) could be and should be separated out from the eroticization of fidelity and trust. This has its roots in bohemianism, which saw personal sexuality as compromised by the demands of conventionality, including marriage. The British cultural historian Elizabeth Wilson has recounted how late nineteenth-century German bohemianism transformed romantic beliefs about erotic passion as destiny and mingled them with psychoanalysis to form a new politics of sexual freedom that spread through cosmopolitan cities in the early twentieth century (Wilson, 2000: 179–187). Now sexuality could be seen as a liberating and ecstatic force. Some of this was domesticated, in the form of the eroticization of married sex, but a strand of political thought took up Freudian themes concerning the dangers of repression, and in particular the family as an institution that caused psychological damage.

Mixed with existential philosophy and popularized by beat generation culture, this sexual politics was given intellectual credibility by Freudo-Marxians such as Reich and Marcuse. I want briefly to discuss Marcuse's *Eros and Civilization* because it represents the most sophisticated attempt to advance a politics of sexual freedom on philosophical and political grounds, and also because its ideas directly fed into the sexual politics of middle-class youth and the rock counterculture, not least via Marcuse's teaching at Berkeley, a global center of campus radicalism, and just across the bay from the hippie capital that was San Francisco. Marcuse's aim was to challenge Freud's intense pessimism about sexual relations, whereby the search for pleasure comes into conflict with scarcity in the natural and human environment, resulting in a desexualization of the body as a whole, with all sexual activity concentrated on the genitals. For Marcuse, Freud was describing a particular state of sexual affairs, "repressive desublimation," desublimation because it involved the release of erotic energy, but repressive because it remained controlled by the reality principle and made workers passive, ready to provide alienated labor. Marcuse believed that the development of the forces of production would undermine the historical necessity for such repression. This assumption, that the forces of production would more or less inevitably develop in such a way as to release sexuality from capitalism's need to repress pleasure, was based on an untenable extrapolation of future conditions from the post-war economic boom. His view was not, however, that everyone could just do what they liked in the utopia of tomorrow. Marcuse was arguing that the very categories of perversion and gratification would change, resulting in a polymorphous, more dispersed sexuality. As Alisdair MacIntyre (1970: 50) points out, when Marcuse hints that the categories of gratification would change in this new utopian post-scarcity world, it is hard to avoid asking what we will actually do sexually: massage each other's feet?[7]

In the cultural and political apparatus surrounding rock, such notions of sexual freedom were articulated in a rougher form; in, for example, The Weather Underground's Smash Monogamy campaign, or in invocations of rock's Dionysian transcendence of constraint (such as Jeff Nuttall's *Bomb Culture*).[8] This is the moment where the conjunction of sex and drugs and rock and roll enters the popular cultural mainstream as means of self-realization, drawing on widespread reading of a lineage of thinkers from William Blake and De Sade through Nietzsche to Freud to Sartre, who were interpreted as arguing that civilization was an oppressive charade. A flavor of this can be found in *Power Play* (1970), by Richard Neville, an extended ode to the joys of orgiastic and commitment-free fucking.[9] Neville was a key underground figure, with strong links to rock via the advocacy of figures such as John Lennon and British alternative music hero, the BBC radio presenter John Peel. In music, such notions of sexual freedom were felt to be most powerfully embodied in the counterculture's transformation of blues and blues-based R&B, which through its racialized links to black masculinity had come to be coded as transgressive. Led Zeppelin's "Whole lotta love" is the anthem of this strand of rock. But other widespread rock expressions of supposed sexual freedom were androgyny, dandyism, and bisexuality. For some, glam rock offered a moment in the early 1970s where extremely popular musicians offered widespread images of a different kind of masculinity (see Stevenson, 2006, on David Bowie). We shall see in discussing metal later that there are debates about the degree to which the androgyny of some popular music genres really reflects any kind of challenge to limiting binaristic models of human sexuality. But rock, it should not be forgotten, by no means freed itself of the narcissism that was increasingly pervading popular music and popular culture. As Simon Reynolds and Joy Press (1995: 16) point out in their brilliant and exhaustive

[7]   Perhaps such ideas had an indirect influence on the New Age concept of tantric sex, adopted and advocated by music stars as varied as Sting and P Diddy. Or perhaps not.

[8]   This romantic appraisal of the Dionysian is the basis of Camille Paglia's heroization of The Rolling Stones and other classic rock bands (see Paglia, 1995).

[9]   Neville summarized his 1960s views in a later retraction: "Steeped in the sexism of the time and thrilled at shaming the citadels of repression, I said stupid things. Making love is still better than making war, but orgies are not the key to social justice" (quoted by DeGroot, 2008: 216).

account of gender and rebellion in rock, a band such as The Rolling Stones could combine usurpation of self-adornment with the belittling of women for such frivolousness, for example, the promotional video for "Have you seen your mother baby standing in the shadow?" where Jagger tauntingly lords it over a (former) lover, telling her that she will turn into her mother unless she sets herself free from the shadow of personal and presumably sexual restraint. There were democratizing aspects to the way in which countercultural sexual politics inflected popular music culture but rock's sexual politics were deeply problematic.

3.4 Post-War Pop's Emotional Resources

Without doubt, post-war pop music contained a huge amount of banality and sexism. Pop provides a compromised set of resources for the kinds of emotional self-realization that Nussbaum advocates. Against rock's excessive critique of pop, I want to argue that, at its best, post-war pop dramatized for young people the risks involved in a new, relative sexual freedom, of attraction and rejection, often in an urban context newly freed from the brutal requirements of nature.

I offer some examples here, more or less at random. A more comprehensive survey is beyond my scope here. The point is that these represent types of recorded music that have often been dismissed, by rockist critics, or by those who are interested only in art music. In the 1959 hit "Dream lover," the deep yearning of Bobby Darin's heartfelt vocals is complemented by a pizzicato violin undertow that creates an almost neurotic sense of neediness. In the soft harmonies of doo-wop recordings such as the Fleetwoods' "Tragedy" or its B-side "Little miss sad one," the music is comforting, not only through the tenderness of singer Gary Croxley's vocal, but also through the interplay of male and female voices, which seem to suggest that a wholeness might be restored to the psyche of a girl listener damaged by rejection. In the heart of the commercial beast of music capitalism, in New York's Brill Building, young songwriters such as Carole King were able to articulate the vulnerability associated with the new sexual freedom becoming available in the era of the pill and popular pornography: "will you still love me tomorrow?" as King's song puts it (the title actually lacks the "still"). The 1962 recording by the Shirelles uses a Brazilian *baion* rhythm, where the on beat is followed by a pause and two half-beats, and as Dave Marsh (1989: 77) observes, this encapsulates the hesitancy involved in deciding whether the girl should "believe the magic of your sigh." Meanwhile, lush strings and a "busy pizzicato" convey a rich sensuous excitement, suggesting that if the song is about making a difficult decision, the decision is probably going to be "yes."

To treat popular music as always "about" sex can risk missing this realm of feeling and emotion in popular music, or just as bad, leads to the dismissal of such music as romantic ideology, or as a vehicle of female subjugation. Rivalry, jealousy, and mistrust are of course as much a feature of intimate relations as warmth and tenderness, and pop addressed these too. In Texas Ruby's Texas swing classic "Don't let that man get you down," from 1945, enmity masquerades as friendly advice, as Ruby warns girls that because her man's heart is cold as ice, not to mess with him. And you would not want to mess with Ruby whose rich low alto speaks of strength and resilience, in spite of her supposed heartbreak. And here, in a fine essay, is musicologist Richard Leppert, comparing Patsy Cline's version of "It wasn't god who made honky tonk angels" with Kitty Wells' earlier version:

> She projects not one emotion, as was the case with Wells' original, but several and in quick succession. Like Wells, she laments, but she also vents frustration and even anger. Above all, she is unresigned. ... Cline's delivery constantly alternates mood, duly expressive of her untenable position within the gender dyad that the narrative describes (Leppert, 2007: 55).

Leppert shows how Cline achieves this by moving to the flow of the rhythm in something like her own time, implying her autonomy. And more than that, unlike Wells, Cline sounds as though she is enjoying herself, and thereby refuses the shame offered by the narrative of the song.

There were more adult versions of these dramas too, written for older audiences, and articulating other emotions. Fears about commitment and fidelity were expressed in terms of stories of determination, survival, sacrifice, and abandonment. Bacharach and David's "A house is not a home," as performed by Dionne Warwick in 1964 (not the later version by Brook Benton) is not a love song about teenagers, it is a melodramatic invocation of the commitments involved in sharing a life, and of what it means to be rejected not after a teenage date, or a one-night stand, but after years of joy and pain with another person. The orchestral arrangement draws on the conventions of musical theater to make personal pain into an epic portrayal of fear of loneliness. Gladys Knight and the Pips' "Midnight train to Georgia" is about what it means to see a partner's life dissolve and to support them as they attempt to rebuild it. "L.A.," Gladys almost mutters at the start of the song, before a huge pause which suggests the momentousness of what follows, "proved too much for the man." This is a "stand by your man" song, but only a very harsh ideological reading would see it purely in those terms. It is also about returning to a set of better values, away from the ruthless competitiveness of modern life, represented by the Big City. It evokes homesickness too – an often powerful feeling that art rarely represents (Marsh, 1989).

Pop is not just about the pain and challenges of love; it is also been about the joy of feeling a special connection with another human being, and about the excitement and invigoration of sex. And one of the great achievements of the demand for greater sexual freedom in the 1960s, in terms of music, was that pop could celebrate these things in an adult way without disguising sexual desire behind euphemisms. Marvin Gaye's "Let's get it on" and a great deal of the oeuvre of Barry White play with the singer as seducer. The lyrics of these songs are often about sexual play as much as sexual pleasure – but the performances leave us in no doubt about the delight that might be experienced in the intimacy of these men's bedrooms. Prince inherited this tradition, but combined the promise of sexual ecstasy with a gender-bending kinkiness and a deep funky exuberance. He made sexual borderlines sound hugely enjoyable in an era when AIDS loomed over people's sex lives like an impending storm.

Like so much sentimental music of the final third of the twentieth century, songs such as "Midnight train to Georgia" and "Let's get it on" draw on the conventions of gospel music to express sincerity and emotional depth. As Simon Frith (2001) notes, the dominant form of pop in this period combined features of rock and soul with elements of nineteenth-century parlor songs (see also Van Der Merwe, 1989): easy melodic lines, rising pitch to indicate the release of emotion, and narcissistic self-pity. From soul, singers like Elton John took hesitancy, introversion, and intimacy, in contrast with the extroverted confidence of Victorian ballad singers (Scott, 1989). And from rock came a new dynamism of rhythm, amplification, and texture. The result was the rise to pop pre-eminence of the rock ballad, with the power ballad as the ultimate marker of sincerity. When Whitney Houston sings "I will always love you" or Celine Dion covers "The power of love," they are singing about the way in which the need for attachment can overwhelm us. For skeptics, power ballads are excessively sentimental – and I tend to share that view. But when these songs are performed in public, it is hard for me not to be moved by how moved other people tend to be. The songs might be explicitly about sexual love, but they are easily translated into expressions of other forms of love, such as familial – which is why they are so often performed at funerals.

The rock ballad, like the teen pop hit before it, became the focus of bohemian opprobrium, because of rock culture's sense that real sincerity and authenticity lay in a more earthy expression of desires. But some of the most beloved rock and indie songs have features of the ballad. Radiohead's "Creep" rises from introspective yearning to a crescendo of alienated sorrow. What distinguishes it from "The power of love" is its self-loathing and lack of redemption, expressed most piercingly in the startlingly abrupt guitar chords played at a crucial point in the chorus. "Alternative" has become a questionable term in an era where indie and alternative rock are big-ish business. But songs like "Creep" offer a genuine alternative to those who find power ballads and their tributes to love cloying or restricting. "Creep" is the equivalent of an indie movie that uses all the techniques of the Hollywood thriller or romance to generate emotional interest but which then refuses to give its audiences a redemptive ending. That attitude in "Creep" derives from punk's critical engagement with pop, which I will discuss later.

3.5   Sex and Love on the Dance Floor

Perhaps one of the factors that leads people, like the friend of mine I quoted at the start of this chapter, to make very strong links between music and sexuality, and thereby to downplay love, is that they may have in mind, quite reasonably, a different side of music's role in people's lives, where musical meaning is relatively submerged beneath a general affective sense of sexual atmosphere. After all, music serves as a soundtrack in public spaces (clubs, parties) where sex is a primary aim for lots of people, if not always the actual result. Music made for dancing in such settings often suggests sex in its lyrics and more significantly in rhythms and instrumental and vocal timbres that have come to be associated with sensuality. In a whole range of geographical contexts, Latin music has played something like this role (see Chapter 5 for discussion of the tango, and how it gained its sexual overtones in working-class dance places); this obviously draws on dubious articulations between eroticism and exoticism. Dance genres such as house and hi-energy drew on the drugged-up hedonistic sexuality of queer dance spaces (clubs and converted warehouses) in the 1980s. "Baby wants to ride," a house track from 1987, credited to Frankie Knuckles, provides an extraordinary mixture of mock-religious invocations, political statements about freedom and peace, and sexual come-ons (and the version I have is not even the x-rated version, released in 1988 with more explicit lyrics). It's all over the place. What brings it together is hypnotic kick drums, a repeated synthesizer riff, and the regular insertion of a swelling sound that evokes a passing train horn. The latter picks up on the "ride" of the title, which is clearly sexual. But there is a collective ethos too – the lyrics recall the train metaphor in civil rights anthems like the Impressions' "People get ready" ("there's a train a-coming") and in celebrations of internationalism such as the O Jays' "Love train" ("People all over the world, join in, on the love train"). The record is hardly wholesome, though: it manages to be both uplifting and gloriously seedy.

Pop has constantly drawn energy and inspiration from dance-based genres in order to provide new ways of invoking and provoking sexual feeling, from disco to reggae to house to R&B. However, this should not be thought of as an unmediated expression of sexual feeling. At their best, dance pop records somehow enact the obsessive fascination of sexual desire, and do so with a certain stylishness and wit which can leave you wondering how much was intended, and how much was wonderful accident. In his remarkable though meandering book *Words and Music* (2004), British journalist Paul Morley writes about Kylie Minogue's "Can't get you out of my head":

> Great pop songs about love should try to define what it is to feel love for someone else and should imply how that love will one day come to an end, so there is a kind of melancholy lacing the joy; and the song should achieve this in a way that means that when you listen to it, you can't get it out of your head. You can't get 'Can't get you out of my head' out of your head (Morley, 2004: 27).

So the song is about love and sex and the relation between states of mind, Morley observes, but it is also about itself, and about the fact that it is about itself. And yet

> it is just ingenious enough to wrap the collection of received sounds and stolen rhythms with a seal of novelty, thus making it not a parody or a homage or a copy of something else, but something that has been made modern and knowing enough to add to the history of a certain kind of pop music (Morley, 2004: 27).

Alongside the sentimental, the seductive, the sensual, and the clever, much popular music is based on a more raucous carnivalesque idea of sex as *dirty* or funny, or both. This is far removed from the sensitivity and emotional pain of adolescent pop, or adult songs about the challenges and satisfactions of sexual love. Here the pleasures are more transgressive, as ordinary constraints on what can and cannot be said and felt about bodies and desires are expressed lyrically and also musically. This has been a major element in music consumed by working-class people including hip hop, reggae, ragga, country, or hillbilly.[10] Nick Tosches (1989/1977: 120–156) has shown that behind the bland respectability of mainstream country culture in the late twentieth century, lay a sordid history of vernacular sentiment, including dirty songs that the country music establishment later sought to repress. Hip hop has brought a mixture of sexuality and comic revulsion into popular culture in a way that no other genre currently does. Hip hop, though, has just been one element in a further sexualization of popular music in the wake of the counterculture. I return to this issue later in the chapter.

My argument has been that pop music in the post-war period, pervading everyday life via the media, constituted a rich terrain of commentary on love and sex. The focus on personal relationships may have been disproportionate, and I am sure pop music would be better if it was about more than love and sex, more of the time.[11] But the focus on intimacy reflected not only a business context where sexual desire might sell more records, because of its supposed universality. It was also a result of the fact that music was increasingly being heard in public spaces where groups of young people could gather – or in bedrooms where young people might fantasize more freely than in the cramped shared living spaces endured by previous generations. Such songs reflected the sexualization of love, often oriented by an ethos of commitment, fidelity, and trust. The best pop music registered the problems of maintaining such an ethos, perhaps especially so in an increasingly consumerist and hedonistic society.

[10] The best book on the ambivalent and complex politics of carnival and transgression is by Peter Stallybrass and Allon White (1986), who were drawing on the Russian literary critic Mikhail Bakhtin.

[11] Thomas Scheff (2011) provides a compelling study of popular song lyrics. The book pays too little attention to the ways in which music and performance complicate the emotional meanings of the words. But Scheff analyzes emotions in greater depth than I have seen in any example of popular music studies.

3.6 Critiques of Countercultural Sexual Freedom

By the 1980s, bohemian notions of sexual freedom had come under serious attack, but were also being absorbed into popular culture in new ways, linked to a new culture of narcissism. The fact that even an intellectually brilliant advocate of sexual freedom such as Marcuse was unable to construct a sufficiently robust political edifice for their views made the liberationist sexual politics strongly associated with rock culture highly vulnerable to critique. The conservative attack was divided by the different pulls exerted by the clear economic gains to be had from the commodification of sexuality and a paternalist wing that emphasized the virtues of order and restraint. Many conservative commentators saw the 1960s as an era of sharp moral decline, and have continued to do so ever since. In music theory, the most prominent advocate of this conservative position is the philosopher Roger Scruton, who from a Kantian perspective on the sacredness of the person, advocates erotic love as oriented to the "irreplaceable incarnate subjectivity of the other," defying death through its links to sexual reproduction and its celebration and endorsement of the individual subject. This finds its greatest musical expression in Wagner, whose music emphasizes love as exaltation and preservation of the individual over self-gratifying lust (Scruton, 2003: 130–131). In Scruton's philosophy of sexual desire, this emphasis on exaltation of the individual manifests itself as an argument that masturbation offends against the principle of personal encounter that should regulate sexuality by "creating a compliant world of desire, in which unreal objects become the focus of real emotions, and the emotions themselves are rendered incompetent to participate in the building of personal relations" (Scruton, 1986: 345–346). This may prompt us to push towards a more dialectical conception of musical–sexual politics by realizing just what the often misguided countercultural advocates of sexual freedom might have been up against.

A rather different way of opposing countercultural notions of sexual freedom is represented by the sociologist Bernice Martin, based on a more latent conservatism than Scruton's writing. Martin traced the ways in which, in her view, the legacies of romanticism associated with the middle-class youth counterculture of the 1960s, had come to transform culture well beyond it. Using a Durkheimian framework, Martin argued that the romantic crusade was always an impossible utopian dream because cultural radicals were implicitly seeking to universalize *liminality*, the experience of being on the threshold between different planes or aspects of life. This has relevance for understanding peak experiences of musical collectivism, including gigs and (for some musicians) performances, and also dance parties and raves (on rave politics, see Chapter 4). But it is also relevant for considering music and sexuality. Derived from the work of anthropologist Victor Turner, the concept of liminality embodies the opposite of social *structure*. "At the stage of liminality a ritual characteristically involves either taboo breaking…and/or extremely rich, multi-vocal symbols which embody a wide range of social possibilities, most of which will again be tabooed once the stage of liminality is over" (Martin, 1981: 50). Opposition to structure is fundamental to liminality, as is a sense of commonality amongst those sharing liminal experiences. In these very rare and very delineated moments, "not only is anything possible, at least at the symbolic level, but there is an undifferentiated and ecstatic one-ness with the other liminal participants and often, through them, with humanity in the abstract" (Martin, 1981: 51). For Turner, in complex modern societies, the functional equivalents of liminal rituals are above all to be found in "the arts," but also science and philosophy. In marked contrast with the Frankfurt School's critique of standardization in modern societies, Turner sees capitalism as "a particularly extended case of the multiplication of liminoid possibilities" (51). Martin takes a different and somewhat more moralistic approach, but one that I think is nevertheless interesting in providing a sociological understanding of the limits reached by rock's sexual politics. The whole point of liminality is that it cannot last, and so cannot sustain societies or communities.

Martin focuses on both rock and sexuality, and links the two. Sexuality, because of its especially strong links to ecstatic states, easily stands for the symbolism of opposition to structure and also tends to be hedged by prohibitions which harness it to central institutions of order and continuity. This is one of the political aspects of sex that has not been adequately recognized in the way that music and sex have generally been discussed in recent times. And for Martin, it is sexuality's links to power and control that allow sexual freedom to be presented as particularly progressive. Rock, meanwhile – by which Martin probably means something more like popular music in the wake of rock and roll, including soul and punk – was the main cultural medium through which young people explored the symbolism of liminality in the 1960s and 1970s. Because of its playful, expressive, and non-instrumental nature, rock could easily be set against discipline and functionality, in school and at work. Rock, for Martin, organizes and mediates many aspects of social order, but sexuality, she says "is probably the most important single element…[T]he central paradox of rock is that it uses its most precious symbol of liminality, that is overt sexuality, to reproduce and reinforce the sexual role differentiation of the wider society." In other words, Martin suggests, in offering such liminal experiences as challenging to the established order, rock in fact served conservative functions. But this does not mean that society remained unchanged after the countercultural moment. For Martin, rock "acted as the single most important vehicle for the spread of the hedonistic messages" of what she calls the Expressive Revolution, unleashing narcissism and attendant anxieties. In Martin's analysis, the anxieties produced by "sexual liberation" could only be resolved or assuaged for the rock culture by comedy or shock (though she does not discuss shock nearly enough). This produced a retreat from a notion of sex-as-ecstasy to one of sex-as-dirt, thus undermining countercultural sexual politics. Martin ignores the possibility that different class fractions might have been involved in these varying forms of representation of sex, and she certainly underestimates the degree to which participants in the counterculture sought to balance sexual liberation with devotion to other more mundane forms of good living. Nevertheless, her perspective throws light on why shock and comedy are a key part of the sexual explicitness of a great deal of popular music.[12]

Martin went too far in reacting against the expressive revolution's own sense of itself as a project of emancipation, and at times her tone resembles that of a senior schoolteacher observing the silly ways of the children around her. She seems to assume that the social system works as a unified whole to correct itself – a dubious view associated with structural-functionalism (for more discussion of this way of seeing society, see Chapter 4). Somewhere beyond Marcuse's unfounded utopianism and Martin's Christian Durkheimian pessimism, we need a conception of the ordinary pleasures of music in relation to sex, but one which does not ignore the way that these pleasures are bound up with consumer capitalism and empty hedonism. It is such a conception that I use in examining the post-countercultural sexual politics of music in the next two sections.

---

[12]   Martin, of course, was not alone in her skepticism about the achievements of the counterculture. The same period also saw the publications of various books that were effectively critiques of the narcissism of countercultural modernity, by Richard Sennett (1974) and Christopher Lasch (1978). But Martin took the counterculture more seriously than these other writers.

3.7 Sex and Love in Punk, Alternative Rock, and Metal

The most serious challenge to countercultural rock sexual politics, both within serious analysis of music and in musical culture itself, came from feminism. In popular music studies, one of the earliest and most often cited contributions was Simon Frith and Angela McRobbie's (1990/1978) critique of the polarization of most rock and pop music into two ideal types of musical-sexual politics: the first, "cock rock" – "music making in which performance is an explicit, crude and often aggressive exploration of male sexuality," with Elvis, Jagger, Roger Daltrey, and Robert Plant as examples; and the second, teenybop pop, consumed almost exclusively by girls, and whose representation of male sexuality centered on self-pity, vulnerability, and need, and played on "feminine" conceptions of sex as serious, diffuse, and involving total emotional commitment. These were ideal types with overlaps and internal contradictions, but Frith and McRobbie emphasized a polarization, in which sexual differences and connected gender inequalities between boys and girls were expressed and reinforced in music.[13] For Frith and McRobbie, then, the two different ideologies of sexual love articulated by rock and pop, respectively, were being expressed in a highly unsatisfactory way.

Frith and McRobbie were writing in the period of punk's ascendancy, when new fusions of rock and pop were being attempted, and where the culture was developing a sexual politics quite as complex as anything the high countercultural rock moment had produced. We can identify a number of different modes of sexuality expressed in punk and post-punk culture. Punk's ideology of supposedly telling it like it is could lead to a rejection of hippie sensitivity and feminist critique, which at times bordered on misogyny, for example, in the public statements and some of the recordings of the Stranglers ("London lady"). In other cases, the ethos of sincerity and authenticity manifested itself as disgust at romantic love, a denunciation of sentimentality and of family. One articulation of this view was a widely

---

[13] Frith qualified this account heavily in a later piece, first published in *The New Statesman* (Frith, 1990/1985) following critique of his and McRobbie's original article by others on the constructionist grounds that the task of analysis was to examine how music constructs discourses of sexuality, rather than how it articulates predefined ideologies. In fact it seems quite reasonable to consider the way in which rock performers might partially reflect, as well as constitute notions of sexuality, as long as we hold on to the specificity of the ways they do this as musicians, operating within certain understandings of music, as well as of sex.

quoted statement by John Lydon (then Johnny Rotten, of Sex Pistols) that love was just three minutes – or two minutes, fifty-two seconds in some versions – of "squelching noises." Recordings such as Lydon's "Bodies" (see Gracyk, 2001: 4, for a terrific analysis) and The Birthday Party's odes to abjection and violence, suggested that this disillusion might be experienced as deeply painful. More generally, punk celebrated rebellion founded on homosociality, and the band as group of mates; the Clash and the Jam played with this imagery, and often transcended it. Much about punk was deeply masculinist even as it rejected rock's sexual politics.

But punk had a different side too, bound up in feminism and gay politics, rejecting machismo, and frankly recording vulnerability and rejection. "Ever fallen in love (with someone you shouldn't've)" by Buzzcocks, a band named in honor of dildoes, addressed those issues, but instead of a ballad, the music was a joyous anthem, dissolving private pain into a collective recognition of shared exposure to hurt. Beyond punk's incursions into mass popularity, there were even more radical interventions: Alternative TV's song, "Love lies limp," about male impotence, is as far from the thrusting cock rock of Led Zeppelin as could be imagined. Set to an exhausted reggae rhythm, its anxious guitar riff struggles to leave the same repeated notes. Sex is "a bother," whether with women or men, and the tone is half-humorous, half self-lacerating honesty.

By the 1980s and early 1990s, Anglo-American rock had separated out into two genres, each with very different notions of sexual politics. The first was alternative rock (or sometimes alternative pop) which inherited punk's distancing from sentimental romantic love and from sexual bohemianism. In some forms of indie pop, there was a childlike renunciation of the world of adult sexuality; sometimes the suggestion was that a rediscovery of childhood innocence offered a superior alternative to adulthood. This was not necessarily about regression, as Scott Plagenhoef (2007: 71) remarks of Belle and Sebastian's Stuart Murdoch, who crystallized this aesthetic in the late 1990s: "his examination of emotions through the lens of childhood is less about nostalgia or escapism as it is exploring core human emotions without the distractions, compromises and obligations of adulthood." Other elements of alternative rock represented a hyper-masculine but desexualized rock style, derived from the frenetic energy of punk. By the early 1990s, a new hybrid had emerged, where vulnerability was linked to guitar power, as in Nirvana, or to the energy of electronic dance pop (as in some versions of British indie, such as Pulp). As Matthew Bannister (2006) shows in his study of masculinity in indie rock in the 1980s, indie's attempts to reinvent the relationship of music and sexuality could not shake off aggression and competitiveness – and his view is partly based on frank acknowledgment of his own experiences as part of the New Zealand indie scene of that period. Sara Cohen (1991: 234) recounts how the indie musicians she studied in Liverpool in the 1980s had been bullied at school by male peers for making music, which was associated with femininity "perhaps because of its links with the emotions and with the body." And for some, indie's progressive sexual politics seemed excessively desexualized, and lacking in fun and pleasure. By the early 1990s, at least in the United Kingdom, many young people had rejected indie's melancholy for the hedonism of rave culture. But, as we shall see in Chapter 4, a complex politics emerged in rave. Marcusean themes of polymorphous sexuality were taken up, partly under the influence of esctasy's sensualizing properties but some elements of dance culture rejected sexual bohemianism in favor of a more androgynous notion of collective pleasure.

A very different notion of sexual politics was embodied in metal, which reasserted earthy sexuality without the claims to human emancipation that had accompanied it in the counterculture. To bohemian outsiders increasingly influenced by feminism and queer politics, the mainstream metal of the 1980s and 1990s therefore seemed to manifest a more banal (and less artistically interesting) version of 1970s cock rock. Its carnivalesque elements were, according to some cultural critics, "mere play with oppositional signifiers" (Kaplan, 1987). Against such views, Robert Walser (1993: 134) provided an intelligent analysis of the ambivalence of metal androgyny:

> Androgynous metal's bricolage of male power and female spectacle…are complex responses to crucial contradictions that its fans have inherited…. If male heavy metal fans and musicians sometimes co-opt heavy metal by co-opting femininity, what they achieve is not necessarily the same kind of masculinity as they sought, as the conflicting demands of masculinity and rebellion are mediated through new models and the free play of androgynous fantasy shakes up the underlying categories that structure social experience.

Metal, then, arguably provided a space of play for (working class) audiences to explore sexual identities. This was strictly delineated and temporary, but surely not without significance in the lives of its fans.[14]

---

[14]   Keith Kahn-Harris (2006) suggests that extreme metal genres are marked more by a fear of the abject, which manifests itself in more misogynistic attitudes than those to be found in the fear-and-loathing wing of post-punk.

In other musical genres during this period, including mainstream pop, there was an increasingly explicit sexuality, partly via the increasing prevalence of music video, but also because of the victory of countercultural notions of freedom, in league with commerce, over views concerning sexual restraint (many of them coming from religious leaders) that have increasingly come to be identified with a bygone age. Historian Tim Blanning (2010: 324) credits the "liberating power" of music, alongside many other individuals, groups, and "impersonal forces," in establishing the tolerance towards queer identities manifest in the popular music culture of recent decades. He finds evidence of this tolerance in examples such as the massive tribute to Queen vocalist Freddie Mercury, who had recently died from an AIDS-related disease, at Wembley Stadium in 1991; or the public acceptance of and even affection for Elton John. But the changes go beyond such tolerance to an increasing emphasis upon sexual openness and experimentation as the basis of a fully formed self.

3.8 Sexuality in Twenty-First-Century Pop

The concept of postfeminist popular culture usefully points to some reasons to be cautious in assessing developments in recent decades as a democratization of sexual identities and practices, much less genuine gender equality. Broadly, postfeminism refers to the idea that feminism has been taken into account and is therefore no longer needed (McRobbie, 2009). In the realm of popular culture, Yvonne Tasker and Diane Negra (2007) have pointed out that this entails particular problems of commodification, consumerism, exclusion, and individualism. "Postfeminist culture," they write, "works in part to incorporate, assume, or naturalize aspects of feminism; crucially, it also works to commodify feminism via the figure of woman as empowered consumer" (2). Most relevantly for our present concerns, it also emphasizes "physical and particularly sexual empowerment." Yet it is "white and middle class by default, anchored in consumption as a strategy (and leisure as a site) for the production of the self"; there is a retreat from demands for economic and workplace empowerment of the kind that might constitute a much fuller notion of equality.

One way to explore the sexual politics of music in a postfeminist age is to look at some of the artists that have been most associated with a supposedly excessive degree of sexual explicitness in recent years. To judge from media coverage, it would seem that representations of sex, and provocations of sexual desire, have lost little of their power to provoke concern, anxiety, and even disgust. This is evident in a series of books and articles, academic and non-academic, in the 2000s on sexualization and pornification. Some of the contributions to these debates point polemically to the potential damage that might be caused by exposure, especially on the part of young people, and especially girls, to such representations (Levy, 2005; Dines, 2010). Others provide a more balanced approach (Attwood, 2006; Paasonen, Nikunen, and Saarenmaa, 2007; Smith, 2010) which points to ways in which people, including girls, distinguish reality from fantasy, and in some cases exhibit considerable savviness in their interactions with the media (Buckingham and Bragg, 2004). Music culture has been strangely absent from many of these debates, perhaps because sexual desire is associated so much with the visual. But as we have already observed, musical culture in modern societies is intensely visual, and musical performance is strongly linked to sexuality, and to fears about it. Such fears are apparent in media coverage, which has paid a great deal more attention to sexualization in music – specifically pop music – than has academic and book publishing. In an article for the *Daily Mail*,[15] entitled "How pop became porn" (March 1, 2010), journalist Liz Jones wrote of her exposure to what she claimed was 24 hours of watching MTV's "various numerous channels."

> The woman is naked – or looks like she is. Only a flesh-coloured leotard covers her body. Her long blonde hair tumbles down her back. She's in a cage, sliding her fingers provocatively in and out of her mouth. A scene from a clichéd pornographic film? Sadly not. The woman in question is Shakira, a pop superstar, and the fourth richest singer in the world. The images can be seen in the video for her single, She Wolf, which will be watched obsessively, again and again, by thousands of young men and women, many of whom will form the opinion that writhing in a cage is precisely the way "sexy" women should behave.

The mass purchase of cages for the purposes of sexual gratification in the teenage bedrooms of Britain seems an unlikely consequence of young people watching a Shakira video. While Shakira's attractiveness is not in doubt,

[15]   The *Daily Mail* is one of the United Kingdom's most widely read and influential newspapers – and newspaper readership is much higher in the United Kingdom than in most other countries. I concentrate in detail on it here, because the newspaper typifies one kind of discourse that dismisses the subtle ways in which pop music might enrich life, and inaccurately identifies the ways in which it might detract from it.

the video involves a display of acrobatic dancing skill more than it does the explicit erotic contact of porn: the focus is contortion rather than penetration. The explicit meaning of the song concerns a woman who attends to her man's domestic needs, but feels sexually unwanted. The cage symbolizes her feelings of entrapment. But another sub-text brought out by the video reveals the playfulness of this – later in the video, wearing a dress, and beaming with pleasure, Shakira dances, alone and then surrounded by others in a dance club. The use of vocoder to dehumanize her vocals further suggests someone taken over by a force she cannot control. In a simple and effective way, this pop song enacts the frustration of unfulfilled desire and the pleasures of release – through music and dance, as much as sex. Popular culture, and pop music, will surely always be about such themes, and it is hard to see this video, and this song, in themselves, as evidence of objectification, though they are certainly narcissistic.

Jones' article, a strange mixture of titillation and deep moral concern, was occasioned by the publication of a report, commissioned by the Home Secretary (the UK equivalent of a Minister of the Interior) on sexualization of young people, and its potential links to increasing violence against women and girls, and written by a psychologist and regular *Cosmopolitan* contributor, Linda Papadopolous. The report's findings about music were extremely limited, confined mainly to citations of two papers claiming to show, on the basis of dubious content analysis, that "degrading lyrics" (which somehow they found only in rap and R&B) were "related to" advances in sexual behavior in adolescents (Martino et al., 2006; Primack et al., 2009). That did not stop the report calling for a ban on broadcasters showing music videos with sexual posing or sexually suggestive lyrics before 9 p.m. and an amendment to the law so that music videos would be covered by the 1984 Act of Parliament that regulates video content. Nor did it stop a tide of sensationalist media coverage, much of it concentrating on a number of prominent female singers, accompanied of course by alluring pictures of those singers – presumably these needed to be hidden from any children who might pick up newspapers – including one by Dr Papadopolous herself in the *Daily Mail*, entitled "Why do Rihanna's songs have to tell girls they're 'sluts'?"

Rihanna's songs do no such thing, and nor do her videos. They do, however, celebrate sexual pleasure in an often unsubtle way. "Rude boy's" lyric "can you get it up? Are you big enough?" is a taunt, a challenge, rather than a simple expression of availability. The attitude is "You're lucky – I'm getting to let you have me" and the affect-less voice indicates her own self-control. The female singers identified by much media coverage as responsible for sexualization (rather than the corporate system of cultural production that creates the marketing tools) are in fact considerably more interesting, inventive, and ambivalent than they are portrayed. This tradition of challenging men has a long history, long before second-wave feminism emphasized female empowerment in popular culture (listen to Julia Lee's "Don't come too soon," from the 1940s).

In this and other ways, the sexual explicitness in twenty-first-century pop involves new versions of older themes. As Eva Illouz (1997: 7) suggests, "love remains one of the most important mythologies of our times" and this is still apparent in a great deal of pop. Rihanna's "Umbrella" is a sad and tender love song after all. Perhaps the strangest star of all modern female pop stars, Lady Gaga, seems actually to undermine sexual desire through her extreme styling. Gaga's world is one of depthless, remorseless, and entertaining aestheticization, mixed with touches of identity politics. *New York Times* critic Jon Caramanica reports Gaga's emergence at the end of a Madison Square Garden live show, "sparklerlike contraptions on her chest and crotch, spitting out tiny, angry, smoldering bits" ("Girl pop's Lady Gaga makeover," July 21, 2010). In the wake of Lady Gaga's success, Caramanica suggested, "[t]he space for women in pop to try out new aesthetic identities hasn't been this vast in some time." Gaga is at her most interesting, it seems to me, when she addresses sexual anxiety through such humorous performance, rather than when making earnest statements about empowerment.

Music videos, along with hundreds of other performances where women singers and dancers reveal their bodies, and men do not, presumably have some role in reflecting and perpetuating gender and sexual inequality. Many music videos are staggeringly banal, and are full of clichéd images of fleshly female submission and strutting male singers. And even the most inventive of the great female stars of the twenty-first century are embedded in a culture of profound commodification. In that respect, it was all too predictable that in the much-hyped video for Lady Gaga's "Telephone," there would be repeated and unsubtle product placement of a cell phone. Nor should we underestimate the ways in which individualistic narcissism produces potential problems for the psyche in modern societies. There are more intelligent understandings of the problems of contemporary sexuality and sexual representations than those offered by sensationalist journalists. Rosalind Gill, for example, has argued that there has been a shift in the way that (patriarchal) power operates from an external, male judging gaze to a self-policing narcissistic gaze. I would argue that this represents a higher or deeper form of exploitation than objectification – one in which the objectifying male gaze is internalized to form a new disciplinary regime (Gill, 2007: 258).

This self-policing is related by Gill to the distorted forms of self-realization that were discussed in Chapter 2. Especially for women, in the neoliberal era, "the self has become a project to be evaluated, advised, disciplined and improved or brought 'into recovery'" (262). Contemporary musical cultures are clearly implicated with this dubious individualization. But they offer other things too, and not only in the world of "alternative" music, with its sometimes asexual and often pretentious musings. As my earlier readings have shown, even seemingly explicit pop records and videos are concerned with the nature of desire, and the nature of intimate relationships. Again, we need to consider love as well as sex.

3.9   Black Music and Racialized Sexuality

Pop has close links to dance music, and dance music is especially associated with African-American genres. The result has been that pop is also linked to racialized sexuality, even as the very meaning of "race" changes in modern societies. To tell the story of sex and popular music as I have so far, in terms of the rock/pop dialectic (even while acknowledging the influence of blues, R&B, soul, and funk on rock and pop), fails adequately to address the crucial juxtaposition of sex and race in modern culture.

As Paul Gilroy (2000: 178) has commented, there is a danger that critical intellectuals, in discovering the special potency of popular cultural styles, might rush "too simplistically or too swiftly to either condemn or celebrate." Nevertheless, in an article first published in 1994 and reprinted in his book *Against Race* in 2000, Gilroy provided a powerful commentary on "the apparently sex-obsessed culture" of contemporary African-American culture. His suggestion was that the repudiation of ideas of collective black freedom and progress, combined with the assertive pursuit of sexual pleasure provided a "dismal moment in which public politics becomes unspeakable and bio-politics takes hold." For Gilroy, R&B singer R. Kelly is the exemplar of this moment of the privatization and somatization of community. In this conjuncture, "[R]acialised sex is an ephemeral residue of political rebellion"; the pursuit of collective freedom gives way to the

"the androcentric and phallocentric presentation and representation of heterosexual coupling," "a racialised biopolitics of fucking," based on a "mood in which the person is defined as the body and in which certain exemplary bodies" – Mike Tyson, Michael Jordan, Naomi Campbell – become questionable symbols of community.

Gilroy is sometimes criticized for an overly nostalgic critique of contemporary Black Atlantic culture[16] but in fact his contribution ends with a thoughtful consideration of the ambivalence of a figure who might seem to exemplify the view that 1990s hip hop had rejected community in favor of nihilism (West, 1992): Snoop Doggy Dogg. Why, Gilroy asks, would a young African-American choose, in the 1990s, "to present himself to the world with the features, with the identity, of a dog?" (Gilroy is thinking of his album cover as well as his name). This may be "an accurate evaluation of the social status of young black men" but more than that, "[i]n opting to be seen as a dog he refuses identification with the perfected, invulnerable male body that has become the standard currency of black popular culture," as exemplified by R. Kelly. What is more, Snoop's emphasis on bestial sex directs attention to "radically alienated eroticism," which perversely might bring ethical grounding to "the debased black public sphere. We need to talk more, not less, about sex," comments Gilroy, alluding to Salt-n-Pepa's more wholesome take on the subject.

Whether or not Gilroy is right to find intimations of redemption in the ludic nihilism of gangsta, his analysis hints at the complexity behind what might too easily be dismissed as misogyny (though of course there are undoubtedly many instances of misogyny in rap – and in white rock too). Eithne Quinn's superb book on gangsta rap shows how it also represents deep continuities with the past, defying simple notions of decline, or complete transmogrification. The representation of black masculinity in contemporary rap, and his performance of sexual power, draws on highly complex legacies: the figures of the pimp, the hustler, the "badman" (Quinn, 2005).

With their intense focus on sexualized bodies, hip hop and contemporary R&B raise political questions concerning the meanings of sexual freedom and transgression in this highly racialized context. In the division between these two genres, there are echoes of the 1950s to 1970s rock/pop division, but in an age in which there has been a general sexualization of nearly all popular music. R&B is more sexualized than teenage pop ever was; and hip hop, marked as the more subversive and socially significant

---

[16] I return to Gilroy's perspective on the decline of black publicness in Chapter 5.

form, just as rock was in the mid-century, is far more reliant than was rock on ideas of sex as dirty and/or funny that I discussed earlier. These notions were present in rock to some extent, especially in metal, but they were suppressed in rock culture's pompous commentaries on its own importance. In hip hop, they are central, and are responsible for some of the banal accusations of misogyny that are applied to hip hop more than any other aspect of contemporary popular culture, without stopping to ask why rappers might speak of sex in the way that they do. There are times when some critics seem guilty of forgetting that performers are involved in the creation of narratives and fantasies. In many cases, the aim of all kinds of outrageous statements in hip hop is to make the listener respond in amazement: "*What* did he just say?" That does not mean that representations and stories are without consequences, and we certainly should not ignore the possibility that some listeners might find their pre-existing homophobia and misogyny confirmed or permitted by hip hop stories. But middle-class educated critics should know better than to think that articulating a viewpoint can be equated with believing and advocating it. Public statements and actions by hip hop and R&B artists – by *any* artists – that affirm homophobia and misogyny are much more deleterious in this respect.

Music's changing relations to sex and sexuality reflected and helped to constitute an increasing sexual "freedom" in Western societies. The spread of bohemian notions of sexual freedom via the rock counterculture was particularly important. But the partial democratization of intimate life is accompanied by commodification and individualization and by deep anxieties produced by narcissism and the hedonistic pursuit of pleasure. Nevertheless, as I have tried to show, popular music culture has provided numerous resources for pleasurable exploration of sexual identities and a rich commentary on everyday emotions.

4

Sociability and Place

4.1 Ways of Being Together: Forms of Publicness

Music, and its sibling cultural practice dance, more than any other kinds of communication, seem linked to sociality and community. This suggests that any consideration of music's value needs to address a question fundamental to any understanding of modern society: how might we flourish *together*?[1] That question becomes more complex and difficult in the modern world, when people are constantly surrounded by strangers, and when distant events, institutions, and people can have a major impact on our lives. In such circumstances, commonality, community, and solidarity are vital but controversial concepts. The last few decades have seen an intensification of longstanding tensions between forms of politics that claim to emphasize the value of individual and business freedom and those that concentrate on commonality. The victories of neo-liberal forms of thought and policy have surely strengthened the forces of competitive individualism. In spite of this, the notion of the common good survives as a key ethical principle. There are good reasons to be suspicious of attempts to dissolve difference in the name of dubious principles of universality. And

---

[1] The question of how we might live together in large groups called "societies" is of course the fundamental issue of sociology, a discipline which can be glossed to mean "knowledge of friendship." Yet the sociology of music has been surprisingly reluctant to conceptualize, in any sustained way, the relations between music and collective experience. Ethnomusicology has been rather better at this – see the survey by Gregory (1996) of the main traditional social "uses" of music identified by ethnomusicology. On this, see also Merriam (1964), Nettl (1983), and the useful survey by Clayton (2009).

Why Music Matters, First Edition. David Hesmondhalgh.
© 2013 David Hesmondhalgh. Published 2013 by John Wiley & Sons, Ltd.

invocations of "community" have been notoriously abused in politics. Yet without *some* notion of commonality, as Nick Couldry writes, "any refounding of democratic politics seems impossible, even unimaginable" (2006: 64). People's feelings towards distant others may often be only superficially compassionate, and may even be sentimental and self-serving. But the capacity for solidarity with strangers remains crucial.

How then might music relate not only to sociality but also to solidarity, community, and commonality? We saw in Chapters 2 and 3 that music's highly valued ability to feel intimately connected to the self is rarely unblemished by the problems that afflict society and the self. An underlying assumption in the next two chapters is that we need to understand music's potential for sociality and community as ambivalent too. Music can reinforce defensive and even aggressive forms of identity that narrow down opportunities for flourishing in the lives of those individuals who adhere to such forms of identification, and in those affected by such choices. But it can also enable life-enhancing forms of collectivity, not only in co-present situations but across space and time.

Important concepts in respect of any such discussion of the problems and benefits of collectivity are *publics* and *publicness*. These concepts connote more than just collective life. In their contrastive pairing with the private realm or privacy, the terms also incorporate a sense of openness, visibility, and accessibility (Weintraub, 1997). That sense of openness to others is one that I believe we should value, and should defend against conservatism's tendency to privilege the freedoms of individuals and businesses over solidarity, community, and equality (rather than balance them in a way that maximizes flourishing). Yet the terms "publicness" and "publics" have been used in such a bewildering variety of ways that some conceptual clarification is necessary. Political theorist Jeff Weintraub (1997) cogently and helpfully distinguishes between two rather different meanings of publicness. As they are highly relevant to the next two chapters, I will discuss them here. The first understands publicness in terms of *sociability* among people who do not know each other – the kind of public that you would find at a large club, or a football stadium, or even a shopping mall. Sociable publics can take mediated forms as well as co-present ones, as when we listen to the same song on the radio at the same time, or watch the same televised event. The second meaning conceives of publics and publicness via a notion of political community grounded in citizenship, in ideals of collective participation in decision-making, and where the central value is aspiration towards some kind of collective *deliberation* and, ultimately,

Co-present

Festivals	Political meetings
Concerts	Conferences
Shows	Seminars
Sporting competitions	Workshops
Carnivals	Demonstrations and rallies
Parades	

Sociable publicness ─────────────────── **Deliberative and activist publicness**

Social networking sites	Social networks oriented towards deliberation
Broadcast cultural and sporting events	Newspaper opinion letter pages
	Broadcast political debates

Mediated

Figure 4.1   Forms of public and publicness

action. Like sociable publics, deliberative publics can take co-present and mediated forms, but more usually involve the latter.[2]

In this book, I follow Weintraub by differentiating *deliberative publics* from *sociable publics*, and I add to this by distinguishing co-present and mediated forms of each.[3] Figure 4.1 schematically lays out four types of publicness: co-present sociable publicness, mediated sociable publicness, co-present deliberative publicness, and mediated deliberative publicness. It gives examples of each. In this chapter, I concentrate on music's relations with co-present sociable publicness; Chapter 5 concentrates on mediated sociable publicness, and it also addresses music's relations to deliberative publicness.

It needs to be recognized that some kinds of sociable event hover on a line between "private" or closed, and "public" or open. So I also address in

[2]   Weintraub also discusses how liberal economics tends to treat the "public" purely as the realm of state administration (administrative publicness – a third meaning of the term).
[3]   In using the term "deliberative," I mean to invoke the ideal of greater participation in democratic life, but I avoid the term "participatory publicness" because of the danger that this term might confuse sociable participation, for example, the kinds of musical participation discussed later in this chapter, with democratic participation (the relation between the two is a major topic of Chapter 5).

"Private" intimate sociable events	Small parties where everyone knows each other	Social networking interactions among "friends"	Small events open to anyone but where many people know each other	Larger, open events	Broadcast events	"Public" open sociable events

Figure 4.2 A continuum of private and public events

this chapter the ways in which music might enhance life by intensifying feelings of warmth and solidarity between friends and among family members, in "semi-private" settings such as parties. Figure 4.2 summarizes the idea that the relationship between private and public events might be best understood as a continuum, rather than as a dichotomous pair.[4]

To sum up, I engage in this and the next chapter with a vital aspect of why music matters: its ability or otherwise to enhance feelings of shared experience, attachment, and solidarity towards other human beings. The concept of publicness is important to this. In this chapter, the emphasis is on music's ability to enhance or otherwise co-present interactions between people in particular places.

4.2 Celebrations of Musical Participation and Their Limitations

I begin with what many people consider to be the most valuable and important experiences of collectivity and communality through music, those involving participation and shared experiences of performance.

What value do people find in musical participation? When music psychologists have answered this question, they have treated it almost entirely in terms of benefits for individuals (See the discussion of music psychology in Chapter 2). As will hopefully be clear from earlier chapters, I do not deny in any way the importance of individual experience and flourishing. But participation is also significant for what it says about our ability or otherwise

[4] My view is that we need to value good versions of intimacy and privacy, and good versions of openness and collectivity, and we also need to question how the lines between these desirable entities have often been drawn. Such questioning has been a major contribution of feminist thought (e.g., Pateman, 1989: Chapter 6).

to join together with other people in experiences of sociability and community. The concept carries a heavier moral burden than is implied by studies that focus entirely on individuals' ability to accumulate rewards through it. In the political realm, for example, participation has been understood as the royal road to civic agency (Dahlgren, 2009: 80). In music too, analysts have understood the importance of participation as consisting in more than the sum of the rewards to the individuals involved. Indeed, some leading commentators have seen collective musical participation as the pinnacle of music's sociality, and even a model of human solidarity, a way of countering the individualism (as opposed to positive individuality) that a variety of commentators, going back to Saint Simon and Tocqueville in nineteenth-century France (Lukes, 1973), have taken to be a negative characteristic of modern life.

So for some, modernity entails a loss of the kinds of collective activity associated with communal participation in music. And it is understandable that some would feel that modern life has seen a profound individualization of musical experience, when we consider the rise of the Walkman and MP3 players, where individuals use music to cut themselves off from their surroundings and project all kinds of values and imaginings on to the strangers and urban landscapes around them (Bull, 2007). For Simon Reynolds, "the iPod is Radio Me, where there's no nasty surprises and the programmer magically knows what you want to hear" and he opposes it to the community created by good music radio, which allows "connection with people you might have nothing else in common with", and the creation of social alliances (Reynolds, 2011: 118–119). In this chapter, exploring the dialectic of individualization and collectivity in modern societies, I examine the ideas of three significant analysts who are profoundly troubled by individualism and by other (in their view) related aspects of contemporary musical experience: Christopher Small, Charles Keil, and Thomas Turino. All three of these writers place a very high value on forms of musical practice that maximize communal participation. Their work is helpful because they provide eloquent testimony to the life-enhancing possibilities of taking part in musical experience, and potentially illuminate understandings of what is at stake in musical sociality. Consistent with my aims in this book, they also relate the positive potential of music to ways in which dynamics of power and inequality might limit that potential. What I want to argue, however, is that in seeking a type of community that is not feasible in conditions of modernity, they set up a notion of collective flourishing which is only likely to lead to misunderstanding and disappointment. Their virtue is that they demand extremely high levels of beneficial social interaction; their downside is that they miss the more ordinary ways in which good sociality continues to be a feature even of the damaged worlds of capitalist modernity. I deal with Small and Keil in this section, Turino in the next.

Christopher Small and musicking

In his book *Music of the Common Tongue*, Christopher Small argued that rather than a thing or collection of things – a set of great recordings or compositions, for example – music should be understood as *activity*. Music is of course a noun, and most European languages do not have a verb to denote such activity (Small, 1987: 50). So Small coined the term *musicking* to draw attention to the way that musical performance and participation are central to the value of music.[5] His account was really an attack on the hegemony of classical music from the point of view of someone who had been deeply immersed in that tradition (Small was apparently an enormously talented and engaging teacher of that music) but who had come to feel that it offered only limited resources for human flourishing compared with the collective vitality of genres that were then, to compound the problem, dismissed by those who did not know what they were missing. Small's book was infused with a sense that real flourishing can only be achieved through greater levels of equality, and an enhanced sense of people's mutual connections with each other. However, Small's work is limited by denial of some of the complexities of modernity. His perspective seems to me to be typical of a certain way of thinking that locates the value of music in its potential to recover a primitive sociality that has been lost. That primitive sociality is then made the basis of a quest for an ideal future.

This is apparent in Small's eloquent discussion of what happens in good performance. Central to our enjoyment of performance, wrote Small, is a feeling that we have been "in the company of like-feeling people, in an ideal society which musicians and listeners have together brought into existence for that duration of time" (67).

---

[5] Small's concept of musicking is often mentioned or referenced, but his theory of the social value of music is rarely considered in any detail. A later book developed his concept in a set of essays (*Musicking*, 1997), but it is *Music of the Common Tongue* (1987) where his theory is first elaborated.

Given the common concern musicians and listeners have in bringing into
existence an ideal society, a set of social relationships, then the more subtly,
comprehensively and imaginatively the relationships between the sounds are
explored, the more it will strengthen the feeling that those social relations are
valid and important, and will thus intensify the participants' sense of being
and well-being (68).

The idea that musicians and listeners have a *common concern* with bringing
into being an ideal set of social relationships is striking. It is not clear though
whether Small means that, objectively, we would all benefit from bringing
into being such ideal societies, or whether musicians and listeners are
especially involved in attempts to do so, because something in music and
dance particularly encourages, or manifests, such a yearning for ideal relationships. Small seems to mean the latter because he goes on to discuss how,
through its links to ritual, music could provide "public images of sentiment"
(Small was quoting the anthropologist Clifford Geertz) that allow us to
establish common identity.

Underlying Small's approach is a leftist version of a tradition of thought
associated with the great French sociologist Emile Durkheim, whereby
people have a powerful pre-existing inclination towards communality and
collectivity, but modern industrial societies instead encourage alienation,
individualization, and anomie. For Small, music and dance, which at their
best were embodied in cultural practices of the African diaspora, could
counter the human damage wrought by modernization and industrialization because of the way they embodied the integrated, holistic, and adapt-
able nature of African societies, where relations between individuals and
communities were more oriented to good living. By contrast, the classical
music tradition that Small had grown up with, but had come to question,
reflected the individualized, disciplined, overly stable, impersonal, and
functional social relations of industrial society (Small, 1987: 69).

Applied to the music of the African diaspora, Small's account underestimates the way in which the music of the African diaspora itself is modern,
as well as non-modern – an issue addressed in the discussion of nationalism, diaspora, and cosmopolitanism I undertake in Chapter 5. In celebrating Afro-diasporic music's affirmation of an ideal collectivity, Small
seems to have in mind performances which encourage bodily and collective
participation on the part of dancing audiences. He contrasts funk and
reggae performances with the staidness and deadness of classical music
concerts. However, Small blurs *performance* and *participation*. To what

extent does the (modern) divide between performers and audiences (producers and consumers) affect their supposedly shared quest for an ideal society? Small does not adequately incorporate the difference between performers and audiences into his analysis. What is more he seems to assume that modern performances of Afro-diasporic musicians recover pre-modern forms of collectivity more than they do. And he has little to say about the important fact that the music of the African diaspora has been most lastingly and powerfully manifested in recordings, which involve rather different notions of collectivity and community than live perfor-mances, but which may themselves have considerable value. In bemoaning individualization, he seems to downplay the role of the imaginary forms of community allowed by recordings and other media such as radio – the issue invoked by Reynolds earlier. A final problem is that Small may understate the way in which less participatory forms of performance might also enhance human life. Out of a strong reaction against the particular forms that classical music takes, he seems to downplay the value of contemplation, and of the slow unfolding of emotion over time. Classical music too might, in certain circumstances and perhaps in more indirect ways, enhance collective as well as individual lives. I think that Lawrence Kramer is right when he claims that music of all kinds embodies the drive for attachment, but classical music dramatizes and reflects on it in the act of invocation (Kramer, 2007: 33). An understanding and appreciation of classical music may be difficult to develop, and may be more accessible to relatively privileged social groups. But that does not make them per se less valuable. Small appears to reverse the terms of classical music's supposed cultural hegemony, so that its plea-sures are dismissed as bourgeois and therefore worthless.[6]

Perhaps the major problem with Small's account was that the relations between bodies of musical activity and the societies that they derive from are surely more complex than he allowed. He assumed music mirrors the structure and values of the societies and cultures that produce it. In this respect, his account is vulnerable to criticisms that have been made of a great deal of nineteenth- and twentieth-century thinking, whereby culture was understood as "a way of life" that is then reflected in songs, dances, and other expressions. Such notions, which appear in a variety of genres of anal-ysis, from the work of folk music collectors to 1980s' subcultural theorists, tend to neglect particularities and overemphasize structural coherence

---

[6] This seems to be the result of a polemical overstatement of his position, as apparently Small continued to gain great personal reward from classical music until the end of his life.

(Middleton, 1990: 167). They underplay hybridity, contradictions, and strange displacements. They potentially (and unintentionally) efface the agency of musicians, as reflectionism makes the efforts of musicians seem as though they are merely the natural expression of social structure.

Charles Keil: Engendered feeling

In spite of these problems, there is something vital in Small's writing that should not be overlooked: his emphasis on the way that more participatory forms of music may enhance human life, and the way that certain musics might be based more on such values than others, at least some of the time. The same is true of ethnomusicologist Charles Keil. His work too is limited by certain underlying assumptions about the relationship of music and society, but this time derived more from a kind of Freudo-Marxian emphasis upon the collective release of inhibition.

In 1966, Keil wrote a piece of great originality and lasting influence, which contrasted two different orientations towards music, one founded on "embodied meaning" and the other on "engendered feeling."[7] Embodied meaning was a term that Keil had taken from the musicologist Leonard Meyer. As we saw in Chapter 2, Meyer's (1957) book *Emotion and Meaning in Music* had developed a theory of music which saw musical communication as mainly based on the emotions produced by relationships between elements in a piece of music rather than from reference to objects or emotions in the world. According to Meyer's perspective, affect was produced by musical techniques that played on listeners' sense of anticipation and suspense – and musical meaning was embodied in these relations. To be clear, the term "embodied" does not refer therefore to a more bodily relationship to music, through performance and dancing. Such somatic aspects of music were actually a feature of the "engendered feeling" mode of musical communication – and as we shall see, Keil felt this kind of music had a much greater contribution to make to humanity. This view is evident in Keil's perspective on a related and significant argument in Meyer's book, where Meyer develops an aesthetic based on the benefits of deferred gratification as a musical structure unfolds over time. It was this aspect of

---

[7] This essay and others by Keil are most easily to be found in a wonderful collection of writing by Keil and his friend Steven Feld, *Music Grooves* (1994), supplemented by dialogues between them, and so in my discussion I cite the versions of Keil's ideas to be found in that book.

Meyer's argument in particular that Keil sought to challenge.[8] The jazz Keil loved was oriented towards engendered feeling, not embodied meaning based on deferred gratification. What is more, Keil believed that this orientation to engendered feeling was actually shared by most of the world's music (see Keil, 1994/1966: 156). He drew up a table of contrasts between two different attitudes and orientations towards music-making (see Table 4.1 – from Keil, 1994/1966: 55). This table makes clear that Keil's preference was strongly for the groove-driven, bodily, participatory aesthetic of the engendered feeling mode. A later essay made this element more explicit still. Participation, wrote Keil in 1987, "is the opposite of alienation from nature, from society, from the body, from labor, and is therefore worth holding onto wherever we can still find some of it." Such participation was encouraged by rhythmic and textural "discrepancies" in groove-based music – such as "within a polka drummer's snare-drum beat and between that beat and of four or five other bass sources, each of which will be shaped by a personal touch" (99).

But how did such participation relate to social and historical forces? Keil had a more sophisticated understanding of music–society relations than Small, as is apparent in a later essay, "People's music comparatively," which focuses on the struggles of peoples – "ethnic segments of the working class" such as African-Americans or Polish Americans – "to keep control of their social identities in music" (see Keil, 1994/1966: 202). Keil wisely rejected accounts that see certain forms of vernacular music, such as the blues and polka, as folk musics that spring up from the untrammeled creativity of a people. Instead, he focused on the intensely *mediated* nature of such "people's music" – a term he preferred to "folk," with its connotations of the rural and illiterate, or "popular" music. For example, the blues, wrote Keil, needed to be understood as "originally or primarily" an urban phenomenon, which reflected certain white ideas about blacks, and which were "most influential in both black and white cultures as a recorded or mass-mediated form" (200), and yet which were still powerful, life-enhancing forms.

Unlike Small, then, Keil did not rely on a mapping of musical styles on to social structures; and he paid much more attention to issues of mediation

[8]   Here is Keil on his reaction to Meyer, whose classes he attended at Yale: "Hearing Lenny spin out his theories of syntax and style and meaning and music having to earn itself by deferred gratification. It was driving me nuts … I was deeply angry about this version of what music was about because it didn't explain John Coltrane *at all*" (Keil, 1994/1966: 11–12). See Huron (2008) for a music psychologist's later development of Meyer's ideas.

Table 4.1   Keil's model of embodied meaning and engendered feeling
(Keil, 1994/1966)

	Embodied meaning	*Engendered feeling*
Mode of construction	Composed	Improvised
Mode of presentation	Repeated performance	Single performance
Mode of understanding	Syntactic	Processual
Mode of response	Mental	Motor
Guiding principles	Architectonic (retentive)	"Vital drive" (cumulative)
Technical emphases	Harmony/melody/embellishment (vertical)	Groove/meter(s)/rhythm (horizontal)
Basic unit	"Sound term" (phrase)	Gesture (phrasing)
Communication analogues	Linguistic	Paralinguistic (kinesics, proxemics)
Gratifications	Deferred	Immediate
Relevant criteria	Coherence	Spontaneity

than did Small. Keil's theory therefore potentially goes beyond Small, to provide a fuller account of the advantages and benefits of participatory musical activity. But as with Small's theory, there is a danger that Keil may downplay some of the adverse aspects of the societies and groups he associates with the values of participation and collectivity, and perhaps especially the relations between social suffering and damaged subjectivity. Keil clearly felt that music in the engendered feeling mode was better for humanity. He acknowledged the problems of fascist and nationalist forms of communality, but he felt that they could be easily differentiated from "participations that really revitalize, equalize, and decentralize" (Keil, 1994/1966: 98) – although he wrote that such differentiation might get more difficult as economic and ecological catastrophe unfolded. In Keil's analysis, participation is the surest route to an egalitarian revitalization of life. Echoing Small, Keil felt that this was closely connected to ethnic and class marginalization: put simply, the poor and the dispossessed were more likely to embody these values. Underlying this aesthetic was a Freudian-Marxian politics:

> In our culture (and perhaps in others where repression and oppression must be fought) it may be that music whose goal is engendered feeling, spontaneity, and the conquest of inhibition is of far greater value than music which aims to reflect our civilization and the repression-sublimation-Protestant-ethic syndrome upon which it is based (75).

Keil's aesthetic is ultimately based on the liberating capacities of pleasurable release of inhibition and repression.[9]

Yet this Marxian-Freudian reading is based on an overly optimistic understanding of human subjectivity combined with a deeply pessimistic analysis of existing society. We can seek a better world, while still acknowledging that conflicts between people and within people's psyches are going to be inevitable. Indeed, a realistic appraisal of such facts might be a necessary (though not sufficient) basis for thinking about what better worlds might be possible. We can explore this by examining the question of repetition, which is essential to Keil's participatory aesthetic, and implicitly, to Small's too. Keil's emphasis on the emancipatory dimensions of groove-driven engendered feeling is radically opposed to certain concerns about the problems of repetition in popular music. There is an everyday version of such concerns. The Dad of a friend of mine hated rock music, because for some reason he focused entirely on the back beat. Of course, this made hearing any rock music more or less unbearable for him. Most listeners know that attention should be directed mainly to other elements, such as the interplay of other rhythms with that back beat, or the melodic and harmonic contrasts at the forefront of the music. Consequently, for my friend's Dad, and for many listeners unfamiliar with the codes of repetition involved in music intended to produce dancing, or to reproduce the evocation of dancing on record, repetition was dreadful.

There is another objection to repetition in music, which applies not only to popular music, but to the overly obvious or oppressive recapitulation of themes in pre-modernist music. This might be described as a more "sophisticated" modernist objection to repetition, and the analyst most associated with this position is Adorno, who found the drive to repetition psychotic and infantile (Adorno, 1973/1948: 178–181). It can be argued that popular music is more marked by repetition than other forms, given the emphasis on melodic development in classical music.[10] Musicologist Richard Middleton (1990) showed that repetition in popular music is much more varied and complex than analysts such as Adorno imply. There is repetition at the level of short phrases and riffs ("musemes," like the "phonemes" of

---

[9]   This mode of thinking is also discussed in Chapter 3.

[10]   See, for example, Adorno (1976: 29). As always, Adorno is more complex than a summary can convey. For example, he criticizes Wagner's use of the leitmotif, which "thunders" in "endless repetitions to hammer its message home" (Adorno, "In search of Wagner," quoted by Leppert, 2002/1932: 532).

speech) and there is repetition of longer phrases and sequences and, as David Brackett (1995: 119) notes, the two often overlap and interact.

For Middleton, however, there is in the potentially elitist objection of Adorno "something we can hang on to": repetition is closely linked to "the primary processes of the psyche" (268) – and so too is music. This means that, in contrast with Keil's hopes that democratizing forms of repetition can be safely and clearly differentiated from nationalism and fascism, Middleton suggests that the grooves that underlie participatory music may not always be innocent. If groove-driven and participatory music is associated with marginalized and even brutalized peoples, as Small and Keil both believe, then alongside the undoubtedly life-enhancing aspects of the music, and the thrilling creation of beauty out of the resources to hand (aspects of African-American music rightly emphasized by Snead, 1984 and others) there may also exist some other, less comfortable elements concerning subjectivity, especially in societies marked by the injuries of class and other inequalities. The brutalizing effects of poverty and marginalization may mean that some aspects of the drive to repetition might be quite ambivalent. If, as Middleton suggests, there are reasons to consider music the primary semiotic process, rooted as it is in the aural relationship of baby and mother (and even further back in the sounds of the womb) and therefore predating verbal and visual communication, then it may rely on connotations that are "prior to any emergence of a subject, locating itself in opposition to external reality". For this reason "the basic pleasure of music may be thought of as narcissistic" (288).

This has a "constructive" dimension: as we saw in considering the work of the English psychotherapist Donald Winnicott (in the context of Nussbaum's use of his ideas) in Chapter 2, repetition can involve the ego mastering reality, as when children learn through reiterated play. In *Beyond the Pleasure Principle*, Freud (1961/1920) built on his observations of one of his grandsons repeatedly throwing a toy out of his pram, and then pulling it back on a string, shouting "fort" (gone!) and "da" (here!), over and over again. But repetition can also be involved in a drive for loss of self: this relates to the desire to be "lost in music," either dancing to trance in a club, or in more religious settings. This can be pleasurable and life-enhancing, and Adorno is surely wrong to see infantile regression only in extremely negative terms; it has positive dimensions too. Freud's discussion suggests that human drives for gratification and pleasure might also substitute for subjectivity, and it hints at the way that the subject itself might seek its own dissolution. Freud saw these dynamics in terms of life and death drives,

Eros the god of sexual love versus Thanatos the god of death, but Middleton's argument was that drives towards vitality and dissolution, life and death are interconnected in a field of tension, struggle, and mediation. That seems to me to be absolutely right, and it takes us back to my discussion of celebrations of individual self-realization through music in Chapter 2. I suggested there that music might be more bound up in difficult psychic processes than its advocates sometimes acknowledge. What Middleton helps us to see is that the repetition that underlies the most collaborative and participatory forms of music might have ambiguous meanings. Celebrations of participatory grooves might miss some of the darker aspects of psychic life.[11]

4.3 That Syncing Feeling

In Small and Keil's accounts, the value of participation tends to be merged with the value of performance. Dancing at a good gig is not the same thing as playing music with other people, but Small in particular writes as though it is. As we saw in discussing Small, there was also some prevarication about the value of recorded music. Small did not adequately differentiate between the feelings and experiences produced when people enjoy music in the same space, and the feelings and experiences embodied in listening to or dancing to recordings by musicians raised in those traditions. Not many of us had the privilege of attending a 1960s Jamaican dance or a 1970s New York block party, but we may feel we gain some sense of the vitality of such events from ska and hip hop recordings.

In a major recent contribution to thinking about the value of musical participation, the ethnomusicologist Thomas Turino (2008) addresses these issues head-on by producing a simple but rich and helpful categorization of four "fields of musical activity" (90–91). Two of these concern live performance: *participatory performance*, emphasizing the participation of all present, and *presentational performance*, where there are clear artist–audience distinctions. Two of them concern recorded music: *high-fidelity recordings*, which reference or represent the feel of live performance, and *studio audio art*, which makes no reference to live performance, and where the emphasis is strongly on music as an art object rather than a social activity. Turino is clear that these different fields can co-exist in certain

[11] See Middleton (2006: 137–197) for later, even more rigorous discussion of some of these issues, using Lacanian theory.

musical genres or practices, and that they represent something of a continuum, from participation to sonic art, with greater stress on social integration at the participation end, and more emphasis on individual creativity and expression at the sonic art end, and the other two fields representing variations of this.

Importantly, given my earlier argument that we need a more diverse and flexible notion of collective experience than can be found in Small and Keil, Turino claims that all the four musical fields should be valued equally: "Since each musical field offers its own benefits for different types of individuals," he writes, "it would be optimal if all fields were equally valued in every society so that any individual could engage in music making as best fit her personal dispositions and habits" (Turino, 2008: 51).

Let us put aside whether any society could ever feasibly balance such a different set of impulses and traditions. A more striking problem with Turino's reasonableness here is that Turino's own preference for the participatory performance form of music-making is very clear. In fact, the most powerful sections of his book represent a celebration of participatory traditions. (These are often based upon his ethnographic fieldwork in Zimbabwe and Peru and his own experiences in playing in a band in the United States, for example, as a zydeco band leader in the Midwest.) His argument is that participation is being displaced by modernization and industrialization, and the valuing of work over leisure (226–231). Such participatory traditions are kept alive in a modern country such as the United States only through the determined efforts of grassroots cultural cohorts (229). In ways that are not altogether clear, such activities are supposed to protect participatory traditions globally from the effects of the mass media. Turino recognizes the potential contributions of the media, and clearly values some of the things that recorded music can bring to audiences. But his evaluation is based on a politics that profoundly values participation over consumption, playing over listening. This is apparent in powerful passages such as the following:

> Although I practice music alone and often play at home for my own pleasure, I greatly prefer to play with others. One of the main things I seek through musical performance is a particular feeling of being deeply bound to the people I am playing with. This sense is created when my partners and I feel the rhythm in precisely the same way, are totally in sync, and can fashion the sounds we are making so that they interlock seamlessly together. The musical sound provides direct, immediate, and constant feedback on how we are doing; when a performance is good, I get a deep sense of oneness with the

people I am playing with. I think that what happens during a good performance is that the multiple differences among us are forgotten and we are fully focused on an activity that emphasizes our sameness – of time sense, of musical sensibility, of musical habits and knowledge, of patterns of thought and action, of spirit, of common goals – as well as our direct interaction (Turino, 2008: 18).

Later, Turino refers to this syncing as "social synchrony," following the anthropologist Edward Hall (1976). For Hall, harmonious social interaction was grounded in a synchrony of movement and body language. This provides a tacit identification and thus comfort (Turino, 2008: 42).

Turino is a worthy successor to Small and Keil, and his advocacy of participation in many ways improves on their earlier efforts. I do not dispute that the societies and cultures that he engaged with are ones in which there were higher levels of co-operative participation, and that this is a good thing.[12] Yet Turino also reproduces some of the limitations of Small and Keil, and adds his own. First, like Keil, Turino acknowledges that "the powers that music has for creating positive community relationships" (Turino, 2008: 190) also have their dark sides, but he draws too strong a line between emancipatory and repressive forms of communality. This is apparent in his choice of the Nazi Party's use of music as an example of music's "dark side." This downplays the complexity and ambivalence surrounding more ordinary modes of musical collectivism.

Second, Turino's comments seem to reflect an anxiety about communication in modern culture, and a deep yearning for unity rather than relatedness. Such anxiety is understandable, and his quest for communality is clearly preferable to neo-liberal forms of individualization. But anxiety can produce neurosis, and the displacement of problems. John Durham Peters (1999: 21) has wisely written of the need to "renounce the dream of communication while retaining the goods it invokes. To say that communication in the sense of shared minds is impossible is not to say that we cannot cooperate splendidly." Peters, like others such as Paul Ricoeur, seeks a middle way between, on the one hand, the belief that communication (through language for Durham Peters and Ricoeur, but the point

---

[12] A classic discussion of the value of cooperative participation is to be found in ethnomusicologist John Blacking's book *How Musical is Man?* (1973), based on his fieldwork with the Venda people of South Africa. "When I watched young Venda developing their bodies, their friendships, and their sensitivity in communal dancing, I could not help regretting the hundreds of afternoons I had wasted on the rugby field and in boxing rings" (45).

applies to music too) can resolve social ills, and, on the other, the post-structuralist sense that meaningful communication is impossible, or at least always misguided. Turino seems to underestimate the "wildness of the signs and tokens around us," to quote Durham Peters (1999: 22), and to see music as valuable primarily for bringing about social integration, an effect compromised by modernization and industrialization. Third, psychoanalysis suggests that the desire for merging with others may well reflect impulses and drives that are more difficult than we might readily be able to acknowledge. Or, to look at this from another angle, the need for merging expressed by Turino might reflect deeply rooted neuroses – social neuroses as much as any personal ones (for we all have them in different ways and to different degrees). The inevitable failure to achieve a yearned-for merging might well generate disappointment, and even suffering. Turino's frank and beguiling writing, to be fair, expresses this possibility, even if it does not integrate it into his framework. In one passage, for example, he writes of how, in many performances he had been part of, the ideal of merging and syncing

> was not fully reached with everyone in the group. It is the desire for this feeling – sometimes actually achieved in the past, but only a future possibility – that keeps me playing music. Yet my desire for this ideal also leads to frustration when it doesn't happen and makes me particularly finicky to play with. Because of my attention to sonic syncing, when people aren't locked in together it feels particularly uncomfortable, awful (Durham Peters, 1999: 19).

I recognize the yearning for unity that Turino expresses here. But it is also a yearning that is almost certain to result in disappointment. That might give us cause to wonder about making such desires too much the basis of a musical aesthetics and politics.

Fourth, underlying Turino's approach is the same kind of homologous, reflectionist thinking that often appears in Small and Keil's writing. The good participatory music Turino hears and observes in certain groups in Zimbabwe and Peru is implicitly presented as reflecting more egalitarian societies. "Participatory performance," Turino writes, "does not fit well the broader cultural values of the capitalist-cosmopolitan formation, where competition and hierarchy are prominent and profit making is often a primary goal" (Turino, 2008: 35). It is presented as emerging only from threatened egalitarian enclaves of capitalist societies. Aside from the negative use of the term "cosmopolitan" (see discussion of this term in Chapter 5), the problem here is that such a view underestimates the complexity and ambivalence of capitalist modernity. If capitalist modernity creates the social fragmentation that concerns Turino, it also may deserve credit for creating more spaces where people can choose, or not, to engage in participatory activities. Echoing Middleton's criticisms of homology theories, discussed earlier, we might ask: what contradictions and displacements are involved in the participatory societies and traditions that Turino discusses? Might it be that other elements of the cultures that Turino analyzes are more profoundly marked by inequality and oppression as a result of egalitarian participation being manifested mainly in the realm of music, dance, and ritual, rather than other aspects of society? I do not deny that many non-Western cultures have an egalitarian character that is eroded by capitalist development.[13] Yet we should not underestimate the downsides of some "traditional" societies.

I am in danger of being much too hard on Turino's terrific book. Its quest for an emancipatory aesthetic is inspiring in many respects. But perhaps the most important challenge it raises is as follows: how to hold on to a normative account that registers the different ways in which music might be valuable in different societies and yet not rely on an impossible notion of community as the only realization of music's potential for sociality. It is true that some societies might have greater degrees of musical vitality, and that greater levels of participation are, other things being equal, an important measure of that vitality. But we need accounts that can find enrichment in the more demotic, mundane, and compromised forms of sociality to be found in modern urban life. Such accounts may also help to steer us away from the danger of projecting on to other societies too many of our hopes and anxieties about modern life, distorting our evaluations. So in what follows I want to base my discussion on plain old modern life, in all its contradictions.

---

[13] Ethnomusicologist Steven Feld discussed the egalitarian culture of the Kaluli people of New Guinea and their musical practices in a series of brilliant publications. See, for example, Feld (1982) and the chapter "Aesthetics as iconicity of style" in Keil and Feld (1994: 109–150). Feld's work on collective emotion (in particular, the use of song to evoke nostalgia, weeping, and anger in Kaluli performance) has important links to the approach to music, affect and ethics in Chapter 2 (see Keil and Feld 1994: 144–146) and offers resources to develop that approach significantly. Sadly I do not have the space to undertake such development in this book, and in any case my focus is primarily on the value of music in modern, "developed" societies.

4.4   Ordinary Sociability I: Singing Together

The sense of sociability and community that music and dance can help to generate in us can be enjoyable, pleasurable, moving, and even joyous. They provide opportunities for forging of new friendships, and the reaffirmation of old ones. Compared with other forms of aesthetic experience, music plays an especially powerful communal role by encouraging people to move to the same sounds at the same time, but in different ways (wilder and more restrained, skillfully and not so skillfully, ironically or sincerely). Music, then, combines a responsive form of individual self-expression with the collective expression of shared taste, shared attachments.

But there are inevitably limits on music's capacity for community. As we saw in the two previous chapters, dynamics of emotional self-realization through music are closely linked to status battles in contemporary societies marked by competitive individualism, and music, precisely because of its links to the emotions, and therefore to privileged modes of modern person-hood involving emotional intelligence and sensitivity, might be a particu-larly intense site for such struggles. Music educators may enthuse that everyone is musical, or that everyone can sing, and they are right to point to the ordinariness of music-making. But music-making is not as widely dis-tributed as the ability to speak language (Toynbee, 2012: 164); it has its own forms of talent, expertise, and specialization. I address the implications of this later. Moreover, as the incident in Box 4.1 suggests, the special plea-sures produced by musical sociability do not stop sociable gatherings being marred by rivalry, envy, and hatred. Music itself has a specific role to play in such psycho-social dynamics, marking boundaries of taste and appropriate movement, and creating a sense of intimacy that may feel threatening or provoke anxiety. In this and the next section, I explore these and other questions concerning the benefits and limits of musical participation. My focus is on fundamental experiences of sociability through music: going out with friends, singing together, and dancing together, activities that require very little expertise or training. I then move to the more specialized and skilled domain of amateur music-making in the following section.

Perhaps the most basic form of musical participation is to sing. This has led a number of studies by music psychologists, seeking to show the bene-ficial impacts of music on people's health and well-being (see Box 2.1), to focus on singing, and singing together. Perhaps the most notable research is that of Jane Davidson and her colleagues, who interviewed participants in

Box 4.1   A night out

In Yorkshire, on the rural outskirts of the Bradford conurbation, I'm with some friends in a pub. We're asked to meet friends at another pub nearby, but as we approach, we groan when we see a sign outside saying "Elvis impersonator live tonight." All of us foresee an evening of conversation drowned out by cheesy amplified noise. Our mates are sat in the middle of the cramped pub. But almost immediately, banter strikes up with the women and men around, who are awaiting the performance with half-ironic anticipation. The crowd is a mixture of working-class drinkers and impoverished professional parents on a rare night out. Elvis is a Dad from the local playgroup; it's a fund-raiser. By the time he arrives on stage, enough booze has been consumed for him to be greeted with unforeseen adulation. His white jumpsuit is appropriately snug and he can sing well enough. Immediately people start to sing along. Talkers are shushed during the quieter songs. The speakers are turned up to their maximum, and the power of Elvis's Vegas repertory comes across through the pre-recorded backings played from the decks by Elvis's wife (who is called Sheila not Priscilla). As the evening goes on, the response becomes more raucous, and the interactions more surreal. A work colleague appears at the other side of the room, and, bizarrely, we serenade each other across the crowd to "You've lost that loving feeling." When the simple chords of "Sweet Caroline" strike up, it's clear what's going to happen, and you can feel it in the room. Reaching out, touching you, [slight pause], touching me. ... The chorus elicits an ecstasy of collective singing, women and men, all at the top of our voices. There are smiles and laughter as some of the playgroup Mums perform their adoration of the overweight local superstar, but there's melancholy at times too. It seems that bitter-sweet lines from the Elvis repertory are invoking thoughts about relationships, past and present. Tell me that your sweet love hasn't died. There are drunken goodbyes, and my friends and I stagger out of the pub, feeling we've had a great night, and that the working week has been obliterated by laughter and bittersweet emotion. Unwittingly, I brush against a man's drink as I'm leaving, and he follows me out to the front of the pub, demanding an apology for his spilt beer. Given his state and his size, I'm only too happy to provide one. The power of

Elviss music, it seems, has brought strangers and acquaintances together, and with a formidable intensity. But my pursuer has reminded me unpleasantly that there are those who feel excluded from such collective pleasures. If music-based gatherings answer to our need for sociality and attachment, and combat loneliness, might they also evoke envy when others miss out? And if such gatherings are a place where people can show that they feel comfortable with others, they can also be sites for some to make it known that they are not to be messed with, and that demands for respect sometimes take unexpected forms.

two very different singing groups: one (Sound of Song, based in Montreal) for people from backgrounds of homelessness, long-term unemployment, histories of substance abuse, and mental illness, and the other (the Senior Singers, based in Melbourne) for people over 70 who lived alone and were receiving home-help care (Davidson, 2011; see also Bailey and Davidson, 2005). Participants reported quite profound impacts. These were strongly physical, and singing was compared to the beneficial effects of swimming and running. Elation and great stimulation were reported: "I go into a different place when I sing: I'm flying, better than any drug. That high makes you feel as though you've run a marathon. You know: exhausted but satisfied" (78). Other studies have attributed this to the controlled deep breathing required by choral singing (Clift and Hancox, 2010).

Emotional aspects were important too. One man in the Sound of Song choir commented: "Man, I think about those bad times and those sad times and those good times with the songs we sing. It brings me to a good place. Before I did the singing group I used to get stuck in my mood and in one of those times" (78). There were both individual and collective aspects to this, and one of the Senior Singers presented this articulately:

Expressing through being in the music is very powerful. It is another way of being. It permits you to be together with everyone in the music – part of the harmony, like one whole thing. But, you're also independent. So, in music you can be small and big, contributing in different ways to the whole. Maybe that's particularly true of singing groups? (79)

Davidson relates such comments as this to a fundamental human need for relatedness. She draws on rather functionalist understandings of such human needs, based on "goal pursuits" and "self-determination" and I will come back to the issue of how to understand the rewards of singing, and other kinds of musical sociality, later. Nevertheless, her analysis of choral singing indicates clearly some of the ways in which collective music-making might enhance life.

One issue raised by these accounts is the degree to which opportunities for such enhancement are available in modern life. Do people sing together less than they used to? It can feel that way when one sees a film such as Terence Davies's *Distant Voices, Still Lives* (1988) with its moving recreations of pub singing in Liverpool in the 1950s, presented as a life-saving relief from the oppression and brutality of cramped working-class homes. Pub singing in the United Kingdom goes back centuries but is extremely rare now outside of karaoke, which I discuss later. Children are still encouraged to sing collectively at schools, not only in assemblies but in classes, and my sense is that the repertoire has broadened ("Livin' on a prayer" alongside "He's got the whole world in his hands"). With the marked decline of church attendance, religious singing has become less a part of people's lives, and many people will have experienced the agonizing discomfort of trying to sing along to unfamiliar hymns at weddings, christenings, and funerals, where there always seems to be one well-trained voice rising above the rest, threatening to release hilarity among the muttering congregation.

Turino, Davidson, and others suggest reasons why the decline of collective singing might be considered a loss and I shall seek to extend their theorizations later. But we should not forget that singing together continues to be present in modern societies. One notable case is football singing in Britain.[14] My son and I are both season ticket holders at an English football club, Blackburn Rovers. The people of East Lancashire, the area where Blackburn is located (and where I was born and raised) can be somewhat shy and reticent, and they sing less than many of the supporters of opposing teams who visit the ground. Nevertheless, when Joe and I first started attending games regularly, when he was eight, it seemed that the most thrilling aspect of the whole experience for him was to be among 20,000 or so people, many of whom were singing. Most chants are snatches of songs and often fade out quickly. Football singing can be horrible.[15] But it can be stirring too, and

[14] There is, apparently, somewhat less singing at football grounds in other countries and other fans admire British fans for the noise they make.

[15] Les Back (2003) has analyzed football singing in terms of how it produces a sense of locality, of "home," for supporters. At the 1990s London clubs he writes about, racist chants were still common. Back stresses that the sense of locality produced by the auditory culture of the football ground is not always exclusive. Racist chanting is much less common now, though homophobia and other forms of hate speech are still prevalent.

often funny. I like the chant directed at players who fall over too easily when tackled, such as the former Manchester United player Cristiano Ronaldo: "Ronny, he's on his arse again, he's on his arse again" to the tune of "Blue moon." Football fans can express collective admiration and even love. The same tune was used for many years to praise one of Blackburn's greatest ever players, the Turkish midfield genius Tugay Kerimoğlu: "Tugay, you are my Turkish delight, you are my Turkish delight, you are my Turkish delight, TUGAY, you are my Turkish delight" – repeated until collective exhaustion sets in. This may not demonstrate any profound engagement with Turkish culture and identity, but it is as near to cosmopolitanism as life in working-class Blackburn may get for now. Liverpool FC fans are often cited as the best collective singers, with their anthem "You'll never walk alone." But in recent years, Manchester United fans have, I grudgingly admit, become the best singers of all, partly because they have developed a repertoire of actual songs, rather than just snatches of chant. Most of these are difficult to make out clearly from across the ground (fans in Britain are segregated according to which team they support, to prevent fights between morons). But they often turn out to be a mixture of funny and deeply offensive. United supporters' song about their then Korean player, Park Ji-Sung, was sung to the tune of "Lord of the dance." Like many football songs, it was primarily intended to insult rivals, in this case Liverpool FC, who, through the distorted lens of Manchester–Liverpool enmity, are portrayed as impoverished thieves: "Park, Park, wherever you may be, you eat dogs in your own country, but it could be worse, you could be scouse [the colloquial term for people from Liverpool], eating rats in your council house." The words do not quite make sense (how can you eat dogs anywhere, and in your own country at the same time?), the poverty jibes are deeply unpleasant, and apparently Koreans rarely eat dog meat. But even rival fans laughed when they heard the Park song. And the feeling produced by such collective singing, it seems to me, is one of *exhilaration*.

Another way in which collective singing also survives in modern societies is at gigs and festivals. Gigs themselves are important collective experiences, where people go to share the same aesthetic experiences together. At gigs where the material being performed is well- known, the gig can turn into a sing-along. It has always seemed to me that one important reason for the continuing popularity of tribute acts is precisely that they allow such collective singing of familiar material. Some people distrust this anthemic quality in popular music, and think singing along constitutes herd-like behavior. Keith Negus (2008: 153), as part of a fine discussion of communal singing at Bob Dylan concerts (which apparently began in the early 1970s and intensified from the 1980s on), quotes two writers who define themselves believers "in corporal punishment for lachrymose community singing." But Negus points out that such singing represents a shared affective response to the emotion of the song, and in the right circumstances that can be moving as well as exhilarating. One surprising pleasure of live music is to attend a gig by a relatively unknown act and to discover that large numbers of other people love the same song as you, and have come to know the words, or at a festival, to discover that a band that you feared might be known only to a few people in fact has attracted a reasonable crowd. When people sing along together, they demonstrate that they share some kind of emotional history in relation to the music, or the performer. At a tea party rally, this may be frightening. In other contexts, it might be deeply sentimental – which is not always a bad thing. But when tens of thousands of people somehow manage to articulate a line like "They haunt this dusty beach road in the skeleton frames of burned-out Chevrolets" at a Bruce Springsteen gig, it seems to me that the emotion being shared involves identification with the idea of the personal damage caused by living on the margins, in New Jersey, or anywhere.

And of course there is karaoke. This involves individual performance, but in my experience this is often secondary to the opportunity for people to sing along together. As is well-known, the origins of karaoke are in Japan where, Hiroshi Ogawa (1998) reports, singers strive hard to approximate the singing styles of the star who originally recorded the track. It could, therefore, be seen as a nightmarish replacement of oral culture by a mechanized, standardized mass culture, but karaoke is considerably more complex than this, both in Japan, and in its global manifestations.[16] Rob Drew's wonderful book, *Karaoke Nights* (2001), provides great insight into a number of aspects of karaoke, in ways that allow us to go beyond a narrow functionalist conception of the benefits of singing, towards a more social notion of flourishing and self-realization. I want to highlight just three aspects of Drew's rich ethnographic material here (all page numbers from Drew's book).

The first is the way that performance provides amateur singers with the resources to explore and expand their sense of self. When mild-mannered

[16]   As Charles Keil recognized in a thoughtful essay (Keil and Feld, 1994: 247–256), in which he interpreted Japanese karaoke as representing a humanization or personalization of mediated music.

Dan performs Guns N' Roses' "Paradise city," writes Drew, it is an "exercise in self-transformation, exposing a hard edge beneath his soft, thirty something surface" (63). When a preppy young woman sings "Me and Bobbie McGee," she takes on something of Janis Joplin's reckless wanderlust (63). This is not just about individuals "trying on" identities. Also involved is the sociality of performance, the ways in which performance involves transcending the self, and taking into account the other – including other ways of being, as well as other people in the crowd.

A second issue Drew raises is the way in which karaoke provides resources for powerful aesthetic experiences of commonality. What various karaoke crowd favorites have in common, Drew observes, is that "they seem to crystallize the experience of the people who celebrate them and, as a result, to constitute these people as members of a common culture" (56). An ideological reading of crowd favorites might be troubled by such "passionate re-enactments of their own collective litanies" (56). And of course, certain songs might carry dubious resonances. But Drew provides generous, and astute, understandings. Corporate office workers in Ohio rant their way through a hard-rock tribute to slacking; in Tampa, Florida, the most popular country number is the bluegrass classic "Rocky top," "a nostalgic evocation of rural Appalachia that acquires new meaning when set against the New South's centerless sprawl" (56). Drew describes the highly charged response to a performance of Prince's "When doves cry" and hears it through the ears of a group who had reached sexual maturity during the AIDS epidemic of the 1980s. "For kids coming of age in an era of diminishing expectations – regarding not only sex, but family, friendships, careers – [Prince's] words must seem emblematic: maybe I'm too demanding, maybe you're never satisfied" (55). Cool eroticism gives way to expressions of confusion and desperation, and the smiles of the boys performing the song turn to grimaces. The way the audience responds to the song indicates strongly shared experiences of disaffection and anxiety, sexual and otherwise.

A third aspect concerns the way in which karaoke permits a kind of public interaction which is highly ritualized and circumscribed, and which therefore has been lambasted by commentators and ordinary folks who seek a more authentic form of intimacy among strangers (see Sennett, 1974 for a critique of such views). Yet the interaction occasioned by karaoke is also "civil and dependable and accessible." It is "about taking on a narrow role in the cause of doing things together" (89).

Karaoke provides no guarantee of civil sociability. In the 1990s, it seems, Japanese karaoke bars were highly segregated along sexual lines: at night, businessmen sang for each other and their hostesses; in daytimes, housewives, working women, and young people performed in booths (Mitsui, 1998; Oku, 1998). In the United States, however, Drew observed female karaoke singers gaining and skillfully repelling unwelcome sexual attention. He also noted that these bars allowed women a pleasurable public visibility: "if ... relatively impersonal, collective activities like karaoke offer freedoms and pleasures not normally available within close relationships, then women have a particular stake in them" (88). Karaoke and various other forms of collective singing activity suggest that a vernacular and at times intense sociality is still present in modern societies, however problematically so.

4.5   Ordinary Sociability II: Dancing Together

Dancing, too, to paraphrase Drew, permits circumscribed interactions in order for people to be together. Chapter 2 discussed some of the ways in which dancing enhances people's lives at the level of individual experience. But dancing often brings about a pleasurable and enriching sense of *shared* agency for those who value it.[17] Dancers may feel guided by the music, but they are also exercising reflexivity, in conforming to the right moves, or in performing their own particular style of dancing. The physicality of dance can make it an immensely appealing aesthetic experience to communities that are excluded from many more reflective cultural forms. Mark Rimmer (2010) writes, for example, about the popularity of an electronic dance music known as "monkey" among working-class young men in the Tyneside area of Northern England. This ferociously fast bouncy music, adapted from the makina techno style popular in (often queer) clubs in Spain and Italy, created an atmosphere of feverish excitement in the clubs where it was played. It resonated with a culture where young men gained esteem from physicality, adventure, and exuberance.

Dance represents a mutual performance, one which can often be relatively easily learned. As they settle into dancing, if the music is good for them, dancers might find themselves expressing themselves more freely, and gradually relinquishing their initial self-consciousness. Freed from the inhibition of excessive self-monitoring, they might feel pride and even elation in their abilities to move in a way that feels, and perhaps looks, right.

---

[17]   Obviously, many people feel uncomfortable, alienated, or terrified by dancing. It seems that sensitive heterosexual men are especially prone to this.

Or there may be a more basic sense that how I am dancing is good enough for me: a safe dancing space will involve the sense that no one will denigrate a person for their dancing style (the lads that Rimmer hung out with avoided the corporate leisure clubs of Newcastle and Gateshead because uninhibited dancing would lead to mockery – and perhaps the unwelcome interest of bouncers). Dancers, perhaps especially men, often adopt irony, partly as a defense, but also to create another shared experience, that of collective laughter – which also involves bodily invigoration and a certain intensity. Ironic or comedy dancing early in the evening might give way to something more serious and intense when a favorite record is played. These are not marginal parts of modern life. They are not "everyday" occurrences, but they are "everyweek" for many young people. As people get older, collective dances might be more infrequent, but that can sometimes only add to their specialness, at weddings and significant birthday parties (usually those with a zero at the end).

There are even genres and movements devoted to maximizing the heightened social interaction made possible by dance. Dance music, from early jazz to swing through R&B, funk and disco, through to hip hop and electronic dance music, is oriented towards amplifying these experiences and pleasures. Musicians, whether playing live, or creating a track that will be made for dancing at parties or in clubs, seek to guide the sense of inter-subjective agency that dance can provide.[18] As Clarke (2012: 340) recounts, in contemporary electronic dance music, producers and DJs often make the beginning of the track "loose" and "spacey," deliberately delaying the comfort of dancers; they then gradually or suddenly articulate a more regular beat or a particular groove. At such moments, there is a release of tension which expresses itself as an energization, as dancers might begin to move more vigorously. That process of articulation or clarification often reaches a climactic point – perhaps involving a kick drum – allowing for a sense of unity among the dancers. Of course, some people may be so narcissistic and self-absorbed that they want mainly to show off, and may not even think about shared collective experience. Others may be lost in their own thoughts. There is an unspoken, ordinary, and yet significant pleasure in sharing such moments and many electronic dance music genres relentlessly seek out those moments of unity.

---

[18]   See Straw (2001a) for an excellent history of dance music, in relation not only to this succession of popular genres, but also to the dance clubs and institutions that are vital to an understanding of changing forms of popular dance. See also Thornton (1995).

In the late 1980s and 1990s, these aspects of dance made it an object of certain political notions about social integration which recall the writings of Keil and Small, discussed earlier. According to these views, rave culture involved the creation of new forms of community based on intensely corporeal and pleasurable activities and the loss of the self within the crowd. There were also important feminist elements to such perspectives, as the pleasures of dancing engaged women and men in ways that seemed to resist traditional gender divisions and hierarchies. Maria Pini (1997), for example, wrote of how rave seemed to offer a certain destabilization of sexual categories, in line with the anti-essentialist thinking of the time. I was harshly doubtful about this kind of thinking back then. I enjoyed the way that dancing in clubs was much wilder and more intense than in the days of post-punk, when dancing was often deliberately stiff. But I was suspicious of the inflation of the politics of rave to a greater level of social significance than it seemed to merit (I expressed some of these thoughts in Hesmondhalgh, 1997). Rave politics seemed in danger of claiming that the politics of dancing were more real than those of social justice – this was an era when the British Left had suffered a series of defeats, notably the Miners' Strike of 1984–1985. Looking back now, I feel more kindly disposed to rave culture's utopian commitment to sociality. Like lots of people who have taken too many drugs, rave advocates talked gibberish at times. But the incoherent political statements some of them made now seem like an attempt to articulate the value of benign collectivity and commonality.[19] My view is still that we need to hold on to the rich ordinariness of music and dance, and not burden them with a political meaning which they end up being unable to carry. The excitement, friendship, and sociality brought about by music have a connection to politics and to making connections across different communities (see Chapter 5). But we need to move beyond an unrealizable drive for social merging, or a view that people can only deeply care about pleasure.

It is important not to give up too much in thinking about the notion of community. Gerard Delanty (2003) rightly argues against various notions of community based on self-contained, homogeneous groups. But if writers such as Turino seem to yearn too much for community, postmodernist notions seem to give up the utopian kernel of sociality too much. (Post) modern community is fragile and temporary, Delanty writes. But in his

---

[19] Sophisticated and interesting explorations of the politics of dance music from the time include Jeremy Gilbert and Ewan Pearson's *Discographies* (1999) and Pini (1997).

rejection of a false nostalgia, Delanty seems to undervalue continuity and sociability. He seems hardly to consider the question of whether there might be forms of community that might enhance the lives of the people who are "inside" them. His example of modern community is commuters who travel to work with each other without interacting but who then come together if anything goes wrong. But this seems to give up on what might be shared in communal experience and locality too much. Surely this comes down to a certain regularity and intensity of interaction. Continuing relationships between people matter. And while not everyone need be a friend, passing nods, brief conversations, and teasing banter are ways in which we live successfully together. We should not underestimate the corrosive effects on sociality of the rise of "non-places" that deny the opportunity for such interactions. My argument here is that music and dance are often involved in encouraging and enhancing positive experiences of community, and continue to be so in the modern world, though in constrained ways.

4.6   Playing Together: Amateur Musicians

Against the admirable but inflated hopes for musical participation evident in writers such as Small, Keil, and Turino, I have been emphasizing the (constrained) possibilities for musical enrichment available in ordinary life in modern societies, and the kinds of participation that untrained and relatively unskilled people can undertake. I now address a domain of shared musical activity which necessarily requires a somewhat higher level of skill and commitment – playing musical instruments together in groups. I want to discuss the kinds of rewards that people – and societies – might get out of such activities. These rewards in principle apply to both amateur and professional musicians, but in considering the degree to which modern societies might allow satisfactions and rewards associated with making music to thrive, each raises rather different issues. In particular, the conditions of professional musicians force us to confront the problems created by the modern division of labor, and by working conditions associated with cultural production. In this section, I discuss the benefits of making music, before focusing on questions concerning access to amateur production. This then leads into a discussion of how we might more adequately theorize the positive aspects of music's sociality. A later section deals with professional music-making.

In discussing singing earlier, we saw some hints of the pleasures and rewards involved when even untrained people play music together. Doing so seriously, even as an amateur, brings even more significant benefits for people. We have already seen evidence of this in Turino's eloquent accounts of what he gained from playing in groups of various kinds. In a discussion of the ways in which music can achieve "flow" (see Chapter 2), Csikszentmihalyi (1990: 111) notes that "even greater rewards are open to those who learn to make music" than to those who learn to listen attentively. Music psychologist Stephanie Pitts (2005: 10) lists the following ways in which the musicians she studied valued their activities highly: as a source of confirmation and confidence; as an opportunity to demonstrate or acquire skills; as a way of preserving and promoting repertoire; as a forum for social interaction and friendships; as a way of enhancing or escaping everyday life; and as a source of "spiritual" fulfilment and pleasure. Gabrielsson (2011: 222–249) records a number of remarkable accounts of strong emotional experiences of musical performing, from classical, folk, jazz, and popular musicians, many of them positive, including feelings of "blissful intoxication" and deep communication with other performers and the audience, but also strange mixtures of happiness and emptiness, deep anxiety, and loss of control.

Like singing, amateur music-making is often thought to be in decline. In his strange essay *Musica Practica*, Roland Barthes (1977: 149) celebrated the sensuality of making music. *Musica Practica* is

> the music which you or I can play, alone or among friends, with no other audience than its participants (that is, with all risk of theatre, all temptation of hysteria removed); a muscular music in which the part taken by the sense of hearing is one only of ratification as though the body were hearing – and not "the soul"; a music which is not played "by heart"; seated at the keyboard or the music stand, the body controls, conducts, coordinates, having itself to transcribe what it reads, making sound and meaning. …

Barthes claimed that such activities, based around the democratizing effects of the piano, had "faded out altogether (who plays the piano today?)."[20]

---

[20]   The answer to Barthes' question may well be: more people than ever before, but many of them are in Asia – which is where most of the world's pianos are produced. A report on the global and Chinese piano industry prepared by Chinese Business Intelligence in 2012 claimed that 450,000 pianos were produced globally in 2010. For a highly informative history of the piano, see Parakilas (2001).

Michael Chanan (1994: 29) claims that "the whole vast modern commercial apparatus of music" has driven out the amateur, and reduces the listener to the condition of compliant consumer. Yet, against Barthes, Chanan also argues that *Musica Practica* "cannot be put down." It remains "the essential feature of the way that music is transmitted from generation to generation" and "even the highly organized mode of production of music under late capitalism cannot do without it" (30).

Writing in the 1980s, anthropologist Ruth Finnegan (discussed in Chapter 2) discovered an abundance of amateur music-making in what might have seemed like the most unlikely of places, Milton Keynes, a "new town" with a national reputation in the United Kingdom for being culture-less and soul-less. Finnegan's book remains the most important social-scientific study of amateur music-making, partly because of its implications for questions of sociability and community in relation to music.

The main worlds that Finnegan analyzed were classical music, brass bands, folk, musical theater, jazz, country and western, and rock and pop. Although only a minority of people were active amateur musicians, Finnegan showed that music affected a vast number of people, either as participants and organizers, or as audiences. Amateur music had great relevance for the overall life of the city and for the way people structured and experienced urban life. Finnegan also indicated the resources needed to sustain a musical life within a city, including local commercial institutions (notably, music shops and recording studios, but also church halls, village halls, and the like) and the remarkable amount of unpaid labor gifted by amateurs.

Finnegan's research suggested that the image of the contemporary city as lacking in cultural ties was deeply dubious – even a supposedly "alienated," culture-less place like Milton Keynes. But she also argued that the notion of community, in which "people are bound by numerous ties, know each other, and have some consciousness of personal involvement in the locality of which they feel part" (299) was also inappropriate for conceptualizing the activities she analyzed. There was considerable anonymity within many of the local music clubs. Many people knew little about their co-members' lives. Nor did audience members generally know each other. But the point of such activities was not to know everyone – this in any case would be impossible in a large, complex town such as Milton Keynes or even one of the neighborhoods within it. Musical clubs and gatherings provided a mixture of different relationships, some close, some more superficial. But there was always the potential to get to know some people better.

Given these facts, Finnegan preferred the term "pathway" to alternatives such as "musical world" or "community," in order to avoid misleading overtones of concreteness, stability, boundedness, and comprehensiveness associated with them. For Finnegan, the concept of pathway had a number of advantages:

- It carried a reminder of the part-time nature of much local music-making – other paths exist alongside the ones chosen, and music was just one way in which people could "find their way" in modern urban life.
- It encapsulated the way that musical activities were not random or created from nothing, but followed existing patterns.

The value of such pathways for those involved with amateur music-making was high. Finnegan reports that the strong impression given, not by everyone, but by person after person in her research, was that

> their music-making was one of the habitual routes by which they identified themselves as worthwhile members of society and which they regarded as of somehow deep-seated importance to them as human beings. ... [These pathways] provided a recognized channel of self-expression in many senses, for drawing on personal networks, for growing up through the various stages of life, for achieving a whole series of non-musical aims in the locality, for sharing with others, and, not least, for providing meaning for personal action and identity (306–307).

There are some problematic aspects of Finnegan's book, which I will come back to shortly. My point for now is that it very effectively undermines simple narratives of decline, and the idea that music in modernity lacks sociality.

4.7 Theorizing Positive Musical Sociality

The previous two sections laid out evidence that certain forms of positive musical sociality continue to exist in modern life, both for unskilled non-players and for more skilled amateurs, in demotic and in relatively "cultivated" forms. There are other positive aspects I could also have mentioned, including the pleasures of attending musical events together (gig-going and concert-going), and even of just talking about music with friends, arguing over which musicians and records are great, and which are not, and why (see Chapter 5). But how should we understand the value of these various instances of what happens when people come together to share music? How might we understand music's potential to bring about or enhance flourishing through social interaction of these various kinds? How, in spite of all their very great strengths, might we move beyond the limited accounts of musical community provided by writers such as Small, Keil, and Turino? My focus on the positive dimensions of music's sociality is deliberate; bearing in mind this is a *critical defense of music*, I will return to the more negative dimensions later. Three possibilities are discussed here. The first route locates music's sociality mainly at the micro level, and centers on music's perceived ability to synchronize time across different people. The second is a particular version of the notion that music is based on a fundamental tendency on the part of humans to be social, as developed in Durkheimian sociology. The third is a more developed version of this, which draws on an understanding of fundamental human needs.

Music, time, and micro-sociality

One source which has frequently been referred to by commentators interested in music's sociality is Alfred Schutz's essay "Making music together," published in 1951. Schutz saw music as exemplifying a "mutual tuning-in relationship, the experience of the 'We,' which is at the foundation of all possible communication" (Schutz, 1951: 92). Music does this, Schutz reckoned, by synchronizing the sense of inner time of the various participants. Schutz provided a way of understanding the relationships between musicians emphasized by Turino,[21] when he writes of how "a musician has not only to interpret his *[sic]* own part which as such remains necessarily fragmentary, but he has also to interpret the other player's interpretation of his – the other's – part and, even more, the other's anticipation of his own execution" (Schutz, 1951: 94). Schutz also had in mind relationships between composers and listeners, with musicians acting as intermediaries. "The beholder, thus, is united with the composer by a time dimension common to both, which is nothing other than a derived form of the vivid present shared by the partners in a genuine face-to-face relation such as prevails between speaker and listener" (90).

---

[21] Surprisingly, given his discussion of syncing and merging, Turino does not make reference in his book to Schutz's essay. A comment by John Durham Peters (1999: 5) is relevant to Schutz's use of a radio metaphor to describe human communication: "Interpersonal relations gradually became redescribed in the technical terms of communication at a distance – making contact, tuning in or out, being on the same wavelength, getting good or bad vibes."

For Peter Martin, Schutz's essay offered an understanding of "how music as a particular kind of medium can be effective in, for example, providing a personal 'narrative,' sustaining a sense of identity, or creating a feeling of 'belonging'" (Martin, 2006: 221). This incorporates music's ability to connect people in emotional and physical, as well as cognitive ways. For Martin, music's effectiveness – and implicitly its value – derives from the ways in which it provides a means for people to link individual consciousness and collective membership (Martin, 2006: 221). He aligns himself with Tia DeNora's emphasis (DeNora, 2003: 45) on what music affords – what it makes possible – rather than on what it means.

This approach helps us to focus on situated activity and in particular the importance of *time* as a basis for understanding valuable aspects of music's sociality. Drawing on some remarks by the Russian composer Igor Stravinsky, John Blacking wrote in 1973 about the contrast between our experience of actual time in ordinary daily experience and music's ability to "create another world of virtual time" (Blacking, 1973: 27). Building on this, and on remarks by the composer and music theorist Jonathan Kramer, Simon Frith claimed that one of music's most important dimensions is that it can encourage us to experience a sense of a *continuing present* (Frith, 1996: 148–149). There are connections here with Csikszentmihalyi's notion of flow, discussed in Chapter 2 – of how we can valuably lose ourselves in absorbing activities, of which music is one; and with the way that Adam Phillips, quoted in Chapter 2, related a healthy loss of self-consciousness to our sense of *aliveness*.

But Schutz's account, like Martin's and DeNora's, is ultimately based on an assumption that music matters because it works for people, providing practical solutions for them. As we saw in Chapter 2, there is a danger that the conception of agency at work in such considerations of music might be too simple. It implies that people are able, a great deal of the time, to make music work for them at will. It seems as dubious to make such assumptions when considering people's attempts to construct good collective experiences and identities, as when we are addressing attempts to live good lives as individuals. In the interactionist sociological tradition Martin and DeNora operate in, social life is understood as intersubjectivity, and this has the unfortunate consequence that "macro" phenomena disappear into thin air, as Layder (2006: 98) puts it. In the sociology of music that derives from such interactionism, music becomes a model of the intersubjectivity that constitutes the social, collapsing the various domains of social life (coherently outlined by Layder, 2006, as psychobiography, situated activity, social settings and contextual resources) into just one of these – situated activity.

Music and fundamental human sociality

A second way of understanding and valuing music's sociality is based on the idea that there is something primal in humans that orients them towards shared experience and that music and dance meet those needs in modern societies in ways that are ultimately beneficial. We have already seen that a version of this idea ultimately underpins Small's preference for highly communal, passionately engaged forms of collective musical experience, with the danger that individual experiences and situations are collapsed into placing a high value on social cohesion and integration. Another version of this idea in social theory originates in the work of Emile Durkheim. In his work on religion, notably *The Elementary Forms of Religious Life* (1976/1915), Durkheim drew on observations of Australian aboriginal peoples to make claims about the basis of religious experience. Early peoples often operated in separate groups, but when they came together, a great "collective effervescence" (226) ensued. The intensity of feeling produced by the social resulted in the distinction between the sacred and the profane, as feelings of delirium were projected on to rituals and totems. For Durkheim, sacred experience was, in essence, the intense social experience produced by collectivity. Such collective effervescence could be dangerous, Durkheim recognized, but modern societies were marked by a devitalization through neglect of the renewal of social and moral order.

Some social theorists, such as Zygmunt Bauman, take a very different view, seeing community and collectivity as full of danger. Bauman locates hope mainly in a pre-social moral impulse in individuals (see Shilling and Mellor, 1998). Others, though, such as the French social theorist Michel Maffesoli detect in modern societies a "revitalization of the sacred, the appearance of new forms of sociality, and the return of an emotionally-grounded category of the moral" (Shilling and Mellor, 1998: 202). (Post) modern life sees an abundance of new collectivities, which Maffesoli called "neo-tribes," based on what is emotionally shared between individuals. These are often aesthetic collectivities based on fleeting participation. This has led some music researchers to look to Maffesoli's neo-Durkheimian theory as a way of replacing subcultures as a concept for understanding collectivities of (young) people in relation to music, dance, and other forms of popular culture. In its postmodernist form, this was based on an idea that young people were increasingly able to choose and to move freely between different identities (Muggleton, 2000) – a long way from the Durkheimian roots of concepts of collective feeling, and a dubious assumption about people's freedom of choice in modern life (see Hesmondhalgh, 2005 for a discussion of some of these theories).

Maffesoli's own approach was intriguing in pointing to the "primitive," somatic, and affective nature of people's desires to be together, and how this took new forms. But both Maffesoli and his adaptations in youth and popular music studies tended to ignore the dangers of the emotional nature of neo-tribal groupings (by contrast with writers such as Stejpan Meštrović (1991) who interprets collective effervescence purely in terms of its dangers). Just as significantly, there was a strong implication in Maffesoli's work that rationality and moral action are nowhere to be found in modern societies (Shilling and Mellor, 1998). This is a problem shared with some Deleuzean approaches to musical collectivity (such as Jordan's (1995) interesting take on rave crowds as "bodies-without-organs") and with Victor Turner's ideas about liminality and *communitas* (discussed in Chapter 3). We should not underestimate the ways in which dancers, football fans, and people singing at gigs are often involved in a certain amount of reflective activity (see my earlier discussion of dancers).

In my view, one of the best discussions of these issues comes from the social commentator and historian, Barbara Ehrenreich, who provides a version of the collective effervescence approach grounded in an understanding of human desire, and capacity, for collective joy. Ehrenreich acknowledges fully that "a restoration of festivity and ecstatic ritual will not get the world out of ecological and economic crisis and that such activities could not be restored with anything like their original meaningfulness." But for Ehrenreich, "the capacity for collective joy is encoded into us almost as deeply as the capacity for the erotic love of one human for the other." Her argument is simply that we need more chances to "acknowledge the miracle of our simultaneous existence with some sort of celebration" (all quotations from Ehrenreich, 2006: 260) – and she shows that music and dance are fundamental to such opportunities.

The capabilities approach

At their best, the two approaches I have discussed so far allow us to value ordinary experiences of intersubjectivity, and extraordinary experiences of collective pleasure, and to explain them. At their worst, they lead to misleading understandings of the social, and of the social value of music. A third and complementary perspective helps us understand sociality and aesthetic experience as part of human flourishing, drawing upon the capabilities approach outlined in Chapter 2. To recall the discussion in Chapter 2, the capabilities approach, as developed by Martha Nussbaum, emphasizes human needs for affiliation, for "being able to live with and toward others," including but not confined to recognizing and showing concern for other human beings, and for "being able to have attachments to things and people outside ourselves" (Nussbaum, 2006: 76–77). The advantage of this approach over the other two approaches so far discussed are that people are understood as reflective and imbued with ethical agency, but also subject to the operation of structural forces, and – in line with object–relations versions of psychoanalytical thought – dependent, vulnerable, and not always with a full understanding of their own emotions and circumstances. Another advantage of this approach is that it makes much stronger links with theories of social justice, and invites normative consideration of which social and institutional arrangements might allow musical sociality and communality to thrive, or not. These are issues that I take up in Section 4.10.

4.8 Spectres of Capitalist Modernity Revisited: Class and Inequality

Having given a positive account of music's sociality so far, I now address how various social, institutional, and psychic factors may diminish music's contribution to people's lives. The first issue I examine here concerns inequality of access to the benefits of making music collectively. I will begin by looking at access to the realm of amateur musicianship, by returning to Finnegan's study of music in Milton Keynes. For Finnegan seems to downplay social class, which seems likely to be a major factor in restricting access to the possibility of musical flourishing, given that musical training generally requires various resources – not just money, but also the desire to invest in a future, in the secure expectation of future self-realization. How generally were life-enhancing activities associated with music-making available in Milton Keynes? Finnegan claims that her research did not reveal "any clear class-dominated patterns for involvement in music generally. Active music-making of any kind was a minority interest, but within that minority were people of many backgrounds in terms of education, wealth and … occupation" (Finnegan, 1989: 312). Finnegan also says that the various genres or worlds she examined were not marked by class characteristics.

This suggests that music might offer a basis for life-enhancing possibilities across social classes, and the class inequality that mars modern societies does not affect music-making in the same way. Because of the importance of her case study, and the significance of these statements, it is worth examining Finnegan's language carefully. In discussing the class composition of the classical music "world" she examined, Finnegan states that "[m]any of those engaged in classical music were from reasonably affluent, educated and privileged families, but certainly not all" (313). But this makes it sound as though explanations invoking class would have to be based on *everyone* involved in a certain pursuit being from the same class, which would be an extraordinarily ham-fisted understanding of class as a social influence. We are surely more likely to be looking at *patterns* of participation, at *tendencies* rather than absolute correspondences. Later, Finnegan claims that the only one of the musical worlds she examined which was closely connected to working-class occupations and backgrounds was country and western ("and even here there were exceptions" (314)). But Finnegan does not consider an alternative interpretation of this datum: that people from the middle classes dominate music-making in general.

Finnegan declares herself troubled by "the preoccupation with so many social scientists and others with 'class' as the paramount factor in western industrial society for transmitting life-styles from one generation to the next" (311) – and the scare quote marks around class indicates her skepticism about the very category. But in distancing herself from sociological explanations based on "grandiose-sounding factors" (312) such as class, Finnegan makes no specific reference to previous studies of music and social class, or even to studies of social class at all. That Finnegan was really not very interested in the implications of social class for people's experiences is also indicated by a passing but revealing piece of sociological understatement. Finnegan concedes that "it is true that a family on a low income found it harder to undertake regular instrumental lessons for their children, but families committed to music still tried to pursue it even from meagre resources" (313). There is a ring of complacency here. Working-class families who wanted to participate in musical training could do so if they were prepared to make the sacrifice. But two questions follow from this, neither of which Finnegan in any way addresses. First, there is the quantitative question of how many working-class people made such sacrifices. Based on my experience of working-class relations to learning music, I suspect the answer is: not many. Second, there is the qualitative question of what the experience of such sacrifice might have involved, how difficult it might have been, and what effects might that have had on people's experiences of participation in Milton Keynes musical life. Finnegan provides no actual figures on how many people from which social class participated in which musical worlds, but instead resorts to quasi-quantitative statements such as "certainly not all" or statements that people from all classes could be found within any world, ignoring the question of how many of each were to be found there. Nor does she define or categorize social class, other than providing a list of the wide range of occupations involved in music-making in Milton Keynes – as if this indicated that class was not an explanatory factor. Of course it may be that Milton Keynes in the early 1980s was a rather successful example of the integration of different social classes. But Finnegan's own figures (26) suggest that the majority of the city's population in any case belonged to "higher" social classes: 80% of employment was in the ABC1 category. This was a middle-class city.

Other sociologists have taken Finnegan's research as evidence that social class does not significantly affect musical practices.[22] Peter Martin (2006: 99) says that Finnegan's "findings raise serious doubts about approaches which reduce such connections [between music and other activities in people's lives] to one-dimensional associations between social class position and musical taste." I hope that the preceding discussion indicates that while Finnegan's research might be used to counter "one-dimensional associations," it certainly does not provide secure evidence that social class was not an important factor in influencing access to music-making.

Given all this, the question arises of how typical Milton Keynes may be as a case study of the enhancement of people's lives through amateur music-making in a particular locale? How many other towns might be as successful and as flourishing in this respect as was Milton Keynes in the early 1980s? At the very least, we should look at other cities to assess the degree to which the dynamics traced by Finnegan might be found elsewhere. It is surprising that, as far as I am aware, no one has followed Finnegan by systematically researching the whole musical life of a city – perhaps also to include professional music-making and musical consumption that she did not consider. Some of the more troubling dynamics of class and racial division that mar modern societies – including smaller towns and cities than Milton Keynes – seemed not to be so marked there as in other cities and towns, and this may have had a significant influence on Finnegan's study. This takes us to the question of place and locality.

---

[22] This has been typical of trends in the sociology of music, which have been overwhelmingly in the direction of interactionism.

4.9   Uneven Musical Development

The importance of place and locality is downplayed in some forms of cultural analysis. In the 1990s and 2000s, the era of debates about globalization and the arrival of the internet in (many people's) everyday life, social scientists and theorists understandably emphasized the fact that local places are increasingly infused by all kinds of economic, social, and cultural flows that come from other places, often very remote. This is a commonplace of ideas about globalization: that the global affects the local. And it is true that things have changed. Many people in the modern world are highly mobile, and move regularly between different places. Nevertheless, most of us can say that we live in a particular place, and most people would recognize that the place where they spend most of their time is a vital determinant of the quality of their lives.

In music too, in spite of the global circulation of musical commodities, place matters. We often use music to evoke a sense of a particular place, reviving memories or stimulating our imagination. In all kinds of genres, from symphonies to ballads to rock songs to rap, some composers and performers invoke where they came from, whether straight outta Compton, like NWA, from Kingston (Bob Marley) or Finland (Sibelius). For others, local reference is muted, but a sense of origin in a particular place becomes embedded in audiences' understandings of a performer: most people know that the Beatles were from Liverpool, and that Liverpool is a port with a rich working-class history. A vital part of the mythology of music concerns certain places at certain times: Vienna in the 1780s and 1790s; New Orleans in the first two decades of the twentieth century; San Francisco in the late 1960s. Alternative rock has been a particularly fertile territory for such mythologization (see Straw, 1991).

But myth can often be a poor basis for genuine musical vitality, even within a particular genre. If a band identified with a certain place makes it, then there is a rush of signings of other bands from the same area; this is what happened following the success of Manchester bands Happy Mondays and Stone Roses. And, as Street (1997: 106) has observed, in the wake of success, as with various Sheffield bands in the early 1980s, the money tends to flow to wherever the record company that signed them is based (in the British case, usually London). Bands often relocate in order to be nearer to expertise and to escape the scene that spawned them (on the complex ways in which the word "scene" has been used in popular music studies, see

Box 4.2   Scenes

The major way in which place has been investigated in popular music studies has been via the concept of scenes, most notably in a classic article by Will Straw (1991), which compared dance music and alternative rock. Elsewhere (Hesmondhalgh, 2005) I have pointed to confusions in the way that the concept of scene has been used. Sometimes it is used to denote the musical practices in a particular genre within a particular town or city; sometimes it is used to denote a cultural space that transcends locality. As Straw himself later asked, "How useful is a term which designates both the effervescence of our favourite bar and the sum total of all global phenomena surrounding a subgenre of Heavy Metal music?" (Straw, 2001b: 248). Straw proceeded to defend the term by observing that the concept persists within cultural analysis for a number of reasons, including its ability to "disengage phenomena from the more fixed and theoretically troubled unities of class or sub-culture (even when it holds out the promise of their eventual rearticulation)" (Straw, 2001b: 248). For Straw, "'scene' seems able to evoke both the cozy intimacy of community and the fluid cosmopolitanism of urban life. To the former, it adds a sense of dynamism; to the latter, a recognition of the inner circles and weighty histories which give each seemingly fluid surface a secret order" (Straw, 2001b: 248). These are good goals, but I remain unconvinced that scene really can do this work, given the incommensurable attempts to theorize it. I find the concept confused rather than productive. But Straw's original 1991 article on scenes is valuable in other ways. It provides an acute analysis of how some genre cultures can retain a sense of cosmopolitan openness (a characteristic he attributed to dance music culture at the time he was writing) while others remained sealed within certain social groups (he pointed to the white, middle-class nature of alternative rock).

Box 4.2). By the time bands become well-known, the musical world they emerged from has often dissipated. If anyone had gone looking for musical vitality in Seattle once Nirvana became globally famous in the early 1990s, they may well have been disappointed.

Shank (1994) provided a fascinating ethnographic study of the rock "scene" in Austin, Texas, in the 1980s. For Shank, the vitality of rock music in Austin derived from a productive interaction of musicians and audiences. A "scene" was "an overproductive signifying community, arising from a certain intensity of commitment." For Shank, such intensity of commitment was a "necessary condition" for creativity, innovation, and critique within a place, for the production of exciting music "capable of moving past the mere expression of locally significant cultural values and generic development – that is, beyond stylistic permutation – toward an interrogation of dominant structures of identification, and potential cultural transformation" (Shank, 1994: 122). This is surely right, and of course such commitment then feeds into infrastructures of production, distribution, and performance (see Kruse, 2003). But such scenes are only one part of the musical life of a city. Many are enclaves of bohemian, middle-class whiteness and in some cases are linked to processes of gentrification. They are often cut off from other "scenes," such as the kind of fecund but chaotic rap scene richly described by Nik Cohn (2006) in the case of New Orleans. This is why the approach of Ruth Finnegan, discussed earlier, is potentially so important, in spite of the problems of her approach. Finnegan looks across different genres and different groups, in a real attempt to look at the vitality of musical life across Milton Keynes as a whole. Too often, judgments by middle-class educated people of the musical vitality of a city are based only on their own preferred genres (usually alternative rock, maybe electronic dance music, hip hop in a few places). On the other hand, it is the case that the "intensity" that Shank prized in Austin is likely to be produced in situations where people have the time, energy, and inclination to spend time together in public space. This means that music oriented towards younger people (in their late teens, twenties, and early thirties) is always likely to be the most productive of regular interaction. On the down side, mobile groups of young people might move on quickly. Schools and educational institutions might be the most important way to create a good enough continuity.

4.10 Elements of Thriving Musical Places

Given these factors, let me now lay out some of the more general conditions that I think are needed to make for thriving music-making and consumption, both professional and amateur, within particular localities. Importantly, this does not only include facilities and resources within particular cities. National and even international arrangements vitally affect what happens at the local level.

- *Live music venues of different kinds and sizes,* allowing for music from a variety of genres. Good classical and jazz venues will need extremely good acoustics and seating, venues oriented towards more contemporary and popular forms will need good standing or dancing space. Venues of different sizes would allow for artists of different levels of standing and popularity to come to the same city. A good number and variety of smaller venues would provide more opportunity for small-scale professional and semi-professional musicians to learn live music skills and to build audiences.
- *A good quality of live music venues,* including venues that do not charge excessive prices for entrance or for food and drink upon entry. Provision of these things helps to generate a sense of pleasurable and sociable belonging, which means that people will come back time and again, and maybe get to know other regular attenders. One major factor in quality would be proximity to other places of entertainment and culture, so that musical venues are not perceived as places isolated from the general flow of life in a city (as when concert halls are located on the outskirts of cities, accessible mainly by car).
- For the aforementioned to be possible, there needs to be *a sympathetic legal and regulatory environment,* usually at the national and local levels. This would include licensing arrangements that allow flexibility in how and when performances take place, including arrangements for licenses to sell alcoholic drink. The legalization of cannabis, and good health information about the psychological dangers of excessive use, would be a major benefit to people's enjoyment of popular music.
- *Good transport infrastructure, street lighting, and high degrees of personal safety,* allowing musicians and audiences to get to and from musical events easily, safely, and inexpensively.
- *National and/or local education systems and curricula that value music highly.* This would include the presence of schools and other educational institutions, such as universities, that support music-making of a range of kinds, by providing venues and encouraging and nurturing the love of a range of musics in children and young people. This would include not putting an excessive value on music that can only be produced with significant resources, such as expensive-to-make pop music, or music

for large orchestras, compared with music that is relatively easy and inexpensive to make.

- *National and local communication systems which value a range of musical genres highly, and provide the means for musicians to build audiences.* Commercial radio and television, because of their reliance on audience maximization for the sake of profit, are unlikely to fulfil this role as effectively as publicly supported broadcasting systems. Good grassroots web sites can play a major role in sustaining scenes, but may have to rely on public support, at least initially.
- *Libraries and museums* that allow people inexpensive access to musical resources, including recordings and books about music, of a range that would not easily or normally be available to various groups.
- *A mixture of "cultures" in a locality*: a mixture of people from different social classes, ethnic groups, or of different subcultures. This may make possible the exchange and cross-fertilization of talent, practices, and ideas about how to produce and consume music, allowing for innovative hybridity, and for people to reach out beyond their particular social groupings to understand a greater range of cultural experiences.

4.11 Quality of Working Life of Professional Musicians

The final issue I want to examine, in looking at some of the factors that might limit music's positive sociality in modern life concerns access to the worlds of professional music-making. Presumably, if music-making brings the kinds of personal rewards and satisfactions that, as we saw earlier, research suggests that it does, then quite a lot of people are going to want to make a living out of making music. And this indeed turns out to be the case. This raises two questions. First, echoing our discussion of amateur musicians, who gets to be a professional musician? Second, what quality of working life might professional musicians achieve? What resources might be necessary to maintain regular satisfactions from being an amateur musician?

A number of sociologists have pointed to the social nature of artistic creative production, but they show that artistic production takes highly ambivalent forms in modern societies. This allows us to understand the context of the sociality involved in music-making more thoroughly. Becker showed that the idea that cultural works emerge from brilliant individuals is at best overstated, and at worst mistaken: "art worlds rather than artists make art" (1982: 198–199), on the basis of interactions between social actors, in a complex and often concealed division of labor. Jason Toynbee (2012) argues against the way that the romantic expressivist model of artistry mystifies musical production and implicitly effaces the agency of musicians by making it seem as though creation is involuntary, emerging from within. He adapts the Russian critic Mikhail Bakhtin's idea that novelists combine a huge variety of voices (heteroglossia) to show that musical authorship is deeply social, for it always involves complex combinations of voices, and so as well as being interactive, "creation is a matter of selecting from a pool of coded voices that are shared within a given musical community" (2012: 169; see also Toynbee, 2000). This does not mean that creation is a happy world of peaceful collaboration, however, as Toynbee fully recognizes. Artistic production, and indeed the very idea of heroic authorship itself were, as Pierre Bourdieu showed, produced not by individuals acting alone but by many individuals whose actions could only be understood according to their place in intensely competitive fields of interaction. Even the very idea of heroic, charismatic authorship was produced within such fields of cultural production – though this had ambivalent consequences, because it also allowed for a much greater degree of artistic autonomy for musicians, writers, and painters. Furthermore, Toynbee argues, the accumulation of profit in the cultural industries, including the music industries, is based on the romantic ideology of authorship, as expressed in copyright law, which relies on the romantic idea that expressions are the property of heroic creators, thus denying the social nature of creativity – and also obscuring the fact that ownership of rights usually belongs to the corporations that finance, distribute, and market music rather than creators.

All this produces a number of complex and contradictory dynamics in industrialized cultural production (see Hesmondhalgh and Baker, 2011; Hesmondhalgh, 2013). The presence of high degrees of autonomy and the fundamental sociality of musical collaboration, among other factors (see Stahl, 2006), make jobs and occupations in music-making highly desirable. What is more, governments of many different kinds seek to boost employment in the creative industries and other knowledge-economy sectors, portraying jobs and occupations there not only as sources of competitiveness and economic prosperity, but also as potential sources of rewarding work. Yet there is a massive oversupply of potential workers, which depresses remuneration for all but the highly successful (who are vastly over-rewarded, because of the "winner takes all" structure of the sector), and creates a labor market marked by a vast reservoir of unemployed and under-employed musicians, many of them well-trained and extremely talented.

Clearly, the result is a context in which the pleasures and rewards of musical collaboration are compromised by structural conditions. Put simply, very few people indeed are able to make a living out of making music. Nevertheless, for those who are able to make it into professional music-making (often supported by music teaching, or by other jobs not involving music at all) do achieve some sense of flourishing in their musical lives. Many of the musicians that Sarah Baker and I interviewed for our research project on creative work in the cultural industries attested to various satisfactions and rewards they gained from musical labor. They experienced high levels of autonomy, interest, and sociality, combined with opportunities for self-realization.

But there was another side too, which belied the idea that creative-industry jobs such as theirs are cool and glamorous. Working hours are famously hard for musicians, and pay is abysmal other than for the talented and/or lucky few who make it. The long periods between regular work can lead to feelings of isolation at odds with the sociality of performance, or even the recording studio.[23]

Another key factor to consider here relates back to the institutional conditions for thriving places that were discussed in the last section. Music as a form of social activity is in some ways rather cheap. Some musical instruments are not very expensive. This gives musical creativity a somewhat decentered feel. Digitalization has arguably extended this by making recording and distribution even cheaper (though see Hesmondhalgh, 2013: 341–348 for an assessment of arguments about digital democratization of music). Yet musical entertainment and the recording industries remain concentrated in certain cities, often capitals and regional hubs, both for consumers and producers. As generations of musicians from the provinces in a number of countries will testify, decentralization in musical production does not extend as far as "making it." The uneven development of capitalist modernity haunts musical production too and limits sustained forms of participatory collaboration of the kind that we should value.

---

[23] See Hesmondhalgh and Baker (2011) for a study of workers' experiences in three industries. Among the key theoretical interventions in the burgeoning field of cultural labor studies that discuss music are Ross (2000, 2009) and Banks (2007).

5

Commonality and Cosmopolitanism

5.1 Mediated Commonality in Modern Societies

What contribution might aesthetic experience make to human life? This question has been a central concern of this entire book. Chapter 1 briefly established that the value of such experience had come under increasing attack in recent years. In critically defending music from such attacks, I concentrated in Chapter 2 on how music might contribute to the flourishing of individuals through enrichment of their emotional and ethical lives; in Chapter 3, on music's relationships to love and sexual intimacy; and in Chapter 4 on music's ability to enhance experiences of co-present sociability and community. This chapter addresses music's relation to ideas of *mediated commonality* in modern complex societies. It asks: how might musical experience bring people together across different communities, groupings, and places? How, and in what circumstances, might music enhance human life by transcending or containing social difference?

In order to address such questions, I now need to provide a fuller account of debates about the value of aesthetic experience, and how they have evolved, than I have provided up to this point. Only via such an account can we understand the significance that has been attached to notions of commonality in relation to art and culture. For "aesthetic" refers to something more than what individuals find pleasing, beautiful, and so on; and aesthetics is a term that refers to something more than an academic sub-field concerned with matters of beauty and taste. Debates about the importance of aesthetic experience have their origins in Enlightenment attempts to understand the collective fate of human beings, and place central emphasis on *aesthetic talk*. However, I will show that these debates only hint at the value of musical experience for collective human flourishing in complex, modern, highly mediated societies. The rest of the chapter therefore seeks to build on such debates by examining a broad range of case studies.

5.2 Aesthetic Experience and Aspirations to Commonality

At the dawn of capitalist modernity, a new way of thinking about symbols and about beauty emerged. In the wake of the advance of science, and its staggering achievements, religion lost its status as the primary guarantor of truth. This raised questions about the very nature of human subjectivity. If it was human consciousness that had made emancipation from nature possible, how might we understand ourselves? Yet science could not supply sufficient resources to understand consciousness itself. For Kant and others, the appreciation of beauty, especially in the realm known as art, took on unprecedented importance as a means of comprehending humanity. A new area of philosophy, retrospectively known as aesthetics, had come into being. For aestheticians who were pessimistic about human life, art was the sole means for "creating illusions that enable us to face a meaningless existence" (Bowie, 2003: 4); for those who looked at humanity with greater hope, art suggested what the world might be like if emancipation from the demands of nature could be fully achieved. A belief in the centrality of art and the aesthetic realm in human life began to pervade much Western thought. As Andrew Bowie has shown, music was central to such debates about aesthetics and subjectivity among philosophers. This was because it seemed to exemplify how self-understanding can never be achieved by linguistic discourse alone.

Humans have created images, stories, and sounds for millennia. The elevation of those forms of experience to the new status of "art" was an ambivalent phenomenon. Art was mystified and idealized, made into a privileged category cut off from the experiences of the vast majority of people. But it also became a major source of opposition to the commercial imperatives of nascent capitalism. The aesthetic confirmed bourgeois society but also gestured towards its redemption (Ryle and Soper, 2002: 14).

In the twentieth century, various writers and thinkers concerned with human emancipation and with the fate of art in capitalist modernity rejected the a-historicism of the post-Kantian tradition of aesthetics (including its Hegelian versions). Yet that tradition's identification of art's utopian potential to foreshadow a better world remained of interest, especially to Marxists. Some sought to reinvent artistic praxis under Communism, though this dream had almost entirely evaporated by 1950 as the horrors of Stalinism became clear. Others, Marxist or not, considered that the game was up, and that art had more or less lost its emancipatory possibilities in a thoroughly instrumentalized and commodified world. The goal of political aesthetics was mainly to make this clear and find fragments of hope, usually in avant-garde modernist art. Music remained an important topic in these debates, notably in the work of Adorno. Such deliberations did not take place in isolation, nor were they confined to philosophy or high culture. There were echoes in everyday artistic practice of the issues explored by philosophers, including in music. For example, despairing of the corruption of creativity by commerce, movements from the folk revival to the hippies to punk to rave, sought to reinvent art by returning it to the people. Such thinking persists in the hope that new digital technologies can democratize culture, by leading to the breakdown of capitalist property relations, or by empowering "consumers" to become "producers."

With the decline of Marxism (in political life and in theory) in the 1980s, and in the wake of an increasing disenchantment with Enlightenment thought, many writers began to reject not only the post-Kantian aesthetic tradition, but also attempts to reconstruct that tradition on Marxian foundations (Bennett, 1990). Some of these efforts took postmodernist and populist forms, holding that the best thing for humanity was for people simply to decide what they liked. Such approaches in effect withdrew from any idea that aesthetic experience might be the basis of meaningful emancipation (rather than pleasure or diversion). It potentially left the formation of taste, and debates about the right and the good, in the hands of states and the cultural industries that had increasingly come to be dominated by large national and multinational corporations. The most sustained and impressive critique of the mainstream of Western aesthetics, however, was provided by Pierre Bourdieu, especially in his 1979 book *La Distinction*, a study of taste in France, based on fieldwork he and his associates conducted in the 1960s, already referred to in Chapter 2. Bourdieu showed how the exercise of aesthetic tastes reinforced social inequality. This in itself was not a novel idea. But no one had previously submitted the assumptions underlying classical bourgeois aesthetics to such detailed critique, in particular the privileging of "pure," supposedly disinterested reflection over enjoyment and pleasure; and no one had provided such a detailed sociological treatment of how taste worked as a mechanism of social power. Bourdieu showed how tastes were linked to particular sets of dispositions associated with particular social classes and how, in their cultural practices, dominant classes accrued "cultural capital" which they could, in effect, use to maintain and leverage their superiority. The cultural practices of the working class were despised, dismissed, and misunderstood.

Bourdieu believed that "nothing more clearly affirms one's 'class,' nothing more infallibly classifies, than tastes in music" (18). This was for three reasons. First, concert-going and playing instruments were less widespread than other discriminating practices (theater, museums, galleries). Second, music involved a cultural flaunting of a particular kind, derived from music's special relationship to interiority: "for a bourgeois world which conceives its relation to the populace in terms of the relationship of the soul to the body" (19), musical insensitivity was a particularly negative form of materialist coarseness. Third, music "represents the most radical and most absolute form of the negation of the world, and especially the social world, which the bourgeois ethos tends to demand of all forms of art" (19). These characterizations show the limitations of Bourdieu's sociology of cultural consumption, which was fuelled by a laudable rage against the profound inequality and complacency of French culture. Music, and musical consumption in modern societies, including I suspect that of France in the 1960s and 1970s, are a great deal more complex than is implied in these statements by Bourdieu. In later work, he developed a position which sought to defend intellectual and artistic production against commerce and postmodernist populism. Nevertheless, *Distinction* represents the fullest possible sociological attack on the role that aesthetic experience can play in everyday life, and on how it can be used to divide people, rather than bring them together, and it is impossible to read it without recognizing how class inequality profoundly mars culture and the arts.

5.3   Redeeming Aesthetic Experience?

Can we redeem the emancipatory potential of aesthetic experience in the light of such critique? Some have continued to believe that such experience might be the basis of some kind of human commonality. An attempt to recover this emancipatory dimension of aesthetics is to be found in the work of the French philosopher Jacques Rancière. Rancière sees art, at least under the "aesthetic regime" of the last 200 years, as offering opportunities to redistribute assigned categories of being, subjectivity and occupation, in a manner that is based on the equality of all speaking subjects. It is not surprising therefore that Rancière has been widely taken up by artists and art critics as an advocate of the potentially empowering effects of art (see for example Kristin Ross's (2007) article in *Artforum*). He seems to offer high cultural theory a route towards a non-reductive political conception of art's powers. Yet, in doing so, Rancière draws on a normative framework that is profoundly hostile to the institutional forms of modernity (Bennett, 2011) and his invocations of art's ability to pull together a common humanity are extremely vague and utopian, as even his defenders would concede (see Davis's relatively lucid commentary, 2010).

A somewhat different attempt to redeem the aesthetic was provided by the British media analyst Nicholas Garnham (2000), who, in a major work on the media and social theory, argued against the reduction of the aesthetic to the social and of aesthetic judgements to ideology. To do so, he reconstructed a Kantian argument for the importance of the aesthetic domain in human life. According to this view, art has the capacity to bridge the sensual and the rational, and to allow an escape from necessity, facilitating the creation of alternative worlds where the potential for the combination of happiness and virtue can be projected. From this position, explained Garnham (drawing on Andrew Bowie's work), derive two different theories of the value of the autonomy of art. The first was that of the German romantics, concerning art's resistance to rationality, and its potential expression of creative plurality. This led ultimately to notions of an aesthetic orientation to life as a whole, which carried with it a danger of depoliticization and even solipsism.[1] The second tradition emerging from Kant, much preferred by Garnham, is the Hegelian theory of praxis, where symbolic forms are seen as an objectification and projection of interaction between subjects, on the one hand, and other humans and nature on the other. Here art could be seen as a realm "within which the possibilities of social emancipation could be experienced and thus held open, if only as a utopian possibility" (Garnham, 2000: 156). Garnham's view is grounded in a critical Enlightenment goal of emancipation dependent upon aspirations to commonality, radically at odds with the poststructuralist anti-essentialism that was fashionable in the 1990s. Garnham wished to hold on to aesthetic experience and aesthetic debate as key elements in a continuing quest for commonality across difference. Garnham is much more alert than Rancière to the idea

---

[1] Though see Shusterman (2000) for an interesting defense of this idea.

that aesthetic experience's potential for commonality might be based in common species-being – an extremely unfashionable position within Left thinking about culture at the time Garnham was writing. According to this view, the pleasures of art can be understood as rooted in certain psycho-biological constants; not permanent, metahistorical categories but relatively stable ones, certainly more stable than sociocultural configurations.[2]

Now Garnham is considerably more sociological than Rancière (who shows great hostility to sociology in some of his writing). For Garnham, the problem of aesthetics, of the evaluation of symbolic forms, is "part of the wider problem of creating viable communities for autonomous agents under the conditions of modernity" (Garnham, 2000: 162). Aesthetic experiences, Garnham argues, might operate as *social learning experiences* that might bring people together as much as divide them. Against Bourdieu and post-structuralists such as John Frow, Garnham sought to move away from "a position where aesthetic evaluations are necessarily ideological" and inter-pretative communities are necessarily pitted against each other in incommen-surable value regimes. Instead, he wrote, evaluation might be "a social learning experience" involving "the development of common values within a public sphere of critical debate." Garnham makes a crucial move here, in bringing in the notion of public spheres, or forms of publicness, as a way of beginning to specify how different communities might be brought together across difference. The problem is that Garnham is extremely vague on how this hap-pens. His treatment of debates about publicness is conducted entirely in terms of a fairly traditional conception of politics as questions of government and citizenship (which is the way that questions of "the public sphere" have mostly been treated). The relation of *aesthetic* evaluation to political evaluation, and how the former might be the basis of "the development of common values" were left almost completely unspecified in Garnham's account.

So attempts to redeem aesthetic experience seem to flounder. Two major intellectuals from very different traditions both leave us cast somewhat adrift, by conducting their discussion at too high a level of abstraction. In addition, they do not adequately consider the social institutions that might allow for aesthetic experience to be made the basis of forms of publicness

---

[2] The importance of such biological continuities, and their relation to the value of aesthetic experience needs more careful consideration than it has been given by sociologically and culturally inclined scholars. There are better and worse versions of this position, which there is no space to address here. See, in the context of music, Kathleen Marie Higgins (2012, Chapter 3).

that allow such experience to fulfil its historical role of providing a commonality that might allow humans to flourish collectively. However, Garnham does offer some kind of clue for where we might turn for some more concreteness, and interestingly, he does so by referring to the work of a music critic and sociologist, Simon Frith, and in particular Frith's argument that talk about music might transcend social differences and high and low culture. In responding to culture, "people bring similar questions to high and low art" wrote Frith (1996: 19). Frith's view was that cultural judgements across different social classes, genders, and ethnicities tend to work around rather similar axes of evaluation: believability, coherence, familiarity, usefulness, and "spirituality" ("does this experience uplift me, make me a better person?"). Whether or not Frith's list of shared criteria are the right ones (they seem plausible to me, even if I would express them slightly differently), this at least brings more concreteness to the idea that aesthetic experience might contribute to commonality in positive ways. In the next section, I examine some examples of musical talk, to explore the idea that such aesthetic discourse might be the basis of common under-standing. My argument is that talk can provide only limited insight into the value of aesthetic experience.

5.4   Talk About Music, What It Tells Us, and What It Doesn't

There is a remarkable lack of material that simply considers why people value the music they like.[3] So let us consider what some brief examples of musical talk might tell us about some of the issues raised by the preceding discussions. Do the evaluation of symbolic forms serve to enforce power relations and maintain divisions between interpretative communities? Or can evaluation, and the search for pleasure in beauty (and other facets of art and entertainment), serve as a kind of social learning experience, and one oriented to a common humanity, or at least to connections across social difference? If aesthetic discourse is as culturally, ethically and politically important as Garnham implies, what does it sound like in relation to music?

---

[3] The *Music in Daily Life* project (Crafts, Cavicchi, and Keil, 1993) was a rare example of a study where people talked about what music they liked and why. But the researchers attempted no interpretation of the fascinating material they collated; the book consists almost entirely of excerpts from interview transcriptions.

A few years ago, I made some efforts to address these questions, drawing on the research project that I discussed in Chapter 2, where I and colleagues from the Open University interviewed a number of people about their musical values, tastes, habits, and practices. This material showed that people from various backgrounds greatly value music's ability to articulate emotion, and that there was often a strong intersubjective dimension to this – people valued what this said about relations between people. But does this translate into understanding of and empathy with other social groups? Here is a 41-year-old social worker from London, of Nigerian background.

> I am not particularly religious but I think that the second piece of music which I bought, classical as it was, was Handel's *Messiah*, and I have played that *ad infinitum* until someone nicked it from the house, and now I have to wait until Easter. But when they sing about the trials and tribulations of Jesus at the time, you can really hear it in their voices, they are really mourning their loss and I just find it beautiful and I can't imagine how somebody could take the time to construct a piece of music like that, I think it all the way through the whole thing.

What is striking here is how the music is used to envisage what it is like to be other people, even though they are different (religious rather than secularist). Olle thinks that she can hear the feelings of loss and about other people's imaginary identifications with heroic suffering. Music allows her to understand the difference between herself as a non-religious person and those who have a faith, and not to dismiss or despise those other people.

There were other cases too in our interviews where people saw music as a means of powerfully reflecting on the suffering of others, sometimes in a more explicitly political way. Maria, a 58-year-old retired teacher from Birmingham, born and raised in Greece (and whose first language is Greek not English) told us:

MARIA: I mean people use music to express various things, beauty, oppression, love, so I love for example Shostakovich and when I hear his music is when I would feel enraged by, say, injustice in the world or whatever. Instead of talking politics, say, with you [...] I would just put this on and listen and I could hear the harshness of the regime, the oppression people felt, it is all in his music.

INTERVIEWER: Does it make you angry?

MARIA: If he was to express anger, it is very least of that because a human
          being was able to take all those and give it to you and so you relieve
          some of your anger if you like, because it's becoming acknowledged
          and you have the medium to get it through your system. You also
          identify with that person and you say "yes I know about that," or
          "there is so much experience a human being can have." So I could
          feel very enraged about, say, an injustice but if I hadn't lived myself
          in that system I could only know [it] from books and I could have
          my views but not the direct experience, but when I play the CD for
          example and listen to that, you just feel "I have some kind of direct
          experience of what it meant to be under that regime."

Maria seemed initially to be saying that political anger can be assuaged
through playing Shostakovich. But also apparent here is Maria's view
that music is able to express suffering in a more direct and immediate
way than other cultural forms of expression. Shostakovich experts might
question whether Maria is right to hear the music in this way.
Nevertheless, there is a strong sense here of music as an enabler of
compassion and empathy.

Of course, there may be a darker side to the psycho-social processes
involved in empathy and solidarity through music. For example, individuals, even when making positive judgments, are prone to perceive qualities
in a performer, or in an audience or social group associated with a particular
piece of music, which may simplify or distort the experiences the reality of
that group. This is the problem of *projection*. Projection is a feature of all
our imaginary identifications, and can have healthy and unhealthy dimensions, but here I am interested in some of the rather less healthy simplifica-
tions involved in certain sorts of projection, which can be starkly revealed
when people talk about music. For example, one of our interviewees
explained why she preferred blues and jazz – especially blues – to other
kinds of music:

There's an authenticity to them.[4] It's people singing because they want to sing,
not because they want to make money. I think a lot of the old jazz and blues
people, they didn't make money from it. They sang because they had to sing
didn't they?

---

[4]   It is worth noting that this was the only time any of our 40 interviewees used the word
"authenticity."

This view of black musicians as driven by a primitive impulse to sing for the sake of singing is a distortion of history. It is a reflection perhaps of the double burden that black musicians have to bear: not only as the victims of racism, but also as the repositories of utopian dreams of various kinds about uncommodified culture. Does this kind of projection undermine Frith and Garnham's view of the potential of aesthetic discourse to create commonalities across cultural divisions? Not necessarily. The issue about aesthetic experience and commonality is about *potential*, after all. This interviewee's deep love of the blues might make her *potentially* more amenable to discussion about the problems of taking this view of black music than otherwise.

Enthusiasm, then, should not be equated with the overcoming of social barriers. Equally, a lack of enthusiasm for certain kinds of music cannot be automatically equated with social closure. In some cases, someone might seem to be dismissing music considered pleasing or beautiful by others. But sometimes there is more going on in judgments that might be dismissed as "elitist" than might initially meet the eye or ear. Ashley, a 19 year old student, felt that music was, in general, "going in the right direction," with the exception of pop acts such as Britney Spears and the *Pop Idol* phenomenon.

> I just, I don't really like the way it's designed, in the way that *Big Brother* was designed as well, so that the population will like it. I don't like the way that they can assume the population will buy it and that they do. I think it's sad that everybody is so fickle really and I mean…I'm not…I think that people who were in *Pop Idol* they were all obviously very talented and I'm not saying that they weren't, but, one, it's not my type of music and two, I just don't like the way it's all so set up. You know, "this is the road to glory." "Here we are, here's your ticket."

This may seem very dismissive of the "population," of the masses. For some readers versed in cultural studies, Ashley's comments indicate the most traditional of elitist judgements and, beyond that, a failure of imagination. According to this view, Ashley does not realize that people might gain relatively innocent pleasures from such music. This may be true, but I think that to read Ashley's comment in this way misses the anxiety involved in what he is saying – and importantly in the present context, this is an anxiety felt on behalf of others. There is also anger here, and it seems that this anger is directed not at the "population," with their fickleness, but at those who "design" what presumably, in Ashley's view, should be a more spontaneous experience, or perhaps a more democratic one. For what Ashley seems to be pointing to is the power held by those who control the production of aesthetic experiences, as they say "*this* is the road to glory," on *our* terms. In terms of the debates that are framing my consideration of the material here, there is evidence in Ashley's words of a *yearning* for better social connection.

It's by no means the case that any kind of negative comment can be redeemed in this way as a sign of a search for potential solidarity. Here is Serena, a 58 year old aromatherapist and reflexologist from South Wales, answering a question about whether music today is better than 5, 10, 20, or 30 years ago.

> I am sure this is a terribly biased opinion but no I don't think music is as good nowadays as it was then. I think it is marketed. I think it is all too commercial and I think the creativity now is too manufactured and I go back to the Beatles really when it came from the heart, and it was [hesitates] I don't think it was simpler but it is done through computers now and they can be very clever with technology and I don't think the youngsters necessarily need the raw talent that they had and I think the pop stars are manufactured and produced to order. So I tend to be a bit cynical about it.

Such criticisms of "commercialism" will be familiar to anyone who has discussed modern music, or indeed modern culture. Questioning such oppositions of creativity and commerce, talent and technology, is familiar territory in cultural studies and the sociology of culture. This excerpt followed a section of the interview in which Serena had said that she was tolerant of the music of her children (who were in their late teens at the time of the interview). And yet shortly after that, she talked about her dislike of the kind of music that her children enjoyed – in her words, heavy metal (which is a category some of our interviewees used to mean "loud guitar music"). It struck me in reading the interview transcript and in listening to the tape of the interview, that Serena's discomfort with heavy metal (and in fact with any kind of music that expressed strong emotions) reflected a real uncertainty about her children's lives. In this Serena is not unusual, and she is certainly not "at fault." Her difficulty in making a connection to her children through music could well be, at least in part, a product of the way in which children sometimes use music, perhaps more than other media, to differentiate themselves from their parents. My point though is that if aesthetic discourse has any significance or potential in terms of representing or enabling greater commonality across social difference, then it has to be remembered that aesthetic experience and discourse may also reinforce social divisions – between young and old, in this case, or elsewhere between different ethnic groups or sexes or social classes. In this respect, while endorsing their attempt to move beyond the sociological pessimism of Bourdieu and his ilk, I find it hard to be as hopeful as Garnham and Frith (and maybe even Rancière too, who does not really address "ordinary" aesthetic experience and discourse) about aesthetic talk.[5] We need to find other ways to understand the role of aesthetic experience in bridging social difference in valuable ways.

There is a problem in any case in seeking musical experience's potential for emancipation too much in talk, in aesthetic deliberation, however valuable such deliberation might be in principle. As Frith himself suggests, a great deal of valuable musical experience does not rely on talk, but on action, on moving, playing, dancing. The aesthetic experience of music "gives us a way of being in the world, a way of making sense of it" (272) and "music is especially important for our sense of ourselves because of its unique emotional intensity – we absorb songs into our own lives and rhythm into our own bodies." But at the very same time, music is intensely social: "music response is, by its nature, a process of musical identification; aesthetic response is, by its nature, an ethical agreement" (272). Other cultural forms allow for such emotional alliances, but music provides us with a particularly intense "subjective sense of being social." It "both artic-ulates and offers the immediate *experience* of collective identity" (273). Its effects on our understanding of our identities may have conservative as well as liberating effects, but music "can also suggest that our social circum-stances are not immutable (and that other people – performers, fans – share our dissatisfaction)" (276). Although this falls some way short of the emancipatory hopes of Garnham and Rancière, Frith, then, offers a much more grounded account of the value of aesthetic experience in constructing collectivity. And, although, as we have seen, Garnham uses Frith to argue that evaluation can transcend social difference, this may be to ignore some realities concerning the ways in which people from different backgrounds currently relate to music. For, when people are asked to talk about topics, they struggle to articulate what they actually feel – a difficulty in analyzing people's values and beliefs about any area of life, but perhaps especially so in the case of music, where much experience is non-verbal, affective,

---

[5] The content of discussion threads about music on sites such as YouTube does not bode well for aesthetic talk, either, but this might say as much about computer networks and com-munication as about aesthetic talk in itself.

somatic. In his study of the monkey sub-genre in Tyneside, discussed in Chapter 4, Mark Rimmer (2010) writes that young men drawn to this music discussed it very little, although they swapped tapes, and made their own tracks. This was a working-class culture in which action was valued over talk, and where music functioned not so much to provide emotional self-realization, but to constitute individuals as members of a tightly bound community. One lad responded to a question by Rimmer about how monkey changed his mood by saying that using music in this way was for "daft lasses that listen to a love song and get all upset over it n'all you know" (Rimmer, 2010: 271).[6]

It does seem to be the case that many people find in musical experience powerful and moving evocations of collectivity and solidarity. My excursion into "ordinary" listeners' discourse about music mentioned earlier provides some insight into how some people think about their use of musical experience in terms of *making connections with others*. But we should be wary about overloading aesthetic deliberation with hopes of a historical role for aesthetic experience in modern life.

5.5   Music, Politics, and Publicness

There is another way in which we might understand the relationship between music and collective flourishing. At this point, I can almost hear the voices of certain friends, with strong political convictions, saying: "But what about music and *politics*?" In countless discussions with such friends, two assumptions often crop up: (i) only by changing the world for the better can we all flourish, individually and collectively; and (ii) music's most important role is to advance political struggles for greater equality. I agree with (i), but I disagree with (ii). Let me explain why.

Music's relationships to politics have too often been reduced to a limited number of topics. One is protest songs. Many such songs are powerful, moving, and even inspiring.[7] But they form a relatively minor part of the music of the world. To concentrate on them excessively consigns too much

---

[6]   Close studies of working-class musical experience are too rare. Another excellent one is Aaron Fox's *Real Country* (2004), about how voices and songs are at the heart of the working-class relationship to country music in a small Texas town.

[7]   See Dorian Lynskey's (2010) fine study of 33 protest songs, though all bar three are from the United States or the United Kingdom.

music to a residual political status. Another topic that has been extensively discussed in relation to music and politics is the coming together of musicians, perhaps especially star performers, in public performances that are linked to campaigns for change.[8] The most notable examples were perhaps the Live Aid concerts of 1985, which aimed to raise awareness of mass poverty in Africa, and to raise funds to prevent further deaths. Closely related to this are the political campaigning efforts of certain stars, such as Bono, singer and songwriter for the Irish rock band U2 – including Live 8, the 2005 concerts that followed up the earlier 1985 ones.[9]

We need to move away from these much-discussed and often highly mythologized moments in considering music's relations to democracy and politics, and the broader question of music's relation to collective human flourishing. And, in the context I write (Britain in 2012) we also need to avoid reproducing rock culture's mythologization of itself. Countless books, television programs and articles (print and on-line) have told versions of the same story: rock and roll's rebellion against convention in the 1950s and rock's bringing together of a generation of young people to challenge power in the 1960s. Punk, rave, grunge, hip hop, and other later phenomena are then depicted as further rebellions, either against a previous generation of rebels or against the prevailing conditions of their times. Rock was socially important and played a huge role in the lives of millions of people. In the 1960s, it involved attitudes and values that were the cause of genuine conflict between generations and often between classes. But it was also often a site of pompous, self-aggrandizing pseudo-revolt, as we saw in Chapter 3. And in the twenty-first century, a liking for the rock music of the 1960s and 1970s means more or less nothing, in terms of "resistance" or "counter-hegemony." Conservative journalists, senior politicians, University Vice Chancellors and Presidents – lots of them love rock music; many of

---

[8] For a good collection of pieces on various international dimensions of political movements, popular music and mass concerts, see Reebee Garofalo's *Rockin' the Boat* (1992).

[9] These and other aspects of the relationships between music and politics have been discussed in detail by John Street, most recently in his book *Music and Politics* (2012). His view that "music *embodies* political values and experiences" (Street, 2012: 1) is consistent with my own. However, I would not go so far as Street in arguing that the "boundaries between the two realms of music and politics…are largely illusionary" or that music "does not just provide a vehicle of political expression, it is that expression" And when he claims that music "*organizes* our response to society as political thought and action," I would want to know more about which responses are not organized in this way, and which other forms of communication might be involved in such organisation.

them now love "indie" too. Music's relations to collective flourishing are more subtle and incremental than a focus on mythologized moments of rebellion would suggest.

To be more precise about music's relations to politics, and to collective human flourishing, we should return to the idea of deliberative publicness discussed in Chapter 4.[10] To recap, I distinguished in Chapter 4 between two meanings of the concept of publicness: sociable publicness and deliberative publicness (see Box 5.1 for an explanation of why I prefer "publics" and "publicness" to the term "public sphere" and why the concept of counterpublics is also useful). The latter conceives of publics and publicness in terms of collective participation in deliberation about what is right for people, communities, societies, the world; the former understands publicness in terms of gatherings of strangers sharing the same experiences. The claim that music's most important and valuable relationship to collective flourishing is via its contribution to political struggle (claim (ii) mentioned earlier) is wrong because *music makes much stronger contributions to collective flourishing through sociable publicness than through deliberative publicness.*

However, there is an important connection between the two. Drawn to music for the way it can enrich our lives, both through more individualized and more collective experiences, we gain sets of values, attachments, and identifications from musical culture. These values then feed into people's participations in deliberative publicness, for better or for worse. We have already encountered some examples of music's relationship to values and identities earlier in this book. The popular music of the late twentieth century had a role to play in the processes by which diverse sexualities became more accepted and even celebrated in modern life, even as the poison of homophobia remained present in many areas of it. As we shall see shortly, music has been bound up in the promulgation of dubious forms of nationalism. Importantly, as Frith's (1996) perspective suggests, some of the key values promoted by musical culture relate to the value of sociability and community themselves. This can also be understood in terms of

---

[10] The term "deliberative" should not be taken to denigrate the importance of action: the value of deliberation often involves considering what kinds of action need to take place, whether in terms of simply which party or measure should be voted for, or, when democratic processes break down, as they very often do, advocating extraordinary political action, such as attending demonstrations or marches, boycotting certain companies or goods, etc. Ultimately, then, deliberative publics are a fundamental concern in thinking about democracy, and about how everyone affected by certain outcomes might have some sort of say in determining them.

Box 5.1 No such thing as "the public sphere": publics and counterpublics

The term that has been most used to orient debates about how deliberative communication might contribute to better collective life in modern societies is "the public sphere." This has partly been the result of a wide interest in Jurgen Habermas's book, *The Structural Transformation of the Public Sphere* (1989/1962) and in the debates that ensued when it became widely available in English in the 1990s. Although Habermas was interested in both co-present and mediated forms of deliberative publicness, the term "public sphere" has mainly been used to refer to forms of mediated deliberative publicness made possible and/or inhibited by print and broadcast media, and to some extent in more recent years the internet. However, the term "public sphere" is awkward and potentially misleading. The idea of a singular public sphere, whether political, literary or cultural, makes no sense to me; there are always multiple, co-existing and overlapping publics in any modern society, as Habermas himself recognized even in his early work on the concept.[11] For this reason, I use the terms *publicness* and *publics* rather than "public sphere" here.

As Nancy Fraser (1997: 75–77) points out, to have just one public sphere would make it highly likely that one group's particular conception of publicness would be likely to prevail. The term "counterpublics" usefully refers to the creation of collectivities that set themselves against dominant forms of publicness. Fraser refers, for example, to the way in which, during the 1880–1920 period, African-Americans constructed a counterpublic "in the one space they had: the black church" (1997: 75). While such churches may also have provided arenas for (sociable) publicness, Fraser is referring here primarily to a form of mediated deliberative publicness: churches were connected to each other across the nation, and their connections transcended place. This does not mean of course that this form of deliberative counterpublic was without its problems, or that it was thoroughly effective in countering hegemonic

---

[11] Michael Warner (2002: 47) claims that the term "public sphere" is a misleading translation: "the German *Öffentlichkeit* lacks the spatializing metaphor and suggests something more like "openness" or "publicness". I prefer the term "publicness" to "publicity," because the latter is so easily confused with promotional discourse.

forms of politics; but it may well have laid the ground for the Civil Rights movement of the later twentieth century. Such perspectives suggest the importance of culture and communication to politics, and to attempts to transform the distribution of human flourishing.

music's potential, highlighted throughout this book, to articulate people's needs for attachment and collective expression in ways that feel intimate and personal.

Music's particular relationship to politics and democracy can be made clearer by comparing music with the ways in which other cultural and communication forms contribute to public deliberation. Music is not good, for example, at establishing facts, or the truthfulness of one account over another. Books, journalism, and various other kinds of writing are much better suited for this. Nor is music good at explaining or articulating belief systems, or even individual beliefs. So the argument here does not question that music has significant relations to politics. Rather it seeks to understand those relations better. Music, especially when combined with other forms of communication – and it nearly always is combined with other forms of communication – can be very powerful in forging, fostering, solidifying, and challenging values and attachments, for better or for worse. We need not disparage the importance of truthfulness or explanation to believe that there might also be something significant in forms of communication that work in more affective ways.

In many of the debates about deliberative publicness, there has been a very strong emphasis on deliberation in a particular sense. This understands "political" in a narrow way as referring to the realm of decisions about states, governments, and allocation of resources. This has not only limited what kinds of communication might count as "real" deliberation, and thereby restricted what we might think of as constituting valid deliberative publics and counterpublics. It has also prevented analysts of deliberative publicness from adequately addressing the more affective and emotional aspects of politics. It is in the rich forms of sociability enabled by music that our mutual dependence and obligation can be most powerfully felt, and this can inform our contributions to political life, from voting to demonstrating. One of the main values that musical culture promulgates, time and again, is the virtue of sociable publicness. This often involves exclusions, whether conscious or unconscious, acknowledged or not. But the aspiration to collectivity remains vital.

5.6 Communities of Shared Taste? Subcultures, Scenes, and Fans

The previous discussion of sociable and deliberative forms of publicness begins to address a gap I identified in abstract historical discussions of aesthetic experience and its potential to forge human solidarity: the need to consider modern institutions of public communication that enable (or hinder) commonality. Let me now go further with this. In pre-modern societies, most acts of deliberative publicness, where they occurred at all, involved people gathering in the same space at the same time. With the rise of the communications media, especially over the last 100 years, the traditional model of public gathering, where people came together in this way, has given way largely, though not entirely, to what John Thompson calls "mediated publicness" (Thompson, 1995: 126) in which actions, events, images, and words can be recorded and transmitted to others who are not physically present at the time and place of their occurrence. The development of print was one vital stage in the rise of mediated deliberative publicness, the electronic media of the twentieth century another, and the rise of digital media and the internet surely represents a new phase. Mediated deliberative publicness and mediated sociable publicness were made more possible through the rise of the media (Scannell, 1996). As we saw in Chapter 4, some writers risk underestimating the value of mediated sociability because of an attachment to ideals of co-present community. But it can be highly meaningful for hundreds of thousands of listeners to feel, however vaguely, that they are sharing the experience of listening to a great song with many other fellow humans. In fact, it is through media such as television, radio, and the internet that such shared aesthetic experiences are most likely to take place.

To investigate this area further, and in doing so provide a more concrete approach to the question of how aesthetic experience might contribute to collective human life, we need to look at some case studies of mediated musical publicness. I begin in this section by discussing how and in what ways shared musical affiliations have been thought of as a basis for mediated community of a kind that might be considered socially valuable.

One concept that has been used to explore music's capacity to provide community across different spaces is that of *subculture*. For many years in popular music studies, subculture was a key way of thinking about collectivities of people, especially young people. It had its origins in Chicago School sociology's attempts to understand "deviance," especially among young people, in a more adequate way than psychological theories of the "criminal personality." By the 1960s and 1970s, British researchers had started to use the concept in relation to youth and the meanings of popular culture (Hall and Whannel, 1964). Young people were seen as the source of creative revolt against the staid bourgeois culture of their parents' generation. The best work in this new wave of subcultural studies (some of it to be found in the collection edited by Hall and Jefferson, 1993/1976) attempted to understand the intersections of generation and social class. This was a highly politicized form of analysis: popular culture, including music, was considered to be of most interest when it was most tied to resistance and the empowerment of disadvantaged social groups. At its best, such analysis brought out the subtle and complex social meanings of groups such as the skinheads, described by John Clarke (1993/1976: 80) as "an attempt to re-create through the 'mob,' the traditional working-class community as a substitute for the real decline of the latter." More problematically, there was a tendency to treat non-subcultural youth as conformist and uninteresting, and girls, at least initially, were sidelined. Subculturalist treatments of music were rather limited. Members of subcultures were shown to have shared similar musical tastes – which suggests the importance of music in binding together such groups – but subcultural theorists' efforts to explain why members were attracted to particular sounds were often speculative and underdeveloped, as Richard Middleton (1990: 155–166) showed. This was not the main reason that subculture fell from grace in the sociology of popular music however. It was that, as possibilities for multiple social affiliations proliferated, very strong and fixed affiliation to a particular social group became harder to sustain for young people (Kahn-Harris, 2006). Although subcultures of the traditional kind still exist – the example nearly always trotted out at this point is goth (see Hodkinson's good study, 2002) – they are less prominent than they once were. And certainly it became hard to see youth subcultures and their relations to music as evidence of the creative rebellion of youth.

Instead, researchers turned to concepts such as *scene*, with varying degrees of success. I have already criticized the confusing and contradictory ways this term has been used in popular music studies in Chapter 4. One problem was that the concept was used to refer, sometimes simultaneously, to musical phenomena within a particular city, *and* to phenomena that cut across different places, perhaps even internationally. Although the concept lacked coherence, it did lead to some interesting research, such as Keith Kahn-Harris's book on extreme metal. Kahn-Harris in effect treated the global extreme metal "scene" as a subcultural counterpublic with contradictory features. He showed that the extreme metal genre internationally allows its participants a safe retreat from the contradictions of modernity, allowing them to experience the pleasures of transgression "in a relatively safe, secure and autonomous environment" (157). Kahn-Harris, an extreme metal fan himself, was sympathetic to these desires, but he also showed how that such transgression depended upon "a preoccupation with control of the 'abject', which associates the abject with female sexuality, homosexuality and blackness" (161). Extreme metal provides a strong sense of affective community across time and place for its adherents, but this is a form of (counter) publicness that depends on closure.

Another way in which analysts have seen evidence of a valuable collectivity in modern musical culture has in *fan communities*. John Thompson (1995: 221–225) provided an eloquent defense of the "intimacy at a distance" allowed by fandom – not only "non-reciprocal intimacy" between fan and performer, but also among communities of fans. Fans could bond together in "a community with which individuals could feel deeply involved at a personal and emotional level," wrote Thompson (224).[12] Thompson drew for his examples on the weird and wonderful experiences of fandom recounted in Fred and Judy Vermorel's book *Starlust* ("When I make love with my husband, I imagine it's Barry Manilow. All the time.") (Vermorel and Vermorel, 1985: 11). A more developed portrait of fandom is Daniel Cavicchi's *Tramps Like Us*, on admirers of Bruce Springsteen. Cavicchi (1998) argued that fandom extends the feelings of connection and community that audiences can experience at a live performance, which is a rather rare and special event, into their everyday lives. That sense of community is maintained through fanzines, "computer discussion groups" (this was before the era of social media), meetings at concerts, and other social gatherings. Countless studies have since purported to show social media and other forms of internet communication assist in fans' relations to each other, and in their efforts to answer back to industrial control of the stars and products to which they feel attachment. In some

---

[12]   Like other commentators on fandom in the 1990s, Thompson surely overstated the degree to which fandom was stigmatized (at times there was a sense that fans were some kind of persecuted minority, who needed their own version of Amnesty International to protect them from mass culture critics).

cases, this leads to highly optimistic appraisals of the effects of digitalization on audiences and fandom (Jenkins, 2006). Against this, others have pointed to continuing corporate control of the technologies that are supposedly enhancing community in the on-line world. Some analysts have pointed to the sheer amount of work that fans do. Baym, for example, has written of the role of fans of Swedish independent music: "they sift, sort, label, translate, rate and annotate a large, disorganized, and geographically remote set of cultural materials for international consumption" (Baym and Burnett, 2009: 434). It's not at all clear that this kind of "user-generated content" can coherently be called "exploitation," but to portray it as empowering, and as evidence of a democratisation of the music industry, seems even more problematic, as Baym suggests. It seems to me that digitalization continues, but in an intensified form, the kinds of affiliation across time and space that was observed in earlier periods. Researchers such as Kahn-Harris and Cavicchi provide evidence of people making unexpected and often valued connections with strangers through their shared tastes, and very often via mediated rather than face-to-face communication (with gigs providing important opportunities for meeting up). It is also possible that such communities allow for thoughtful and emotionally engaged reflection on values, at least in certain instances. But even though such collectivities are undoubtedly important in people's lives, these examples of mediated communities (subcultures, scenes, fans) represent a rather thin slice of aesthetic experience across modern societies. They therefore provide only a partial insight into the role of aesthetic experience in creating meaningful and life-enhancing community across social difference. In my view, a more fruitful way to examine the question of music's relation to collective flourishing in complex modern societies is via the idea of *the nation*. I do not make this claim because I think that nations and nationalism have some kind of unchanging centrality in the modern world. Their significance has probably declined in the age of globalization. But it remains massive. And I certainly do not think that nations are necessarily good ways to bind people together. The reason I think that nations are a good way to examine the issue of music's relation to collective human flourishing is that they are the central form that societies and communities have taken in modernity, for better and (often) for worse. As nations are deeply ambivalent entities, in the next section I will explain my understanding of the problem of nationalism, and the related problem of ethnic difference, before examining case studies of music in particular nations.

5.7 Nations, Ethnicity, Cosmopolitanism

Unprecedented numbers of people have died violent deaths as a result of wars fought over the last century, and a large number of those wars have involved sentiments of collective identity formed around the nation. But nations have also, in some cases, been means by which new degrees of civic freedom have been made available to large populations, and where aspirations to equality have been put into political action. Many remain understandably suspicious of nationalism and national identity in spite of this.

As urgent a problem as how different nationalities might co-exist in a better world is that of how different ethnic groups might co-exist within particular nations. This involves co-existence within the same space, living in the same cities and towns, and sharing the same economic, political, and cultural resources. But there is also the question of how different ethnic and religious groups might live in the same, increasingly interconnected world. The stakes here seem hardly less than those involving nationalism and, as with nationalism, culture is central. In recent decades, in many places, biological racism has largely given way to forms of cultural racism. Cultural racism holds, for example, that some groups of people are superior to others because of their prior achievements and dispositions (often the result of privileges derived from power and violence), or that forms of culture need "defending" against others. We can also note the continuing presence of a cultural racialism which asserts that global conflicts represent a clash of incommensurable civilizations.

Conservative nationalism in its most developed form (Scruton, 1999) sees the nation as the foundation of collective moral action and thought, and the only viable basis for political community. The term most often used for positions opposed to nationalism today is cosmopolitanism. In its older, philosophical sense, cosmopolitanism holds that "the moral standings of all peoples and of each individual person around the globe is equal. Individuals should not give moral preference to their compatriots, their co-religionists or fellow members of their demographic identity groups" (van Hooft, 2009: 4). This position (advocated by Kant in the eighteenth century, and defended in classical form by Nussbaum, 1996, amongst others) needs to be distinguished from a vernacular use of the term to refer to "not restricted to any one country or region...free from national limitations or attachments" and "having characteristics suited to or arising from an experience of many countries" (*Shorter Oxford English Dictionary*, 520). I will discuss later how certain conceptions of "aesthetic cosmopolitanism" tend to blur the two meanings of the term, the ethical and the vernacular. Here I am mainly concerned with the common but rather tricky opposition of nationalism and ethical cosmopolitanism. In contemporary thought, there are stronger (Nussbaum, 1996) and weaker (Appiah, 2006) versions of cosmopolitanism. Faced with the challenges of multicultural societies, a variety of proponents offer some kind of "civic nationalism," often opposed to "ethnic nationalism," whereby loyalty might be given to a set of political arrangements rather than a pre-existing entity. Jürgen Habermas's notion of "constitutional patriotism" can be seen as a version of such thinking. Many serious analysts of nationalism tend to take a position that combines, on the one hand, an acceptance that nations are highly resilient as ways of organizing collectivities with, on the other, cosmopolitan sympathies, and that is the position adopted here.[13] But culture adds further layers of complexity to these debates. Given the widely accepted importance of culture in recent debates about ethnic and national identity, and music's status as a cultural form with marked emotional and affective intensity, music's relationship to human flourishing surely merits careful consideration in this context. In what circumstances has music transcended national and ethnic particularism in ways that might enhance human life in general? In what circumstances have musical cultures provided glimpses of what a genuinely cosmopolitan world might look like? I hope the relevance of these debates to the main topic of this chapter is now clear. It is via the question of the nation and its limits that we can most concretely assess the question of whether aesthetic musical experience might breed commonality across difference. I begin with the question of where we might find evidence of the successful transcendence of nations in culture.

5.8   Rock as Cosmopolitanism?

The immense problems of modern nationalism, combined with the supposedly diminishing importance of nation-states in an era of globalization, have led some writers to look beyond the nation-state for

[13]   While sympathetic to cosmopolitanism, Craig Calhoun (2007: 13) has wondered whether nationalism can be "left behind so easily as cosmopolitans sometimes imagine." Calhoun writes from a position that recognizes that it is often the poor and the marginalized who find collective identity most important for their well-being – this includes ethnicities and religions as well as nations – and that abstract universals may not be the best guide to practical ethics.

evidence of music's powers to connect people together and transcend difference. Many social science and humanities researchers have made the point that music, culture and money increasingly circulate beyond the confines of the nation-state, and that links between culture and nation, or music and nation, are now weakened. According to this view, musical cultures existing within a national space need to be understood as constituted by international or transnational flows of culture made possible largely by the development of media. In this section, I want to examine a particular discussion of such international flows, because of what it might tell us about how *not* to understand nationalism and cosmopolitanism in relation to music.

The account concerns rock music. Jason Toynbee (2002) has written about how rock rose to a kind of *mainstream* status from the 1950s to the 1980s. This never meant that everyone listened to rock, or even that all young people listened to rock. Rock formed a mainstream because it brought together "large numbers of people from diverse social groups and across large geographical areas in common affiliation to a musical style" (150). This was ambivalent. It produced a certain commonality but also regulated difference "according to unequal relations of power" (160). Rock was, after all, apparently classless but in fact rested on "the gradual middle-class adoption of the trappings of working-class teenage life" (153). By the late 1980s, rock had become increasingly fragmented and, in different countries and in different ways, was challenged by other forms such as hip hop, electronic dance music and so on as the "mainstream" of popular music.

In retrospect, though, rock's continuing centrality in the national canons of many countries over the last half a century seems remarkable. Many young people have adapted the attitudes, instrumentation, and generic assumptions (such as the primacy of recording technologies to create an artifact that is then reproduced in concert) of rock music culture to create new national hybrids. Outside the Anglo heartland of rock, local musicians developed rock traditions of their own primarily by singing in their own language, and fusing rock instrumentation with older "national" styles. A number of researchers have written about the fascinating consequences (e.g., Hatch, 1989, on Indonesia). The sociologist Motti Regev (2007a: 317–318) has written about how certain examples of Argentinian and Israeli rock, highly prestigious within their own countries, represent unique aesthetic productions which at the same time incorporate elements of "otherness" ("foreign" instrumentation and production techniques).

Regev interprets this tendency for nations to develop their own "pop-rock" as peculiarly "late modern," because rather than seeking essentialism and purism (as in "early modern" attempts to construct a distinctive national identity), they involve a willingness to implement "stylistic innovations in art and culture from different parts of the world" (Regev, 2007b 125). By including components from outside any given ethno-national culture, as they seek status and recognition, musicians "render their consumers inadvertent aesthetic cosmopolitans" (126). The international flows of pop-rock therefore indicate a world marked by "aesthetic cosmopolitanism."

What is striking in the use of the term cosmopolitanism here is how utterly detached it is from the ethical meaning of the concept, as attributing equal moral standing to all peoples. Regev quotes approvingly Ulrich Beck's definition of cosmopolitanism as a condition in which the "otherness of the other is included in one's own self-identity and self-definition" (quoted in Regev, 2007a: 318). The danger is that such a definition equates cosmopolitanism with a kind of cultural hybridity which is closer to the vernacular use of the concept outlined earlier: "having characteristics suited to or arising from an experience of many countries." In fact, though, the (interesting) cases Regev presents, from Israel and Argentina, seem to be examples of national music that rarely cross national boundaries to be heard by people in other countries – a curiously nationalized version of cosmopolitanism. More importantly for my purposes, Regev's empirical claims about increasing levels of hybridization are linked to dubious normative claims. For "the second age of modernity" (Beck, 2000), in which such aesthetic cosmopolitanism has developed, seems a rather benign entity. According to Regev, the purism and essentialism of the first age of modernity have been superseded by a "fluidity and conscious openness to exterior influences" (Regev, 2007a: 318).[14] This allows pop-rock musicians to find an "expanded radius of creativity" (Regev, 2007b: 131). Yet it is not apparent from Regev's account that the integration of foreign styles and tastes into local hybrid styles involves any engagement with the otherness of foreign styles in a way that would meaningfully establish commonality and equal moral standing across peoples (though this may be the case in some instances).

---

[14]   The class politics of the sociological framework that Regev uses seem to have been left behind. That framework is Bourdieu's, but in Regev's theory it is divorced from Bourdieu's interest in the pursuit of interests by different class fractions. The more general framework is that of Ulrich Beck. Calhoun (2010) criticizes the blurring of the normative and the empirical in the work of Ulrich Beck and his associates on cosmopolitanism.

Accounts by other researchers suggest that the supposed fluidity of international flows of rock music involves some difficult aspects. Jeroen de Kloet (2008) writes of how Chinese rock musicians must constantly struggle to assert their authenticity in the face of assumptions by both domestic and foreign audiences that "Western" rock is superior. Brent Luvaas (2009) portrays Indonesian indie musicians as "caught in the middle," unwilling to incorporate signifiers of locality or nationality into their music, and therefore unable to differentiate themselves in the marketing machinery of the global popular music industry. This is not at all to deny that rock music might in many cases be the basis of flourishing musical lives across the world. But whether the global flows of rock culture represent any kind of emancipatory cosmopolitanism, as Regev suggests, is another matter.

Nor is it clear that Regev's characterization of "early modernity" is accurate. Were entire generations of musicians really involved in pursuing essentialism or purism? This may have been true of some attempts to build national folk repertoires. But as we shall see in the next section, there was sometimes more hybridity and cross-cultural communication at work in some projects of nation formation than we may assume in looking back from our supposedly more hybridized twenty-first-century world. This is important in the present context, because it suggests that the role of musical experience in creating dynamics of collectivity in modern nations may be more complex than at first appears. However, this can only be assessed by returning to the vital issue of the institutions that support and maintain publicness.

5.9   Complexities of Music and Nation

With the development of European capitalist modernity in the eighteenth and nineteenth century, the nation and the state began to co-exist or compete with god and sovereign as the basis of political community. A range of musics – art, folk, and popular – became bound up with European nation-states and nationalisms (Bohlman, 2004. In the era of European nation formation, from the early eighteenth century to the early twentieth century, there were heated debates among the bourgeoisie about which national musical styles (French, German or Italian – the British were generally considered inferior) were best, and about how national folk song expressed the common culture of the people (Blanning, 2010). Music became increasingly tied to the articulation of newly emerging European national identities. This was the period in which songs such as "God save the king," "Rule Britannia," "the Marseillaise," "Nun danket alle Gott" became powerful expressions of patriotism and national pride.

Musical nationalism was part of more general attempts by European bourgeoisies to assert values of freedom and equality against religious dogma and aristocratic feudalism. Yet it was also linked to the dissemination of popular nationalisms that lent support for the colonialism and imperialism of the 1850–1950 period, with all its deeply damaging legacies. With the spread of nationalism and capitalism in the late nineteenth century, there was a massive proliferation of national songs, and increasing efforts to canonize national traditions of music through education curricula, national archives, and so on (Bohlman, 2004). At the same time, ethnic groups who felt excluded or marginalized within existing nation states developed their own ethnic repertoires embodying aspirations to nationhood. In the early twentieth century, the industrialization of cultural production coincided with the establishment, across the world, of the idea of the nation-state as the only conceivable way of organizing a polity. Radio, film, and television came to crystallize a set of connections between nation and music that have endured in many countries. In places where elites were seeking to establish loyalties in conditions where rural populations had little or no concept of state or nation, broadcasting became a vital tool for using music and speech to unify the nation. In all this, the communal features of music discussed in Chapter 4 played a vital role. And of course music was instrumental – no pun intended – in helping the leaders of nations to pursue the appalling business of armed conflict. How many young men were inspired to fight and ultimately die in the First World War by expressions of national sentiment that were felt particularly strongly in singing to or marching with patriotic anthems?[15] Given that nationalism seems so clearly linked to the massive intensification of killing and destruction witnessed in the last century and a half, and given music's powerful links to nationalism, it is hard not to see the relations between music and nation as troubling.

Yet we should not dismiss all attempts to create national identity through music as evidence of the ideological use of music by states to reinforce power or to implement violence against citizens of other states. The case of Afghanistan illustrates some of the complexities. Seemingly that country

---

[15]   For a study of ways in which music has been used to incite and arouse violence, see Johnson and Cloonan (2009).

represents a disturbing failure of efforts to achieve a national identity that will transcend ethnic difference – evidence of the doomed nature of nationalist modernity faced with stubborn tradition. However, the past 30 years of appalling violence, based on a clash between secularism and a variety of religious values, and on inter-ethnic rivalry, should not lead us to dismiss all earlier efforts to transcend ethnic difference in nation-building. Without in any way downplaying the conflicts involved in efforts to "modernize" Afghanistan from the 1920s to the 1970s, it seems clear that the neo-colonial maneuverings of the Soviet Union and the United States in the last quarter of the twentieth century made a difficult situation far worse. In the mid-twentieth century, music provided, in some areas of the country at least, a forum where people (mainly men) from different ethnic groups could engage in cross-cultural communication (Slobin, 1976). As John Baily (1994) makes clear, what emerged as a national music in Afghanistan cannot be reduced to the operations of national ideologues. National music synthesized elements of the music cultures of the two main ethnic groups in Afghanistan (Pashtun and Tajik), and systematized and improved them in the light of Hindustani theory and practice, developed in dialogue with the musical culture of neighboring India. National radio, between the 1940s and 1970s, was crucial in popularizing this mixture, which consisted of rhythmic music played with lute and drums, Persian ghazals and folk songs from various regions updated in the kiliwali style. We need to allow for a certain autonomy of music in particular moments of modern nation building, and not assume that national music projects will always serve exclusion and violence. "National music" sometimes turns out to be more complicated than a simplistic ideological critique would indicate.[16]

5.10 Strange Journeys: Working-Class and Ethnic Musics Become National Musics

I now want to explore a different dimension of music's articulation of national identity in order to examine music's potential for commonality across difference. Let me outline a series of events that seems to have

---

[16] The Taliban ban on music therefore goes beyond an antimodern reaction against expressive culture. It can also be seen as representing an attempt to clamp down on communication across difference. On music censorship in Afghanistan before and after the Taliban, see Baily (2009).

occurred with some regularity, across many different nations in modernity. A musical style or genre emerges that is highly valued by a particular social group of relatively low status in that society, especially groups of lower-class ethnic minority people in cities. Perhaps because of the particular intensity of feeling and meaning associated with such musics, some members of other groups also come to value that music, nationally and sometimes internationally (the media are vital to this dissemination) yet the spread of such musics is often the focus of social anxiety on the part of elites. In time, however, if the music persists, and particularly if it becomes the focus of interest across social classes, the music is later adopted by official state institutions, often to illustrate the diversity and even tolerance of a nation's culture – by which point the music (and any associated dances) is far removed from its origins in chaotic and often poverty-ridden performance contexts.

This is pretty much what happened with jazz and blues in the United States, and to a lesser extent with polka. I think it has now happened with rap. But there are instances of roughly this dynamic in many other countries. Why are powerful musics so strongly associated with the poor and dispossessed in modern life? One reason might be as follows. Some groups of people may be deprived of the kinds of cultural resources, such as education, which might allow them to gain respect and recognition through displays of knowledge, learning or verbal articulacy. In situations where literacy is systematically or even inadvertently denied to peoples, for example, it is perhaps not surprising that a people might turn to orally transmitted culture as a means of expressing meaning and seeking recognition from each other. Music is more easily transmitted through oral, informal, and unofficial practices than other forms of communication. Music's status in such circumstances might be relatively high within such marginalized groups and so it might attract particular attention and energy from people within the group as a means of social communication. The attractiveness and prestige of such music might then extend to "higher" social classes who may have greater resources, but who are drawn by the demotic energy of these working-class cultural forms and practices. Members of a social group who show particular talent for music might gain strong recognition from others in the same group. This in turn may further feed music's social status within the group.

The music of the Caribbean and Latin America provides a number of interesting examples of – and variations on – this pattern. Tango developed in Argentina in the late nineteenth century, incorporating elements of topical songs and the syncopated, African-influenced milonga dance genre. Peter Manuel, on whose account I draw here, reports that the genre was "strongly associated with the lumpen proletarian world of brothels, thugs and street people" and especially immigrant populations from Spain and Italy, located in the slums on the outskirts of Buenos Aires (Manuel, 1990: 60). As so often, gender was of vital importance. Tango was macho, fatalistic, nostalgic, and often obscene (see Savigliano, 1995). The Argentinian elite – Eurocentric and concerned to develop a distinctive and respectable national culture along European lines – regarded the early tango with scorn because of its class and ethnic origins. But following the take-up of the tango by the British and French bourgeoisie in the 1920s, the Argentinian upper middle class belatedly endorsed the tango, and a posh version developed alongside a changing version of the earthier form. This meant that in the 1940s, the popularity of the tango across different social classes paralleled the co-existence of a class alliance between a populist political elite and a newly mobilized proletariat. The increasingly pervasive communications media – film, radio, television, recordings – were fundamental to this. As the genre entered into decline, it became a museum piece, occasionally brought to life by composers using its rhythms to express a mixing of modernity and tradition. Above all, though, it came to stand for a mythical moment of national unity. "Argentinians," comments Manuel, "regard the tango as the quintessential expression of their own national character" (59) – though the questions might be asked, "which Argentinians?" and "in which circumstances?"

Similarly, *son* is now regarded as the national genre of Cuba, having begun in Eastern Cuba as a hybrid of European Hispanic and Afro-Cuban styles, played mainly by black and mulatto musicians, and having been adopted across class divides in the era when national broadcasting and cinema emerged in the 1930s and 1940s. In Brazil, samba emerged in the second decade of the twentieth century out of the urban slums of Rio de Janeiro, especially as an accompaniment to carnival. The melodies are European, but the rhythms are associated with Afro-Brazilian populations, the descendants of slaves: a hybrid of styles linked to different ethnic groups. But at the same time, a commercial "samba song" emerged in recording, radio, and cinema, and combined with elements of American swing – as in Cuba, ethnic hybridity allowed for a cross-class appeal which then led to the genre becoming the basis of state attempts to claim diversity-in-unity.

These stories of how these musics become absorbed as symbols of national unity-in-diversity are striking, but there are at least two problems with the way I have told them so far. First, they can distort our understanding of music in relation to nations by reproducing the state's own excessive focus on key genres, rather than looking at the complexity of the musical field as a whole. Second, they can set up a simple dualism where an oppositional music form is absorbed and pacified by the homogenizing, hegemonic nation-state. No doubt there are numerous cases where something like this happens. But the association of the original music with dominated ethnic groups and class fractions is no guarantee of political oppositionality; and incorporation by nation-states can be a complex matter too.

To understand these issues better, we can examine the case of tropical music in Colombia. The music of the marginalized Caribbean coastal region of that country (*La Costa*) became central to its popular music repertoire, as anthropologist Peter Wade discusses in a fine book (Wade, 2000). "Race," class and sex were crucial parts of this story. The region was mixed in racial terms, with a high proportion of black and mulatto people. From the early twentieth century these groups increasingly gained employment by serving wealthy white tourists from the highland interior of the country. But there was a white population too, not all of whom were members of the middle class elite. There was little of the racial segregation associated with the USA. Across ethnic groups, the region had a reputation for emotional and sexual openness, sincerity, and a lack of inhibition, all of which were viewed as at odds with the catholic piety of the inland population. La Costa also had much less of the appallingly violent civil strife of the interior.

The popular music most closely linked to Colombian national identity in the first half of the twentieth century was music from the highland interior, urbanized versions of syncopated rural dance songs. In the 1930s and 1940s, in the cities of La Costa, *bambuco* and other urbanized rural styles were displaced by new styles often played by orchestras. This was a product of the global spread of the large jazz ensemble, but the styles were a mix of North American, Cuban, Mexican and Argentinian, and of cross-fertilizations between them. These musical styles were popularized in films consumed by very large numbers of working-class people. They were interpreted by some sections of the middle class and the elites as vulgar and even immoral, partly because of their association with blackness and with working-class taste but that seemed only to make them more desirable to younger middle-class audiences. The musicians came from a liminal social space, incorporating elements of the provincial middle-class and lower-class rural experience. This mélange of coastal musics, popular across different social classes and ethnic groups, began to be understood by costenos and inland highlanders as the distinctive music of the Caribbean region. In the 1940s, this music, still tied to ideas of blackness, spread into the rapidly modernizing "white" interior of the country. Here, costeno culture and recordings could signify irrationality, indiscipline, and primitivism. But they could also signify – in some cases precisely because of that primitivism – the modern, the cosmopolitan and the new. When civil violence erupted in the late 1940s, costeno music also signified the peacable community of the Caribbean. All this meant that costeno music such as *porro* was sometimes interpreted as trivial, but its good-time feel also meant it was associated with the pursuit of pleasure or happiness (*alegría* – happiness, with connotations of joyful pleasure – was the defining feature of coastal music during this period) as a liberation from tradition. Its ambivalence allowed the music, to negotiate between tradition and modernity, and homogeneity and heterogeneity, in a country where hybridity was felt to be crucial to national identity (Wade, 2000: 137–140). The 1950s – an era of appalling violence in Colombia – and 1960s were the golden age of costeno music, and coastal styles were also popular not only in Colombia but across much of Latin America: *cumbia,* and then, with even greater commercial success, *vallenato* (with strong links to the drug trade) in the 1970s. Coastal music became the national popular music of Colombia. This was further entrenched when, in the 1990s, the state sought to legitimize itself by portraying Colombia as a nation of successful multiculturalism. This coincided with a wave of nostalgia for the 1960s and 1970s era of coastal or tropical music. The nostalgia was not caused by state multiculturalism, but it has to be understood in that context, claims Wade; there is an articulation between the two.

The initial success of *música tropical* in the 1940s and 1950s was seen by many as a commercial appropriation by the national recording industry of this vibrant mix of regional styles, and it has continued to be interpreted in this way by many in Colombia (184). In the 1950s and again in the 1990s revival, the music of peaceable *alegría* could be seen as an attempt to cover over the inequality, violence and oppression rampant in the country. But Wade's interpretation is more forgiving and allows for the partial autonomy of music. The costeno identity of this music remained intact through these changes. Rather than a veil drawn by instrumentalist hegemonic powers, the popularity of revived and reinterpreted cumbia can be seen as a refuge sought by "citizens harrowed by years of violence" (229). Wade relates this to the temporary empowerment provided by dancing to music understood as "joyful" and "sexy" – "the embodied transformation from potential corpse to empowered lover." The case of Colombia suggests that the passage of popular musics – musics of the people – from margins to national styles is too complex to be interpreted as either a counter-hegemonic triumph or an appropriation of people's music by business and the state, or even as a kind of contradictory mixture of the two.

To explore these issues further, still in the context of our discussion of music's capacity to create commonality across difference in modernity, I want to discuss an example from a very different nation-state, Turkey.

5.11   Sentimental Citizenship

The modernizing secular state in Turkey following the end of the Ottoman Empire in 1922 sought to create a split between private and public, with religion confined to the former realm. But, according to ethnomusicologist Martin Stokes (2010), "collective habits of self-identification as Muslims" were never erased and Turkish nationalism continued to have a strong religious undercurrent. Stokes explains that the military coup of 1980 was intended to control both communists and Islamists, the twin rivals of the modernizing, relatively secular Islam of Turkey in the 1970s. Religious sentiment was driven underground in the aftermath of the coup, re-emerging in the form of cassette recordings of sermons that featured weeping, and in a new form of Islamist song based on *arabesk* – the main Turkish version of the hybrid popular forms associated with the marginalized and working-class, especially migrants to the Western cities from the South-Eastern regions.

What Stokes shows is that in modern Turkey, a number of significant musicians, working in this environment, were able to provide some kind of shared space across the class, religious, and political divisions that fractured the country. Turkish musical figures shaped "an intimate, as opposed to official, idea of the nation" (16). Stokes claims that "public discourse about love has mediated the underlying tensions and contradictions" of modern Turkey and that Turkish musicians have played a vitally important role in these public discourses and transformations (34).

One of Stokes's rich case studies concerns the Turkish singing star Zeki Müren. There was an outpouring of national grief when Müren died in 1996 and Stokes suggests why: "When he sang, he spoke to inhabitants of the Turkish republic as a fellow citizen. The entire *millet*, the national community, felt the pain of his death" (35). He was described as "the model citizen." Yet this is perhaps surprising given "Müren's flamboyant (though never verbally declared) queerness."[17] Response to this evident queerness was ambivalent: many affected innocence or ignored it; some later attacked his unwillingness to come out. But Müren's queerness was also widely read, especially following his death, as "a sign of sincerity in an insincere, cynical age or, conversely, of worldliness, wiliness, and urbanity in an age that prefers crass moral simplicities. It could be read as love uncoupled from family and reproduction, and thus given freely to the nation" (36).

We need to understand cultural and media institutions to grasp the events that Stokes narrates. Two of the major public arenas for musical performance in many Middle Eastern and Asian countries have been the nightclub and the cinema. In a series of sentimental films made between the late 1950s and 1970s, Müren played a young musician struggling against the odds and trying to do the decent thing. Partly fuelled by his screen success, Müren became the superstar of the booming nightclub world of Istanbul in this period, singing an astonishingly mixed repertoire: urban and palace music from the nineteenth century, early twentieth-century "art music," rural folk music, and hits from Egyptian and Hindi film musicals. The style was high camp and modern, with spectacular costume, but Müren also demonstrated great religious decorum, and became enormously popular among women as well as men. Central to Müren's impact, writes Stokes, was his voice, commonly described as "soft" or "like velvet," but allied to a "taming" of wild lyrics. His was above all a "civil voice," decent, polite, enchanting, based not on assailing listeners (as in the arabesk genre, which had its own version of intimate citizenship) but on cajoling, caressing and persuading. It was felt to possess the quality of *uyum*, implying reasonableness, thoughtfulness and social-mindedness. It demonstrated "citizenly respect for the principles of intelligibility and transmission, as well as for listeners and bearers of musical tradition" (59). The embodiment of these civic virtues in his voice allowed Müren to thrive in the Turkey of the 1950s and 1960s, a period of "liberal reaction against the authoritarian political traditions of the early republic" (63). Following Müren's death, his work was reinterpreted nostalgically in the 1990s – just as happened with the coastal music of Colombia discussed earlier. Forty years on, Müren's queerness was much more explicitly debated than it had been during his heyday, but now in the context of what might constitute properly civic

---

[17] Turkish public life has made space for queer culture, "not only in music and dance, but in other scattered areas of public life" (36).

behavior by men. Müren was felt to embody sensitivity and emotion, but also the strength to "face down the hyprocrisy of the modern order and its self-deceiving sexual imperatives."

5.12   Music, the Nation, and the Popular

The case studies I have examined in the last three sections suggest that the relations between music and nation are complex. The problems of nation-hood should not mislead us into dismissing all relations between music and national identity as regressive. The centrality of the nation to collective life in modern societies also makes it an important testing ground for music's relations to shared flourishing. There are good reasons to think that the idea of a national music can be profoundly ideological, in that it can serve the interests of the powerful at the expense of more general human well-being and freedom. But as Adorno (1976/1966: 155) suggested, it may also be the case that music, "more than any other artistic medium," registers some of the contradictions involved in the idea of the nation. It is notable too that love and sex play significant roles in the complex minglings of musics within a particular national communication space. Even when appropriated as part of nation-building projects, it seems that music can consistently provide hints, or perhaps better, *reminders*, of more complex notions of identity and belonging. It has done so in particular by prompting listeners and participants to appreciate, in a feelingful way, how poverty and lack of freedom can tear apart the supposedly collective enterprises of nationhood, and yet also how social suffering and marginalization produce a set of experiences that might be denied to the more privileged.

In such instances, it's possible to see the utopian kernel in the idea of popular culture, where "popular" might mean something like "belonging to the people," rather than "commercialised homogenised mass." This utopian invocation of collectivity cannot be freed of the dangerous associations with dubious populism, and morally bankrupt invocations of the term, such as Margaret Thatcher's declaration on her resignation as British Prime Minister that she had returned power to the people. As Richard Middleton (2012) has eloquently shown, the concept of the popular is compromised, contested, and even embarrassing. It has certainly fallen from favor in social science and even cultural studies, following its heyday in the 1970s and 1980s. Yet without some invocation of collective will, based on an idea of "ordinary" shared experience beyond the privileged confines of the wealthy and powerful, it is hard to imagine any possibility of making the world better.[18] This, then, suggests that music, in some of the forms it has taken in modernity, has offered hints that aesthetic experience might still have some lingering elements of the unifying properties that post-Enlightenment thought attributed to it.

For the aforementioned case, studies suggest that musical creativity is not only possible among deprived and marginalized groups of people, but that it might even thrive there, even if that creativity is open to appropriation and commodification. The music of marginalized, and often despised groups, is often taken up by nation-states, and such adaptations sometimes involve dubious projections, which misrepresent the agency and skill of the musicians and dancers involved.[19] Yet many of the main musical forms adopted as national musics seem to show clear traces of their origins in poverty and marginalization. The traces remain.

5.13   Music of the African Diaspora: Life-Affirming Collectivity in Decline?

Drawing on a variety of case studies, the last three sections have provided a relatively hopeful account of music's ability to transcend ethnic, sexual, religious, class and other divides, even in contexts where the problems of nationalism were abundantly apparent. Throughout, it was clear that musical developments within nations have always been affected by events elsewhere – nations have rarely been sealed-off entities (limit cases include contemporary North Korea and Japan from 1650 to 1850). However, we need to return to the question of musical flows beyond the nation state. Given my earlier criticisms of accounts that misattribute a meaningful cosmopolitanism to stylistic hybrids in rock music, where might we look for understandings of international musical flows which might be truer to the ethical roots of the term "cosmopolitanism" and which will indicate

---

[18]   In my view, more than any cultural studies writer, musicologist Richard Middleton has provided the best discussions of the complex political and cultural meanings of the term "popular," drawing on writers such as Stuart Hall and Antonio Gramsci (see, e.g., Middleton, 2000, 2006, 2012).

[19]   For another example, see Jason Toynbee's discussion of Jamaica, including the National Dance Theatre's "licensed slackness for the respectable middle classes" (Toynbee, 2007: 68). Slackness in this context is a Jamaican term for sexual profanity and explicitness, strongly associated with working class dancehall culture (Cooper, 1993).

how musical experience *might* at times be the basis of some kind of life-affirming commonality?

One place to look and listen is the music of the African diaspora. This has been a particular focus of interest for researchers who wish to understand the significance of music, on a more cosmopolitan and global scale, beyond the sense that culture happens "within" national boundaries. The degree of interest in Afro-diasporic traditions stems from dynamics already discussed: music's seeming ability to provide the basis for collective experience and identity (see Chapter 4) and its relation to the downtrodden and marginalized nature of the groups that produce and (at least initially) consume it. For even more than the tango or son, discussed earlier, the genres and styles associated with the African diaspora in the Americas, and elsewhere too, have become not only internationally famous, and also the basis of some kind of cosmopolitan understanding of the links between intimate personal experience, collective identity and social living. I am thinking primarily but not exclusively of blues, jazz, funk, soul, R&B and hip hop, but also the rich legacy of the Caribbean including calypso, reggae, and their later mutations. Yet the story I tell here also brings a note of pessimism to balance the more hopeful accounts mentioned before. We shall see that the achievements of a rich musical culture are vulnerable and fragile in an era of neo-liberal globalization.

A preliminary aside on terminology is needed. Various controversies surround the use of terms such as "black music" and "African-American music." It is undoubtedly true that "white" people have contributed to the entity known as black music, and to all the various genres that tend to be categorized within it: blues, jazz, soul, funk and hip hop. It is also surely the case that these genres drew in a number of ways on non-African musical features and styles. There have been various conflicting attempts to conceptualize what makes for continuity in these black musical traditions, with some emphasizing the "retention" of African musical features very strongly, and others claiming that what matters is continuity of *attitude*. There are certainly better and worse versions of the arguments about these terms. Yet it seems to me reasonable to use the terms "black music" and "African-American music" if only because of the fact that so many prominent exponents of these genres were African-American (and African-Americans still generally endorse the use of the adjective "black"). Significant problems regarding boundaries persist, but the more interesting questions concern the relationship of these genres to emancipation, freedom and flourishing. The genres named earlier are immensely rich sources of music that almost seem to demand pleasurable and intimate experiences of collectivity and sociality, and yet which have constantly linked to forms of commonality, solidarity, and identity that transcend co-presence.

There is no doubt that some of the significance of these genres derives from the fact that the United States became the cultural–industrial hub of the world in the twentieth century. Yet the potential of various Afro-diasporic genres to enhance collective flourishing was surely not eliminated by the dynamics of cultural imperialism. Many writers have been struck by the marked discrepancy between the downtrodden and impoverished nature of African-Americans as a group, and the remarkable global success and circulation of music made primarily by African-Americans, and of stylistic traits influenced by their work. In 1966, Charles Keil wrote that "it is simply incontestable that year by year, American popular music has come to sound more and more like African popular music." (Keil, 1991/1966: 45). Half a century later, the reliance of the most globally popular music on innovations by musicians and producers whose ancestors were forcibly removed from Africa as slaves continues, but in very different political contexts from those of the civil rights era when Keil was writing.

Here we return to the territory already explored in Chapter 4, when I considered the contribution of Christopher Small to our understanding of the value of musical participation and performance in people's lives. Small developed his theory of the value of music for collective experience out of a history of music in the African diaspora of the Americas. In his 1987 book *Music of the Common Tongue*, Small argued that music and dance provided a basis for the survival and even cultural flourishing of the people of the African diaspora, in the face of racism, slavery and imperialism. They did so by allowing people socially defined as "black" to construct and assert a flourishing sense of community and collective identity in the face of their de-humanization and exploitation.[20]

This alone makes those traditions that have been labeled "black music" of great importance in considering music's role in allowing communities to diminish suffering and enhance flourishing across time and place. But Small argued that African-American music has also provided resources for enhancing human life beyond the diasporic community. His explicit aim was to recognize and celebrate the central contribution which "Africans and

---

[20]   Like notable African-American writers such as W.E.B. Du Bois and Ralph Emerson, Small sees the fact that Afro-diasporic music was the music of slaves and their descendants in the Americas as fundamental to any understanding of its significance.

people of African descent have made to the very mainstream of human culture, that is, to the human race's awareness of itself and of the way in which we relate to the world in which we live." (Small, 1987: 1). As we saw in Chapter 4, Small's view was that they did so by developing forms of music and dance which provided a basis for community, ritual, and myth. In the fragmented and individualized world of modern industrial societies, other groups also turned to such forms in order to find a sense of community and identity that they otherwise would lack.

Like Small, Paul Gilroy regards Afro-diasporic cultural forms as having a "special power" derived from the nature of their relationship to capitalist modernity. For Small, as we have seen, that power involved a relationship to community based on the way that these African-based cultural forms inherited features of African musicking founded on performance and participation. For Gilroy, in his classic study *The Black Atlantic*, their significance was based on a *doubleness*: "their unsteady location simultaneously inside and outside the conventions, assumptions, and aesthetic rules which distinguish modernity" (Gilroy, 1993: 73). They were modern because of their hybridity (a product of complex flows), because they "struggled to escape their status as commodities" (73) and because they were informed by a sense of artistic practice as an autonomous domain. But at the same time these black expressive forms were anti-modern. They challenged the modern hierarchies whereby scientific thought and reflection are ranked above art (in this Small and Gilroy are in accord) and the "privileged conceptions of both language and writing as preeminent expressions of human consciousness" (74). Music in the black expressive tradition had been refined and developed so that it provided an enhanced mode of communication, which fused technology and art in powerful, life-enhancing ways. This modern and anti-modern doubleness put music "at the very heart of forms of diasporic consciousness that have defined themselves against nationalism" (73) – not only the kinds of nationalism associated with the development of the nation-state, but also "black nationalism," aimed at creating a separate nation for black people, and in Gilroy's view, founded on an "essentialist" understanding of black identity. Translated into music, this black nationalist viewpoint saw music as an expression of traditions rooted in a shared, organic, ethnic essence. Taking music seriously, as Gilroy argued that both black nationalism and its anti-essentialist postmodern adversaries had failed to do, allowed for an appreciation of the syncretic complexity of all modern culture, and of expressive culture's constant tendency to reinvent tradition, rather than merely conform to it. In a probably accidental echo of Small's references to how musicians and listeners sought versions of an ideal society, Gilroy saw recordings as a search for "an ideal communicative situation" (102).[21] This was not based so much on face-to-face presence as on the evocation, in recordings, of intimate interactions of performers and crowds. In later work, Gilroy turns even more towards a position that celebrates the cosmopolitan political potential of key forms of diasporic music, against the essentialism of black nationalist rhetoric, but in ways which increasingly distance his analysis from categories of race (see Gilroy, 2000).

Gilroy, in my view, provides a compelling account of the way in which Afro-diasporic music enhanced human flourishing across black and white communities. However, as we have already seen in Chapter 3, when we discussed the sexual politics of rap, Gilroy sees the era of neo-liberalism as having eroded the life-enhancing potential of black music. These quotations from his recent book *Darker Than Blue* (2011) represent potent elegies for what has been lost:

> The counter-cultural voice of black Atlantic popular music has faded out. Song and dance have lost their preeminent positions in the ritual and interpretive processes that both grounded and bounded communal life...If any oppositional spirit endures, it is a residual trace of what that historic formation accomplished when music was more central to the everyday lives of people, when it could articulate protest and dissent and, in particular, testify to the ability of the young to imagine better alternatives to a hopeless, broken world (121).

> My sadness at these changes is [...] connected to a desire for the restoration of a public culture in which art and social life, those different dimensions of our complex practice as a collectivity, could dissolve easily and pleasurably into each other (123).

Marketization and commodification explain the fading. "Political outlooks were reshaped by patterns of interaction in which racialized subjects discovered themselves and their agency through their social life as consumers rather than as citizens.... The racial community's journey toward human

---

[21] There is also probably a conscious echo of Habermas's quest for an escape from "systematically distorted understanding" through a more rational and deliberative and less instrumentalist use of language, oriented towards "the ideal speech situation."

and civic recognition involved the retreat of publicity and the privatization of their culture" (11–12).[22]

Gilroy is able to recognize critical and utopian potential in more recent black cultural production, even in rather surprising places, as we saw in considering Gilroy's thoughts on Snoop Doggy Dogg in Chapter 3. Yet clearly Gilroy's view here is that the ability of Afro-diasporic music to promote the kinds of interaction and solidarity that would genuinely enhance collective flourishing has, for now, been lost.

There is no simple moral to draw from this story, concerning the fate of music's ability to contribute to commonality. It may be that there are other musical phenomena emerging that will provide different versions of that hope. Perhaps appropriations of digital technologies will provide new emancipatory counterpublics. Certainly we would be wrong to think that hope resides only in the past. In clubs and dance halls and bedrooms across the world, experiences of musical sociability and intimacy may be laying the grounds for new ways of inculcating a sense of what we have in common with others – the grounds for any meaningful kind of politics, and any worthwhile form of living.

5.14   A Critical Defense of Music

I began this book by describing its fundamental aim as being to construct a critical defense of music, one that might help to combat the way the value of music has been dismissed, trivialized or misunderstood. Chapter 2 located the value of music in its capacity to contribute to human flourishing, concentrating in particular on music's special relationship with affective experience. I suggested there some of the ways in which that capacity might be severely constrained by systemic and psycho-social factors. Chapter 3 extended consideration of the affective power of music into intimate relations via a historical and multitextual discussion of post-war popular music. Popular music was defended against excessively harsh criticism of its relations to love and sex. Again, though, I highlighted ambivalence, by showing that popular music has been closely bound to deeply problematic aspects of modern subjectivity. Chapter 4 defended music from criticisms that derive from unrealistically ambitious aspirations for its capacity for

---

[22]   These ideas are discussed in more detail in Chapter 5, when the sexualization of contemporary black American expressive culture is discussed.

creating community. I tried to provide evidence that, even in our damaged modern societies, music has a valuable tendency to provide a basis for rich, feelingful experiences of sociability. Picking up on the capabilities approach discussed in Chapter 2, I showed how music can thereby help to meet fundamental needs for attachment and solidarity with others. But it can only do this in the right social, economic and institutional conditions. I pointed to major problems of unequal development, cultural labor markets, and class inequality. Chapter 5 looked at music's capacity for creating community beyond co-present groupings, and shared locales, across complex, highly mediated societies. Aesthetic experience, I argued, cannot match the redemptive hopes that post-Enlightenment thought invested in it. But it cannot be reduced to an economic or discursive power game either, whatever some forms of critical theory imply. Musical culture develops values and identities that sustain the ideal of living well together, and this can contribute in important ways to political life too. Music has proven to be a valuable binding force across social difference in a number of places and times in modernity. At times it has been the basis of an inspiring and deeply felt cosmopolitanism. These capacities of music remain susceptible to erosion. Music's ability to enrich people's lives is fragile, but I believe it can be defended better if we understand that fragility, and do not pretend it floats free of the profound problems we face in our inner lives, and in our attempts to live together.

So how can we ensure that music's value is maximized, that more people flourish better through music? I would like to think that answers to this question have been strongly implied throughout this whole book, by pointing to the constraints on music, as well as its potential. I'd love to be able to bring it all together, and lay out what should be done, in practical, policy and political terms, to fulfil music's possibilities. But that would need another book, and I need a break. I'm going to lie down. And then I'll go with friends to see Patti Smith perform live in Leeds, where I hope she'll remind me vividly and emotionally, as her recordings often do, of why freedom, solidarity, and love matter.[23]

---

[23] She, and her band, did.

Acknowledgments

Parts of Chapter 2 previously appeared in Martin Clayton, Trevor Herbert, and Richard Middleton (eds), *The Cultural Study of Music*, 2nd edn, Routledge, and as "Towards a critical understanding of music, emotion and self-identity", *Consumption, Markets and Culture*, 11 (4), 329–343 (2007). Fragments of Chapter 5 appeared in "Audiences and everyday aesthetics: talking about good and bad music", *European Journal of Cultural Studies*, 10 (4), 507–527 (2008). These earlier pieces have been substantially revised. Table 4.1 first appeared in Charles Keil's "Motion and feeling through music," in the *Journal of Aesthetics and Art Criticism*, 24, 337–49 (1966). It is reproduced with the permission of the author and of Wiley-Blackwell.

My friend and colleague Stephen Coleman suggested the title of this book after a previous title, *The Value of Music*, was rejected by Blackwell. I thought of adding "a social science approach" as a sub-title, but I worried that it would put people off.

Stephen also supplied helpful thoughts on Chapter 5. Dai Griffiths, Jason Toynbee, and an anonymous reader provided comments on the whole of a first draft. Their generous responses are hugely appreciated. Jason Cabanes, Christiaan De Beukelaer, and Carlo Ponti provided assistance. Jayne Fargnoli commissioned the book and tolerated its slow evolution towards something rather different from what I proposed many years ago.

This book was written in difficult times, in gaps between obligations and struggles that often felt challenging. Music, friendship, and love helped a lot. I want to mention just a few people here, where music and memory are strongly wedded (one example each). Alison Bentley (busking in the Turf Tavern, 1981); Dai Griffiths ("Andy's got a brand new record collection");

Dave Swann (the killer mix tape that included my introduction to Gram Parsons); Graham Caveney (*Red Roses For Me*); Helen Steward (my brown-eyed girl); Joe Hesmondhalgh (aged seven, his first festival, on the floor playing air guitar on his back); Ian Kershaw (oh no, not "Love will tear us apart," nobody can dance to that); Jason Toynbee (Orbital live in Coventry, 1994); Julie Hesmondhalgh (dancing to "Oliver's army," with her mates, 1979); Maureen Hesmondhalgh (Radio One playing in the kitchen); Nilly Sarkar (Maria McKee live, Kentish Town, 1993); Patrick Costello (jazz and socialism); Roger Lewins (that clip of Stevie Wonder playing "Superstition" on *Sesame Street*); Rosa Hesmondhalgh (word perfect on the Black-Eyed Peas' "Shut up, " aged eight); Simon Finch ("The passenger" at the Cat's Whiskers in Burnley); Steve Parker, Robin Lancaster, Simon East, and Duncan Cooper (Brudenell belters and other great Leeds gigs); Steve Swann (conceding I was right about Nirvana); Teresa Gowan (Glastonbury 1989, camping in the rave field); Tim Ward (who owned only three albums, all pretty good, but played over and over and over again).

A number of other people also opened musical doors for me, often without realizing it. Some are friends, some are people I see only once in a while, some I've completely lost touch with, and some are gone now. I'd like to mention the following people here: Rick Wojcik, Tim Wall, Bill Brewer, Caspar Melville, Lorraine Leu, and Nabeel Zuberi. I'm lucky to have some great colleagues at the University of Leeds and that helps me cope with the burdens of working life; even better, a number of them are music lovers. In addition, a community of music scholars, many of them involved in the International Association for the Study of Popular Music, have provided advice and support and sometimes just good musical conversation down the years. If I tried to name them all, I'd risk offending people I accidentally omitted, but I must thank the following for their generosity when I was starting to study music: Georgie Born, Dave Laing, John Street, Simon Frith, Will Straw, Keith Negus, Chris Ballantine, and Les Back.

My Dad, John Hesmondhalgh, died in January 2013, after years of struggling with Parkinson's and a serious eye condition. He liked music but had little understanding of my fascination for it. He found my writing incomprehensible. But he was a lovely man, who understood the importance of sympathy, sociability, and community. I am not sure if it means anything to "dedicate" this book to his memory, but I want to end it by recording my love for him.

References

Adorno, T. (1973/1948) *Philosophy of Modern Music* (trans. A.G. Mitchell and W.G. Bloomster), Sheed and Ward, London.

Adorno, T. (1976/1966) *Introduction to the Sociology of Music* (trans. E.B. Ashton), Continuum, New York.

Adorno, T. (2002/1932) On the social situation of music, in *Essays on Music, Selected, with an Introduction, Commentary and Notes* (ed. R. Leppert, trans. S.H. Gillespie), University of California Press, Berkeley and Los Angeles.

Ansdell, G. (1995) *Music for Life: Aspects of Creative Music Therapy with Adult Clients*, Jessica Kingsley, London.

Appiah, K.A. (2006) *Cosmopolitanism: Ethics in a World of Strangers*, Allen Lane, London.

Attwood, F. (2006) Sexed up: theorizing the sexualization of culture. *Sexualities*, 9 (1), 77–94.

Back, L. (2003) Sounds from the crowd, in *The Auditory Culture Reader* (eds M. Bull and L. Back), Berg, Oxford, pp. 311–328.

Bailey, B. and Davidson, J. (2005) Effects of group singing and performance for marginalized and middle-class singers. *Psychology of Music*, 33 (3), 269–303.

Baily, J. (1994) The role of music in the creation of an Afghan national identity, 1923–73, in *Music, Ethnicity and Identity: The Musical Construction of Place* (ed. M. Stokes), Berg, Oxford, pp. 45–60.

Baily, J. (2009) Music and censorship in Afghanistan, 1973–2003, in *Music and the Play of Power in the Middle East* (ed. L. Nooshin), Ashgate, Aldershot, pp. 143–164.

Banks, M. (2007) *The Politics of Cultural Work*, Palgrave, Basingstoke.

Banks, M. (2012) MacIntyre, Bourdieu and the practice of jazz. *Popular Music*, 31, 69–86.

Why Music Matters, First Edition. David Hesmondhalgh.
© 2013 David Hesmondhalgh. Published 2013 by John Wiley & Sons, Ltd.

Bannister, M. (2006) *White Boys, White Noise: Masculinities and 1980s Indie Guitar Rock*, Ashgate, Aldershot.

Barthes, R. (1977) *Image, Music, Text* (trans. S. Heath), Noonday Press, New York.

Baym, N.K. and Burnett, R. (2009) Amateur experts: international fan labour in Swedish independent music. *International Journal of Cultural Studies*, 12, 433–449.

Beck, U. (2000) The cosmopolitan perspective: the sociology of the second age of modernity. *British Journal of Sociology*, 51 (1), 79–105.

Becker, H. (1982) *Art Worlds*, University of California Press, Berkeley.

Bennett, T. (1990) *Outside Literature*, Routledge, London and New York.

Bennett, T. (2011) 'Guided freedom: aesthetics, tutelage and the interpretation of art', *Tate Papers* 15, http://www.tate.org.uk/research/publications/tate-papers/guided-freedom-aesthetics-tutelage-and-interpretation-art (accessed February 22, 2013).

Berlant, L. (1997) *The Queen of America Goes to Washington City: Essays on Sex and Citizenship*, Duke University Press, Durham.

Blacking, J. (1973) *How Musical is Man?* University of Washington Press, Seattle.

Blanning, T. (2010) *The Triumph of Music: The Rise of Composers, Musicians and Their Art*, Harvard University Press, Cambridge, MA.

Bohlman, P.V. (2004) *The Music of European Nationalism: Cultural Identity and Modern History*, ABC-CLIO, Santa Barbara.

Boltanski, L. and Chiapello, E. (2005) *The New Spirit of Capitalism* (trans. G. Elliott), Verso, London.

Born, G. (1992) Women, music, politics, difference. *Women: A Cultural Review*, 3 (1), 79–86.

Born, G. (1995) *Rationalizing Culture: Boulez, IRCAM, and the Institutionalisation of the Musical Avant-Garde*, University of California Press, Berkeley.

Born, G. (2005) On musical mediation: ontology, technology and creativity. *Twentieth-Century Music*, 2 (1), 7–36.

Born, G. (2010) The social and the aesthetic: for a post-Bourdieuian sociology of cultural production. *Cultural Sociology*, 4 (2), 171–208.

Bourdieu, P. (1984) *Distinction* (trans. R. Nice), Routledge, London.

Bowie, A. (2003) *Aesthetics and Subjectivity: From Kant to Nietzsche*, Manchester University Press, Manchester.

Bowie, A. (2007) *Music, Philosophy, and Modernity*, Cambridge University Press, Cambridge, UK.

Boym, S. (2001) *The Future of Nostalgia*, Basic Books, New York.

Brackett, D. (1995) *Interpreting Popular Music*, Cambridge University Press, Cambridge, UK.

Buckingham, D. and Bragg, S. (2004) *Young People, Sex and the Media: The Facts of Life?* Palgrave, Basingstoke and New York.

Bull, M. (2007) *Sound Moves: iPod Culture and Urban Experience*, Routledge, Abingdon and New York.

Calhoun, C. (2007) *Nations Matter: Culture, History, and the Cosmopolitan Dream*, Routledge, New York and Abingdon.

Calhoun, C. (2010) Beck, Asia and second modernity. *British Journal of Sociology*, 61 (3), 597–619.

Cavicchi, D. (1998) *Tramps Like Us: Music and Meaning Among Springsteen Fans*, Oxford University Press, New York.

Chambers, I. (1986) *Popular Culture: The Metropolitan Experience*, Methuen, London.

Chanan, M. (1994) *Musica Practica: The Social Practice of Western Music from Gregorian Chant to Postmodernism*, Verso, London.

Clarke, J. (1993/1976) The Skinheads and the magical recovery of community, in *Resistance Through Rituals*, 2nd edn (eds S. Hall and T. Jefferson), Routledge, London.

Clarke, E. (2012) What's going on: music, psychology and ecological theory, in *The Cultural Study of Music*, 2nd edn (eds M. Clayton, T. Herbert and R. Middleton), Routledge, London, pp. 333–342.

Clarke, E., Dibben, N. and Pitts, S. (2010) *Music and Mind in Everyday Life*, Oxford University Press, Oxford.

Clayton, M. (2009) The personal and social functions of music in cross-cultural perspective, in *The Oxford Handbook of Music Psychology* (eds S. Hallam, I. Cross and M. Thaut), Oxford University Press, Oxford, pp. 35–44.

Clift, S. and Hancox, G. (2010) The significance of choral singing for sustaining psychological wellbeing: findings from a survey of choristers in England, Australia and Germany. *Music Performance Research*, 3 (1), 79–96.

Cohen, S. (1991) *Rock Culture in Liverpool: Popular Music in the Making*, Clarendon Press, Oxford.

Cohn, N. (2006) *Triksta: Life and Death and New Orleans Rap*, Vintage, London.

Cook, N. and Dibben, N. (2010) Emotion in culture and history: perspectives from musicology, in *Music and Emotion: Theory, Research, Applications* (eds P.N. Juslin and J.A. Sloboda), Oxford University Press, Oxford, pp. 45–72.

Cooper, C. (1993) *Noises in the Blood: Orality, Gender and the 'Vulgar Body' of Jamaican Popular Culture*, Macmillan, London.

Couldry, N. (2006) *Listening Beyond the Echoes: Media, Ethics and Agency in an Uncertain World*, Paradigm, Boulder.

Coward, N. (1930) *Private Lives: An Intimate Comedy in Three Acts*, Methuen, London.

Crafts, S., Cavicchi, D. and Keil, C. (1993) *My Music: Explorations of Music in Daily Life*, Wesleyan University Press, Middletown.

Craib, I. (1998) *Experiencing Identity*, Sage, London.

Crouch, C. (2011) *The Strange Non-Death of Neoliberalism*, Polity Press, Cambridge, UK.

Csikszentmihalyi, M. (1975) *Beyond Boredom and Anxiety: The Experience of Flow in Work and Games*, Jossey-Bass, San Francisco.

Csikszentmihalyi, M. (1990) *Flow: The Psychology of Optimal Experience*, Harper and Row, New York.

Cusick, S. (1994) On a lesbian relation with music: a serious effort not to think straight, in *Queering the Pitch: The New Gay and Lesbian Musicology* (eds P. Brett, E. Wood and G.C. Thomas), Routledge, New York and London, pp. 67–84.

Dahlgren, P. (2009) *Media and Political Engagement: Citizens, Communication, and Democracy*, Cambridge University Press, New York.

Danielsen, A. (2006) *Presence and Pleasure: The Funk Grooves of James Funk and Parliament*, Wesleyan University Press, Middletown.

Davidson, J. (2011) Musical participation: expectations, experiences, and outcomes, in *Music and the Mind: Essays in Honour of John Sloboda* (eds I. Deliege and J. Davidson), Oxford University Press, Oxford, pp. 65–90.

Davies, S. (2010) Emotions expressed and aroused by music: philosophical perspectives, in *Handbook of Music and Emotion: Theory, Research, Applications* (eds P.N. Juslin and J.A. Sloboda), Oxford University Press, Oxford, pp. 15–43.

Davis, Oliver (2010) *Jacques Rancière*, Polity Press, Cambridge, UK.

DeGroot, G. (2008) *The Sixties Unplugged*, Macmillan, London.

de Kloet, J. (2008) *China with a Cut: Globalisation, Urban Youth and Popular Music*, Amsterdam University Press, Amsterdam.

Delanty, G. (2003) *Community*, Routledge, London and New York.

DeNora, T. (2000) *Music in Everyday Life*, Cambridge University Press, Cambridge, UK.

DeNora, T. (2003) *After Adorno: Rethinking Music Sociology*, Cambridge University Press, Cambridge, UK.

Dewey, J. (1980/1934) *Art as Experience*, Perigree, New York.

Dines, G. (2010) *Pornland: How Porn has Hijacked our Sexuality*, Beacon Press, Boston.

Drew, R. (2001) *Karaoke Nights: An Ethnographic Rhapsody*, Altamira, Walnut Creek.

Durkheim, E. (1976/1915) *The Elementary Forms of the Religious Life* (trans. J.W. Swain), George Allen and Unwin, London.

Ehrenreich, B. (2006) *Dancing in the Streets: A History of Collective Joy*, Metropolitan Books/Henry Holt and Company, New York.

Featherstone, M. (1991) *Consumer Culture and Postmodernism*, Sage, London.

Feld, S. (1982) *Sounds and Sentiment: Birds, Weeping, Poetics and Song in Kaluli Expression*, University of Pennsylvania Press, Philadelphia.

Filmer, P. (2003) Songtime: sound culture, rhythm and sociality, in *The Auditory Culture Reader* (eds M. Bull and L. Back), Berg, Oxford.

Finnegan, R. (1989) *The Hidden Musicians: Music-Making in an English Town*, Cambridge University Press, Cambridge, UK.

Finnegan, R. (2012) Music, experience and emotion, in *The Cultural Study of Music*, 2nd edn (eds M. Clayton, T. Herbert and R. Middleton), Routledge, Abingdon and New York, pp. 353–363.

Foucault, M. (2000) Technologies of the self, in *Essential Works of Foucault, 1954–1984, Vol. 1: Ethics*, Penguin, London.

Fox, A. (2004) *Real Country: Music and Language in Working-Class Culture*, Duke University Press, Durham.

Fraser, N. (1997) *Justice Interruptus: Critical Reflections on the 'Postsocialist' Condition*, Routledge, New York.

Freud, S. (1961/1920) *Beyond the Pleasure Principle* (trans. J. Strachey), Hogarth Press, London.

Frith, S. (1981) *Sound Effects*, Constable, London.

Frith, S. (1990/1985) Afterthoughts, in *On Record: Rock, Pop and the Written Word* (eds S. Frith and A. Goodwin), Pantheon, New York, pp. 419–424.

Frith, S. (1996) *Performing Rites: On the Value of Popular Music*, Oxford University Press, Oxford.

Frith, S. (2001) Pop music, in *The Cambridge Companion to Pop and Rock* (eds S. Frith, W. Straw and J. Street), Cambridge University Press, Cambridge, UK, pp. 93–108.

Frith, S. (2002) Music and everyday life. *Critical Quarterly*, 44 (1), 35–48.

Frith, S. and McRobbie, A. (1990/1978) Rock and sexuality, in *On Record: Rock, Pop and the Written Word* (eds S. Frith and A. Goodwin), Routledge, London, pp. 317–332.

Gabrielsson, A. (2011) *Strong Experiences With Music*, Clarendon Press, Oxford.

Garnham, N. (2000) *Emancipation, the Media, and Modernity: Arguments About the Media and Social Theory*, Oxford University Press, Oxford.

Garofalo, R. (1992) *Rockin' the Boat: Mass Music and Mass Movements*, Beacon Press, Cambridge, MA.

Giddens, A. (1991) *Modernity and Self-Identity: Self and Society in the Late Modern Age*, Polity Press, Cambridge, UK.

Gilbert, J. (2004) Signifying nothing: culture, discourse and the sociality of affect. *Culture Machine*, vol. 6, http://www.culturemachine.net/index.php/cm/article/viewArticle/8/7 (accessed September 5, 2012).

Gilbert, J. and Pearson, E. (1999) *Discographies: Dance Music, Culture and the Politics of Sound*, Routledge, London and New York.

Gill, R.C. (2007) *Gender and the Media*, Polity Press, Cambridge, UK.

Gilroy, P. (1993) *The Black Atlantic: Modernity and Double Consciousness*, Harvard University Press, Cambridge, MA.

Gilroy, P. (2000) *Against Race: Imagining Political Culture Beyond the Color Line*, Harvard University Press, Cambridge, MA.

Gilroy, P. (2011) *Darker Than Blue: On the Moral Economies of Black Atlantic Culture*, Harvard University Press, Cambridge, MA.

Gracyk, T. (2001) *I Wanna Be Me: Rock Music and the Politics of Identity*, Temple University Press, Philadelphia.

Gregg, M. and Seigworth, G.J. (eds) (2010) *The Affect Theory Reader*, Duke University Press, Durham.

Gregory, A.H. (1996) The roles of music in society: the ethnomusicological perspective, in *The Social Psychology of Music* (eds D.J. Hargreaves and A.C. North), Oxford University Press, Oxford, pp. 123–140.

Griffiths, V. (1988) Stepping out: the importance of dancing for young women, in *Relative Freedoms: Women and Leisure* (eds E. Wimbush and M. Talbot), Open University Press, Milton Keynes and Philadelphia.

Grossberg, L. (1984) Another boring day in paradise: rock and roll and the empowerment of everyday life. *Popular Music*, 4, 225–258.

Grossberg, L. (1990) Is there rock after punk?, in *On Record: Rock, Pop and the Written Word* (eds S. Frith and A. Goodwin), Routledge, London, pp. 92–104.

Grossberg, L. (1992) *We Gotta Get Out of This Place*, Routledge, New York and London.

Habermas, J. (1989/1962) *The Structural Transformation of the Public Sphere* (trans. T. Burger), Polity Press, Cambridge, UK.

Hall, E. (1976) *Beyond Culture*, Anchor Books, Garden City.

Hall, S. and Whannel, P. (1964) *The Popular Arts*, Hutchinson, London.

Hall, S. and Jefferson, T. (1993/1976) *Resistance Through Rituals*, 2nd edn, Routledge, London.

Hallam, S. (2001) *The Power of Music*, The Performing Rights Society, London.

Hatch, M. (1989) Popular music in Indonesia, in *World Music, Politics and Social Change* (ed. S. Frith), Manchester University Press, Manchester, pp. 67–87.

Hennion, A. (2012) Music and mediation: towards a new sociology of music, in *The Cultural Study of Music*, 2nd edn (eds M. Clayton, T. Herbert and R. Middleton), Routledge, London, pp. 249–260.

Hesmondhalgh, D. (1997) The cultural politics of dance music. *Soundings*, 5, 167–178.

Hesmondhalgh, D. (2005) Subcultures, scenes or tribes? None of the above. *Journal of Youth Studies*, 8 (1), 21–40.

Hesmondhalgh, D. (2006) Bourdieu, the media and cultural production. *Media, Culture and Society*, 28 (2), 211–232.

Hesmondhalgh, D. (2013) *The Cultural Industries*, 3rd edn, Sage, London.

Hesmondhalgh, D. and Baker, S. (2011) *Creative Labour: Media Work in Three Cultural Industries*, Routledge, London.

Higgins, K.M. (2011) *The Music of Our Lives*, new edn, Lexington Books, Lanham.

Higgins, K.M. (2012) *The Music Between Us*, Chicago University Press, Chicago.

Hochschild, A. (1983) *The Managed Heart: Commercialization of Human Feeling*, University of California Press, Berkeley.

Hodkinson, P. (2002) *Goth: Identity, Style and Subculture*, Berg, Oxford.

Honneth, A. (2004) Organized self-realization: some paradoxes of individualization. *European Journal of Social Theory*, 7 (4), 463–478.

Horton, D. (1957) The dialogue of courtship in popular song. *American Journal of Sociology* 62 (6), 569–578.

Huron, D. (2008) *Sweet Anticipation: Music and the Psychology of Expectation*, MIT Press, Cambridge, MA.

Illouz, E. (1997) *Consuming the Romantic Utopia: Love and the Cultural Contradictions of Capitalism*, University of California Press, Berkeley.

Illouz, E. (2007) *Cold Intimacies: The Making of Emotional Capitalism*, Polity Press, Cambridge, UK.

Jackson, P. (2004) *Inside Clubbing: Sensual Experiments in the Art of Being Human*, Berg, Oxford.

Jay, M. (2006) *Songs of Experience: Modern American and European Variations on a Universal Theme*, University of California Press, Berkeley.

Jenkins, H. (2006) *Convergence Culture*, New York University Press, New York.

Johnson, B. and Cloonan, M. (2009) *Dark Side of the Tune: Popular Music and Violence*, Ashgate, Farnham and Burlington.

Jones, P. (2004) *Raymond Williams' Sociology of Culture*, Palgrave, Basingstoke.

Jordan, T. (1995) Collective bodies: raving and the politics of Gilles Deleuze and Felix Guattari. *Body & Society*, 1 (1), 125–144.

Juslin, P.N. and Sloboda, J.A. (eds) (2001) *Music and Emotion: Theory and Research*, Oxford University Press, Oxford.

Juslin, P.N. and Sloboda, J.A. (eds) (2010) *Handbook of Music and Emotion: Theory, Research, Applications*, Oxford University Press, Oxford.

Kahn-Harris, K. (2006) *Extreme Metal: Music and Culture on the Edge*, Berg, Oxford.

Kaplan, E.A. (1987) *Rocking Around the Clock: Music Television, Postmodernism, and Consumer Culture*, Methuen, New York and London.

Keat, R. (2000) *Cultural Goods and the Limits of the Market*, Routledge, London and New York.

Keightley, K. (2001) Reconsidering Rock, in *The Cambridge Companion to Pop and Rock* (eds S. Frith, W. Straw and J. Street), Cambridge University Press, Cambridge, UK.

Keil, C. (1991/1966) *Urban Blues*, University of Chicago Press, Chicago.

Keil, C. (1994/1966) Motion and feeling through music, in *Music Grooves* (C. Keil and S. Feld), University of Chicago Press, Chicago, pp. 53–76.

Keil, C. and Feld, S. (1994) *Music Grooves*, University of Chicago Press, Chicago.

Kramer, L. (2007) *Why Classical Music Still Matters*, University of California Press, Berkeley.

Kruse, H. (2003) *Site and Sound: Understanding Independent Music Scenes*, Peter Lang, New York.

Lasch, C. (1977) *Haven in a Heartless World*, Basic Books, New York.

Lasch, C. (1978) *The Culture of Narcissism*, Norton, New York.

Layder, D. (2006) *Understanding Social Theory*, 2nd edn, Sage, London.

Leppert, R. (2007) *Sound Judgment*, Ashgate, Aldershot.

Levy, A. (2005) *Female Chauvinist Pigs*, Free Press, New York.

Lukes, S.L. (1973) *Individualism*, Harper and Row, New York.

Luvaas, B. (2009) The deterritorialisation of Indonesian indie pop. *Cultural Anthropology*, 24 (2), 246–279.

Lynskey, D. (2010) *Thirty Three Revolutions Per Minute: A History of Protest Songs*, Faber, London.

MacIntyre, A. (1970) *Herbert Marcuse: An Exposition and a Polemic*, Viking, New York.

MacIntyre, A. (1984) *After Virtue: A Study in Moral Theory*, University of Notre Dame Press, Notre Dame.

Malbon, B. (1999) *Clubbing: Dancing, Ecstasy and Vitality*, Routledge, London.

Manuel, P. (1990) *Popular Musics of the Non-Western World*, Oxford University Press, London.

Marsh, D. (1989) *The Heart of Rock & Soul: The 1001 Greatest Singles Ever Made*, Plume, New York.

Martin, B. (1981) *The Sociology of Contemporary Cultural Change*, Basil Blackwell, Oxford.

Martin, P.J. (1995) *Sounds and Society*, Manchester University Press, Manchester.

Martin, P.J. (2006) *Music and the Sociological Gaze: Art Worlds and Cultural Production*, Manchester University Press, Manchester.

Martino, S.C., Collins, R.L., Elliott, M.N., et al. (2006) Exposure to degrading versus non-degrading music lyrics and sexual behavior among youth. *Pediatrics*, 118 (2), 430–441.

Massumi, B. (1995) The autonomy of affect. *Cultural Critique*, 31, 83–109.

Maus, F.E. (2012) Music, gender, and sexuality, in *The Cultural Study of Music: A Critical Introduction*, 2nd edn (eds M. Clayton, T. Herbert and R. Middleton), Routledge, London.

McClary, S. (1991) *Feminine Endings: Music, Gender, and Sexuality*, University of Minnesota Press, Minneapolis.

McClary, S. and Walser, R. (1994) Theorizing the body in African-American music. *Black Music Research Journal*, 14 (1), 75–84.

McGuigan, J. (1992) *Cultural Populism*, Routledge, London.

McRobbie, A. (1991) *Feminism and Youth Culture*, Macmillan, Basingstoke.

McRobbie, A. (2009) *The Aftermath of Feminism*, Sage, London and Los Angeles.

Merriam, A.P. (1964) *The Anthropology of Music*, Northwestern University Press, Evanston.

Meštrović, S. (1991) *The Coming Fin-de-Siècle*, Routledge, London.

Meyer, L. (1957) *Emotion and Meaning in Music*, University of Chicago Press, Chicago.

Middleton, R. (1990) *Studying Popular Music*, Open University Press, Philadelphia.

Middleton, R. (2000) Musical belongings: western music and its "low-other", in *Western Music and its Others: Difference, Representation and Appropriation in Music* (eds G. Born and D. Hesmondhalgh), University of California Press, Berkeley, pp. 59–85.

Middleton, R. (2006) *Voicing the Popular: On the Subjects of Popular Music*, Routledge, New York.

Middleton, R. (2012) Locating the people: music and the popular, in *The Cultural Study of Music*, 2nd edn (eds M. Clayton, T. Herbert and R. Middleton), Routledge, London, pp. 275–287.

Mithen, S.J. (2005) *The Singing Neanderthals: The Origins of Music, Language, Mind and Body*, Harvard University Press, Cambridge, MA.

Mitsui, T. (1998) The genesis of karaoke: how the combination of technology and music evolved, in *Karaoke Around The World: Global Technology, Local Singing* (eds T. Mitsui and S. Hosokawa), Routledge, New York, pp. 29–42.

Morley, P. (2004) *Words and Music: A History of Pop in the Shape of a City*, Faber, London.

Muggleton, D. (2000) *Inside Subculture: The Postmodern Meaning of Style*, Berg, Oxford.

Negus, K. (2008) *Bob Dylan*, Equinox, London.

Nettl, B. (1983) *The Study of Ethnomusicology*, University of Illinois Press, Urbana.

Neville, R. (1970) *Power Play*, Cape, London.

Nussbaum, M. (1996) Patriotism and cosmopolitanism, in *For Love of Country: Debating the Limits of Patriotism* (ed. J. Cohen), Beacon Press, Boston.

Nussbaum, M. (2001) *Upheavals of Thought: The Intelligence of Emotions*, Cambridge University Press, Cambridge, UK.

Nussbaum, M. (2006) *Frontiers of Justice*, Harvard University Press, Cambridge, MA.

Ogawa, H. (1998) The effects of karaoke on music in Japan, in *Karaoke Around The World: Global Technology, Local Singing* (eds T. Mitsui and S. Hosokawa), Routledge, New York, pp. 43–52.

Oku, S. (1998) Karaoke and middle-aged and older women, in *Karaoke Around The World: Global Technology, Local Singing* (eds T. Mitsui and S. Hosokawa), Routledge, New York, pp. 53–80.

Paasonen, S., Nikunen, K. and Saarenmaa, L. (eds) (2007) *Pornification: Sex and Sexuality in Media Culture*, Berg, Oxford.

Paglia, C. (1995) *Vamps and Tramps: New Essays*, Penguin, London.

Parakilas, J. (2001) *Piano Roles*, Yale University Press, New Haven.

Pateman, C. (1989) *The Disorder of Women*, Polity Press, Cambridge, UK.

Peters, J.D. (1999) *Speaking into the Air: A History of the Idea of Communication*, University of Chicago Press, Chicago and London.

Peterson, R.A. and Kern, R. (1996) Changing highbrow taste: from snob to omnivore, *American Sociological Review*, 61, 900–907.

Pini, M. (1997) Cyborgs, nomads and the raving feminine, in *Dance in the City* (ed. H. Thomas), Macmillan, London, pp. 111–129.

Pitts, S.E. (2005) *Valuing Musical Participation*, Ashgate, Aldershot.

Plagenhoef, S. (2007) *If You're Feeling Sinister*, Continuum, New York.

Primack, B.A., Douglas, E.A., Fine, M.J. and Dalton, M.A. (2009) Exposure to sexual lyrics and sexual experience among urban adolescents. *American Journal of Preventive Medicine*, 36 (4), 317–323.

Prior, N. (2011) Critique and renewal in the sociology of music: Bourdieu and beyond. *Cultural Sociology* 5 (1), 121–138.

Quinn, E. (2005) *Nuthin' But A 'G' Thang: The Culture and Commerce of Gangsta Rap*, Columbia University Press, New York.

Regev, M. (2007a) Ethno-national pop-rock music: aesthetic cosmopolitanism made from within. *Cultural Sociology*, 1, 317–341.

Regev, M. (2007b) Cultural uniqueness and aesthetic cosmopolitanism. *European Journal of Social Theory*, 10 (1), 123–138.

Reynolds, S. (2011) *Retromania: Pop Culture's Addiction to Its Own Past*, Faber and Faber, London.

Reynolds, S. and Press, J. (1995) *The Sex Revolts: Gender, Rebellion, and Rock 'n' Roll*, Harvard University Press, Cambridge, MA.

Rimmer, M. (2010) Listening to the monkey: class, youth, and the formation of a musical habitus. *Ethnography*, 11 (2), 255–283.

Robinson, J. (2005) *Deeper Than Reason: Emotion and its Role in Literature, Music and Art*, Clarendon Press, Oxford.

Ross, A. (2000) The mental labor problem, *Social Text*, 18 (2), 1–31.

Ross, A. (2009) *Nice Work if You Can Get It*, New York University Press, New York.

Rutherford, J. (ed.) (2000) *The Art of Life: On Living, Love and Death*, Lawrence & Wishart, London.

Ryle, M. and Soper, K. (2002) *To Relish the Sublime? Culture and Self-Realisation in Postmodern Times*, Verso, London.

Savigliano, M.E. (1995) *Tango and the Political Economy of Passion*, Westview Press, Boulder.

Sayer, A. (2011) *Why Things Matter to People: Social Science, Values and Ethical Life*, Cambridge University Press, Cambridge, UK.

Scannell, P. (1996) *Radio, Television and Modern Life*, Blackwell, Oxford.

Scheff, T. (2011) *What's Love Got To Do With It? Emotions and Relationships in Popular Songs*, Paradigm, Boulder.

Schutz, A. (1951) Making music together: a study in social relationship. *Social Research*, 18, 76–97.

Scott, D.B. (1989) *The Singing Bourgeois: Songs of the Victorian Drawing Room and Parlour*, Open University Press, Milton Keynes and Philadelphia.

Scott, D.B. (2003) *From the Erotic to the Demonic: On Critical Musicology*, Oxford University Press, Oxford.

Scruton, R. (1986) *Sexual Desire: A Moral Philosophy of the Erotic*, Free Press, New York.

Scruton, R. (1999) First person plural, in *Theorizing Nationalism* (ed. R. Beiner), SUNY Press, Albany.

Scruton, R. (2003) *Death-Devoted Heart: Sex and the Sacred in Wagner's Tristan and Isolde*, Oxford University Press, Oxford.

Sedgwick, E.K. (2002) *Touching Feeling*, Duke University Press, Durham.

Sen, A. (1999) *Development as Freedom*, Oxford University Press, Oxford.

Sennett, R. (1974) *The Fall of Public Man*, Cambridge University Press, Cambridge, UK.

Sennett, R. (1998) *The Corrosion of Character: The Personal Consequences of Work in the New Capitalism*, Norton, New York and London.

Shank, B. (1994) *Dissonant Identities: The Rock 'n' Roll Scene in Austin, Texas*, Wesleyan University Press, Hanover.

Shilling, C. and Mellor, P.A. (1998) Durkheim, morality and modernity: collective effervescence, homo duplex and the sources of moral action. *British Journal of Sociology*, 49 (2), 193–209.

Shusterman, R. (2000) *Pragmatist Aesthetics: Living Beauty, Rethinking Art*, 2nd edn, Rowman and Littlefield, Oxford.

Slobin, M. (1976) *Music in the Culture of Northern Afghanistan*, University of Arizona Press, Tucson.

Sloboda, J. (2010) Music and everyday life: the role of emotions, in *Handbook of Music and Emotion: Theory, Research, Applications* (eds P.N. Juslin and J.A. Sloboda), Oxford University Press, Oxford, pp. 493–514.

Small, C. (1987) *Music of the Common Tongue*, John Calder, London.

Small, C. (1997) *Musicking: The Meanings of Performing and Listening*, Wesleyan University Press, Hanover.

Smith, C. (2010) Pornographication: a discourse for all seasons. *International Journal of Media and Cultural Politics*, 6 (1), 103–108.

Snead, J. (1984) On repetition in black culture, in *Black Literature and Literary Theory* (ed. H.L. Gates), Routledge, London, pp. 59–80.

Spitzer, M. (2009) Emotions and meaning in music, *Musica Humana* 1 (2), 155–196.

Stahl, M. (2006) Reinventing certainties: American popular music and social reproduction. Unpublished PhD thesis. University of California.

Stallybrass, P. and White, A. (1986) *The Politics and Poetics of Transgression*, Methuen, London and New York.

Stevenson, N. (2006) *David Bowie: Fame, Sound and Vision*, Polity Press, Cambridge, UK.

Stokes, M. (2007) Adam Smith and the Dark Nightingale: on twentieth-century sentimentalism. *Twentieth-Century Music*, 3 (2), 201–219.

Stokes, M. (2010) *The Republic of Love: Cultural Intimacy in Turkish Popular Music*, University of Chicago Press, Chicago.

Straw, W. (1991) Systems of articulation, logics of change: scenes and communities in popular music. *Cultural Studies*, 5 (3), 361–375.

Straw, W. (1997) Sizing up record collections: gender and connoisseurship in rock music culture, in *Sexing the Groove* (ed. S. Whiteley), Routledge, London and New York.

Straw, W. (2001a) Dance music, in *The Cambridge Companion to Pop and Rock* (eds S. Frith, W. Straw and J. Street), Cambridge University Press, Cambridge, UK, pp. 158–175.

Straw, W. (2001b) Scenes and sensibilities. *Public*, 22–23, 245–257.

Street, J. (1997) *Politics and Popular Culture*, Temple University Press, Philadelphia.

Street, J. (2012) *Music and Politics*, Polity Press, Cambridge, UK.

Stroud, S.R. (2011) *John Dewey and the Artful Life: Pragmatism, Aesthetics and Morality*, Pennsylvania State University Press, Pennsylvania.

Tasker, Y. and Negra, D. (eds) (2007) *Interrogating Postfeminism: Gender and the Politics of the Popular*, Duke University Press, Durham.

Thompson, J.B. (1995) *The Media and Modernity*, Polity Press, Cambridge, UK.

Thornton, S. (1995) *Club Cultures: Music, Media, and Subcultural Capital*, Polity Press, Cambridge, UK.

Tosches, N. (1989/1977) *Country: Living Legends and Dying Metaphors in America's Biggest Music*, Secker and Warburg, London.

Toynbee, J. (2000) *Making Popular Music*, Arnold, London.

Toynbee, J. (2002) Mainstreaming: from hegemonic centre to global networks, in *Popular Music Studies* (eds D. Hesmondhalgh and K. Negus), Arnold, London.

Toynbee, J. (2007) *Bob Marley: Herald of a Post-Colonial World?* Polity Press, Cambridge, UK.

Toynbee, J. (2012) Music, culture and creativity, in *The Cultural Study of Music*, 2nd edn (eds M. Clayton, T. Herbert and R. Middleton), Routledge, London, pp. 161–171.

Turino, T. (2008) *Music as Social Life: The Politics of Participation*, University of Chicago Press, Chicago.

Van der Merwe, P. (1989) *Origins of the Popular Style: The Antecedents of Twentieth-Century Popular Music*, Clarendon Press, Oxford.

Van Dijck, J. (2006) Record and hold: popular music between personal and collective memory. *Critical Studies in Media Communication*, 23 (5), 357–374.

Van Hooft, S. (2009) *Cosmopolitanism: A Philosophy for Global Ethics*, Acumen, Chesham.

Vermorel, F. and Vermorel, J. (1985) *Starlust: The Secret Fantasies of Fans*, WH Allen, London.

Wade, P. (2000) *Music, Race, and Nation: Música Tropical in Colombia*, The University of Chicago Press, Chicago.

Walser, R. (1993) *Running with the Devil: Power, Gender, and Madness in Heavy Metal Music*, Wesleyan University Press, Hanover and London.

Warde, A., Martens, L. and Olsen, W. (1999) Consumption and the problem of variety: cultural omnivorousness, social distinction, and dining out. *Sociology*, 33, 105–127.

Warner, M. (2002) *Publics and Counterpublics*, Zone Books, New York.

Weintraub, J. (1997) The theory and politics of the public/private distinction, in *Public and Private In Thought and Practice* (eds J. Weintraub and K. Kumar), University of Chicago Press, Chicago, pp. 1–37.

West, C. (1992) *Race Matters*, Vintage, New York.

Whiteley, S. (2000) *Women and Popular Music: Sexuality, Identity and Subjectivity*, Routledge, London.

Wilkinson, R. and Pickett, K. (2010) *The Spirit Level*, Penguin, London.

Williams, R. (1965/1961) *The Long Revolution*, Columbia University Press, New York.

Williams, R. (1977) *Marxism and Literature*, Oxford University Press, Oxford.

Wilson, E. (2000) *Bohemians: The Glamorous Outcasts*, I.B. Tauris, London.

Winnicott, D. (1971) *Playing and Reality*, Tavistock, London.

Wouters, C. (1992) On status competition and emotion management: the study of emotions as a new field, in *Cultural Theory and Cultural Change* (ed. M. Featherstone), Sage, London, pp. 229–252.

Yano, C.R. (2002) *Tears of Longing: Nostalgia and the Nation in Japanese Popular Song*, Harvard University Press, Cambridge, MA.

Index

Printed and bound by CPI Group (UK) Ltd, Croydon, CR0 4YY